ART OF NEWS WRITING TECHNIQUE

ART OF NEWS WRITING TECHNIQUE

Kishore Sharma

CENTRUM PRESS
NEW DELHI-110002 (INDIA)

CENTRUM PRESS
H.O.: 4360/4, Ansari Road, Daryaganj,
New Delhi-110002 (India)
Tel: 23278000, 23261597, 23255577, 23286875
B.O.: No. 1015, Ist Main Road, BSK IIIrd Stage,
IIIrd Phase, IIIrd Block, Bangalore-560085 (INDIA)
Tel: 080-41723429
Email: centrumpress@gmail.com
Visit us at: www.centrumpress.com

Art of News Writing Technique

First Edition, 2010

ISBN 978-93-80540-64-1

PRINTED IN INDIA

Printed at Mehra Offset Press, Delhi

Contents

Preface

News writing is a key skill for journalists, but it helps with other types of writing as well. That's because news writing is about telling a story quickly and concisely. Anyone can learn to do this, with a bit of help. It's called the inverted pyramid. This upside down triangle serves as a guide for how you include information in the story. Using the inverted pyramid means starting with the most important information, then putting the next most important info and so on. It can also serve as a guide for writing each paragraph in the story. Start with the most important point, then the next most important and so on. The inverted pyramid has an interesting history.

Having the most important information at the top meant that readers always got the essential parts of the story. Another way to think of the inverted pyramid is that you start with the facts and then add the background. So, how do you know what background to add? It's easy. You can use the 6Ws.

Strictly speaking, there aren't six Ws, there are actually 5Ws and 1H, but the formula seems to work. That mnemonic reminds us to include the who, where, what, why, when and how of a story. Why is this? Think about how you tell a story to your friends. You might say: 'You'll never believe WHO I just saw!' Then you might go on to tell the story of where the person was, what they were doing, and why it's scandalous. We all want to hear about people - and that's what news is about? Look at any news story and you will see that all of this information is in the first two paragraphs. Anything after that is background to the story.

With the availability and accessibility of PCS, it's natural for us to use one of the popular word processors for all our written output. Fortunately for writers everywhere, there has recently been a lot of headway in all aspects of the field of writing analysis. Perhaps you'll find this unlikely, but I had the good fortune to hear about a one-of-a-kind utility that is capable of automatically repairing your English errors. Without any effort on your part, you can easily take care of possible problem areas in Articles, CVS, emails and other writing assignments. Imagine detecting a preventable (if you'd been careful) mistake just before delivering your Legal document to a client.

Struggling writers everywhere who are searching for ideas on improving their English would be wise to introduce this type of program to their computer's repertoire. If you'd like to make the writing process easier, it's been proven that this tool makes the writing process much more effective. After checking out this technology, I came to the conclusion that it's a real advantage to native English speakers and ESL learners alike. It's my view that it makes any frustrating writing assignment not just less frustrating, but would you believe relaxing?

Author

Chapter 1

Interpretive Analysis, and Expository Writing

In the late 1500s, William Perkins published the Art of Prophecying, a manual attempting to improve the quality of preaching in England. Like most Puritan theologians of his day, Perkins recommended that the sermon be organized in three sections, the "text," the "doctrine," and the "application". According to Perkins' system, ministers should choose an important verse from the Bible, such as "Let there be light," read it out loud, and then explain what it means on several levels.

For example, ministers might interpret the meaning of the Creation in Genesis by breaking down the meaning of light into visual light and spiritual light. Depending on their temper, ministers might unfold eight or nine different interpretations from a single verse. After the permutations of the doctrine have been surveyed, the sermon then shifts to an application of the doctrine to the lives of the congregants.

While Perkins' method of exegesis is hardly unique, it foregrounds an intellectual skill which is crucial, if not central, to academic discourse today. Perkins calls the act of analytic interpretation "prophecying," not because ministers are seeing the future, but because they're performing a vatic function of interpretation-saying. The purpose of these acts of interpretation, Perkins writes, is to "edify" people about the meaning and spirit of the scriptures. Prophecying is a multi-leveled interpretive act of creation. It's what many of us mean when we talk to our students about "unpacking" the meaning of a text.

For those who have taken the hermeneutic turn, (and even for those who haven't), this story is probably a quaint theological example of a cognitive practice that scholars everywhere perform in different ways in their own disciplines. The broad currency of this critical practice, however, is my point: analytic interpretation, the creation of meaning, is what the critical liberal arts disciplines share. In this chapter, I argue that while competence in interpretive analysis is a commonly acknowledged goal of a college education, it is rarely explicitly addressed in the curriculum.

Because interpretive analysis makes specific cognitive and generic demands on writers, our expository writing students would benefit from both theoretical and practical training in these kinds of exegetical skills. As I use the term in this chapter, analysis refers to the technique of critically interpreting an idea or problem by breaking it into meaningful parts. I emphasize meaningful parts because the skill is not simply defined by expertise in division and classification: it's about explaining why those parts are important in respect to different contexts and circumstances. Interpretive analysis is both a habit of thought (a cognitive trick) and a rhetorical protocol (an expressive structure in speech or writing).

In either case, it's the intellectual machinery of conceptual exegesis. At the risk of oversimplifying the activity I am trying to describe, let me suggest that interpretive analysis is typically forecast with rhetorical expressions like, "the judge's decision avoids several thorny legal questions. First, it indicates..."

Presumably, what follows will be an analysis of the ruling. This practice is very similar to what religious authorities around the world routinely perform in explaining the significance of sacred texts.

While we may assume that analysis is an obvious characteristic of critical writing, our less-prepared students have great difficult recognizing it when they encounter it. Patricia Bizzell has pointed out that our two-year and public university students often enter school with a limited familiarity of written genres. The problem, however, is not just recognizing objective tone: our novice students don't habitually register the difference between analytic interpretation and other types of narrative. When they look at academic discourse they see only persiflage: fancy words, convoluted syntax, and the pretentious invocation of authority.

For them, academic discourse sounds like pompous language, not meaningful discrimination. As I shall suggest later in this chapter, our students are not alone. In many of the contemporary debates about academic discourse, the culture wars, and our internecine battles over college Core requirements, humanities faculty have played a losing hand by betting on the content of a liberal arts education.

We've had difficulty justifying our curricula to ourselves and to others. Perhaps, however, as Robert Scholes suggests in the Rise and Fall of English, we would be better off defining our discipline's value in terms of method rather than content.

Literature and writing faculty can play an important trump: as a language-oriented discipline, English teaches the art of creating meaning in texts. No matter what our disagreements over texts or turf (literature vs. composition), the tissue of our professional discourse is interpretive analysis. It's how we express ourselves to each other; it's how we expect our students to express themselves to us. This methodological approach seems to have been lost in the way we describe our discipline.

Analysis is so integral to the Euroamerican liberal arts curriculum that we seldom feel the need to talk about its centrality or complexity. Among the academic disciplines, explicit analytic training is divided awkwardly among Philosophy, English, and Speech departments, all of which encourage students to analyse concepts as a means of creating the raw material for their arguments.

Traditionally, the Philosophy department covers training in analysis by offering courses in critical thinking and logic. Because many schools have removed philosophy and speech from their core curricula, training in written critical analysis has fallen heavily on English departments, particularly on the composition courses that fulfill graduation requirements. But often, the required composition courses in two-year and large public institutions are organized around issues of coming-to-voice, practice with rhetorical modes (like summary, comparison-and-contrast, description, etc.), syntax review, and research skills.

Even in schools that offer a two-semester expository writing requirement, there isn't much time for an introduction to critical thinking. When critical thinking is discussed, it is usually spent teaching strategies of argument, shooing students away from a catalogue of logical fallacies, and trying to make them comfortable with words like enthymeme and warrant.

The core curricula of most colleges and universities thus suggest that habits of interpretive analysis will be absorbed by students from the variety of courses that they take.

Indeed, for each major, students presumably learn how to perform the type of analysis that suits their discipline or future profession. English majors are generally well-trained in habits of literary analysis after four years of college, even if they've hardly paid attention in class. Few of them, however, could selfconsciously explain how analysis is a part of what they do.

Especially in our composition courses, we expect our students to develop their analytic skills, but these skills are rarely the subject of instructional units in our courses or textbooks. The term analysis is seldom listed in a textbook index; most don't even discuss the skill directly at all.

For example, the MacMillan Writer, a widely distributed composition book, offers a chapter identifying some basic maneuvers in expository writing-description, definition, classification, comparison and contrast, and argumentation. Many textbooks devote a chapter to each of these modes of discourse. Almost all contemporary composition books cross-index reading selections under these schemes or offer advice about how to write descriptive or argumentative essays. Practice in these rhetorical modes implicitly trains students to analyse.

The classification of different types of families, for example, asks students to break down a concept that they initially think of as a simple whole. Similarly, many writing textbooks are devoted toward investigating specialized questions of social diversity, gender, the media, or the environment. These texts generally combine exercises in description, summary, definition, compare-and-contrast, and argument with their topics. By working though ideas like "what is nature?" students learn to break down apparently simple questions and to make fine distinctions in meaning.

While faculty can generate excellent assignments from these texts, it's a question of instructor interest and expertise. Surveying the online syllabi of second semester, required writing courses offered at the state universities of Texas (Austin), Florida (Gainesville), Minnesota (Minneapolis), Ohio (Columbus), New York (Buffalo), and California (Irvine), and at the universities of Pittsburgh, Purdue, and Syracuse (a haphazard list, dictated largely by access to web-available syllabi), I found that in most cases, the course textbooks powerfully shape the type of writing assigned. Descriptive essays, compare-and-contrast, and various types of researched arguments are very popular assignments.

Noteworthy exceptions are assignments like analyses of webpages and journals, and local-issue analyses. Some courses offer variously named process, process analysis, or causal analysis papers, which, except for causal analysis, emphasize descriptive skills more than interpretation.

Class activities often centre on the use of secondary sources, grammar, student presentations, and discussions of the reading homework (which is typically where extensive analytic training occurs). But granting that most writing faculty do train their students in interpretive analysis through discussions, class exercises, and ingenious writing assignments, it's odd that this goal is not expressed more explicitly through textbooks, syllabi, or college course bulletins.

The scarcity of course descriptions or textbooks that address interpretive analysis parallels a curious absence in contemporary discussions about academic discourse. Current debates about academic discourse primarily attend to questions of standard written English, jargon, diction, and objective decorum.

Most of these issues only superficially grapple with what goes on in academic discourse. To my mind, an essay written in second-person Spanglish that examines two aspects of what "ju be playin" means in Hamlet would command far more intellectual prestige than a plot summary salted with phrases like "phallic signifier." The Spanglish essay's diction and verb use would certainly need attention, but the lack of analytic invention in the second paper would be a far bigger problem.

In professional academic writing, the informal diction of some journal articles generally belies the sophistication of these articles' interpretive analyses. For example, even when Peter Elbow makes a case for the place of nonacademic writing in the university curriculum, his essay relies heavily on analytic structure, often developing three or four insights to a given problem in each section of his essay.

In addition to questions of decorum, another overemphasized component of academic discourse is the status of argument and evidence.

While the role of argument is undeniably important, I believe it is also a secondary concern. Ideally, a writer's arguments are discovered after an analysis has taken place, and usually a writer's arguments develop simultaneously with the evidence produced through analysis.

In cases where experienced writers know what they want to argue in advance, they often use interpretive analysis as the means of producing their evidence. In either case, a discussion of the importance of analysis as a rhetorical (that is, generic) and cognitive element of academic discourse has yet to be pursued by composition studies as a whole.

There are some recent noteworthy exceptions. David Rosenwasser and Jill Stephen's Writing Analytically, is a sophisticated Writing Across the Curriculum (WAC) primer for introducing analytic approaches to students of highly advanced reading and writing skills.

Although their text is aimed above the heads of students who would benefit from it the most, it defines interpretive analysis, gives concrete examples, and demonstrates the ways it appears in different disciplines. Similarly, Ben Rafoth has proposed several interrogatory methods with which writing centre tutors can help students take more analytic approaches to their writing.

Helen Fox's illuminating text, Listening to the World, points out that the practice of critical analysis entails a highly specialized relationship to the world that most faculty learned intuitively. As a result, some faculty have difficulty negotiating those expectations with students of different cultural origins. The novelty of these texts, however, points out the limitations of recent debates about academic discourse.

TEACHING TOOLS

Because most textbooks address interpretive analysis in roundabout ways, I've had to invent classroom exercises that foreground this skill as a central feature of academic thought and expression. Although my expository writing courses are not oriented around literature, I usually begin the first day of all my writing classes with a crash introduction to hermeneutics.

At the Christian university, I usually begin the semester with a short passage from the Bible that most of the class is somewhat familiar with, such as Abraham's attempt to sacrifice his son, Isaac. I then ask them what it means. The class then offers several interpretations, based on what they know of other parts of the Bible.

Various students might assert that the meaning of Abraham's sacrifice demonstrates:

- Personal faith,
- Loyalty to God,
- The interpretation of God's messages,
- A foreshadowing of Christ's sacrifice, etc.

Within 10 minutes, we have enough to write several pages of text that interpret a single passage from the Old Testament.

I point out that their interpretations often rely on:

- Deciding what parts of the passage are most important (breaking the text apart);
- Connecting the meaning of those pieces to other parts of the text;
- Applying the significance of that passage to other important events in people's lives.

Each of these strategies of interpretation can produce a variety of meanings, and they all enrich our knowledge of what Abraham's sacrifice means.

A student with feminist interests, for example, might ask what the significance of the boychild sacrifice says about early Judaism. One of my students, who happened to be well versed in Old Testament theology, approached the problem from a historical framework, arguing that the story is an early Judaic parable whose function is to criticize the efficacy of human sacrifice. After discussion, I then explain to my students that they can perform this intellectual skill (a mental trick, really) on sacred texts, dreams, historical events, philosophical issues, politics, and math problems.

Granting the multicultural limitations of working with the tableaux of Judeo-Christian theology, sometimes I'll ask the students to get into small groups and I'll give them a troubling situation to interpret:

A drunken and unemployed father finds his child has been brought home by the police for shoplifting. He leans down into the child's face and says, "you're a worthless bum and you'll never grow up to be anything." I ask them where the meaning of this scene is.

The students respond with any number of interpretations, ranging from the dangers of alcohol, to child abuse, to emotional self-pity, to psychological projection. I push them to come up with at least three different interpretations but I emphasize that all of these interpretations exist simultaneously in the same event-it's a question of what the interpreter wants to do with the problem.

Our cultural beliefs about alcohol use or proper child rearing each present interesting frameworks to approach the meaning of this drama. Once, a student prefaced her interpretation by saying, "Oh, Professor Ganter, I feel so sorry for you." The rest of the class smiled because she included me, and a guess about what my childhood was like, in her interpretation of what the class exercise meant. Fair enough!

I might also suggest a socio-political topic the students might be aware of, such as the recent decade of increased police recruitment in New York City.

Some students recognize that:

- It's part of the mayor's attempt to improve the quality of life in the city. Other students, concerned at recent cases of police brutality and our mayor's crackdown on immigrant street vendors and cab drivers, see it as
- A bullying gesture to keep the poor and minorities quiet.
- Others interpret it as part of the mayor's plan to run for federal office on a law-and-order record.

Although some students may feel more kindly toward the mayor than others, this exercise convinces them that a legitimate case could be made for any, or all three of these interpretations. I conclude the discussion by explaining that what they've just done are exercises in analytic interpretation, and it is the skill all scholars perform in their critical writing.

For example, in his famous study of the Declaration of Independence, Garry Wills organizes his book by simply devoting a chapter to each of his interpretative insights. Interpretive analysis is how thinkers produce whole books of meaning from the examination of relatively modest details, problems, or events.

As a brief review of the literature on writing and cognition suggests, the kinds of intellectual moves I've modeled in the preceding class exercises take for granted a formidable range of cognitive and expressive skills (forming generalizations, making inferences, reading comprehension). Teaching the lower order skills on which interpretation is built is crucial, but students also need practice doing sophisticated work in analytic interpretation at the same time. Russel Durst has called attention to the great demands that analytic writing makes on students, pointing out that until the late 1980s, few studies of college writing acknowledged the significant differences between analytic and non-analytic composition.

Durst shows that even when college writers are prompted to write analytic essays, they frequently fall back on discursive modes such as summary. For analysis to take place, Durst argues, students need to be able to place a text "in a broader context, establishing a frame of reference or stance outside of the text". In my writing and literature classes, I ask my students to draw on outside contexts for interpretive purposes, and I also assign readings that demonstrate the skill I ask them to perform in class. I'm fond of beginning my freshman-level composition courses with an advertisement analysis for two reasons.

First, the students are generally comfortable under standing what advertising is supposed to do (purpose), and they also have a broad knowledge of the general range of advertising methods (genre).

Second, as students whose primary relation to the world is shaped by images and television, it is an interpretive exercise they are accustomed to performing in their everyday lives concerning fashion and lifestyle (in contrast to interpreting sonnets, philosophical problems, or political history).

The writing assignment, though, frequently surprises them. I ask them to choose one significant detail from the ad and explain at least three ways that detail helps sell a product. One of my favourite inclass training images is a Newport cigarette commercial, popular several years ago, where an attractive black couple sits on a park bench with a saxophone in their laps.

The man holds the base of the sax while he pushes the mouthpiece into his girlfriend's mouth. How does the saxophone sell cigarettes?

The class quickly recognizes that the sax suggests:

- That these Newport smokers have healthy lungs,
- That Newport smokers have cool hobbies.

It's promoting ideals of health and artistic achievement. Eventually, one of the more courageous students brings up the sexual innuendo of the instrument's placement and the couple's apparent affection for each other.

In this context, the slogan, "Alive with Pleasure," begins to take on a different meaning. In their explications, I ask them to connect their interpretations of the detail they choose to other parts of the ad (such as its bold green border, the slogan), their knowledge of cigarette advertising in general, or the role of consumerism in people's lives.

To interpret why the saxophone in the cigarette advertisement is meaningful, the students have to draw on cultural beliefs about health and the environment, music and highbrow culture, and racial and sexual relations. Although this exercise in conceptual exegesis is admittedly simplistic, it prepares them for later assignments which require the interpretation of less propagandistic, non-visual phenomena.

The key to making these exercises work is to focus initially on interpretation rather than on evaluation. Most of the students are pretty comfortable giving three reasons why metal detectors should or shouldn't be used in school, or whether it is ethical for advertisers to use pornography to sell their products.

While not bereft of analytic aspects, the intellectual terrain of these sorts of questions features several well-trod pathways, and the students don't have to think beyond their preconceptions. That sort of exercise leads to dull five-paragraph essays. Initially, I try to keep the students focused on asking what problems mean, rather than asking them for immediate evaluative judgements or counter arguments. What does the decision to ban certain books from high schools say about the students? School administration? City government?

Fictional literature can provide a useful training ground for analysis because it obliges students to articulate the meaning of given passages for themselves. When my classes read a poem or a story, I ask small student groups to choose a passage from the previous night's reading and come up with three explanations why it's important to understanding the rest of the text.

Their job is to explain several different ways a given passage is interesting or meaningful, and they're encouraged to refer to other parts of the text for support, or to connect the scene's importance to any historical or theoretical frameworks they wish. They then teach the rest of the class. To help them visualize what this assignment is asking for, I ask them to imagine that their younger sibling in high school wants to know why those women start hollering when they drive over the creek bed in Sandra Cisneros's short story, "Woman Hollering Creek."

Their response would sound like this: "well, the yelling is important for a few reasons. First, it shows..." I also employ critical readings that supplement the material under discussion and which demonstrate the skill I want them to perform. Although his vocabulary is daunting to most freshman, Cornel West's writing is well suited to a multidisciplinary writing environment.

More important, however, West's style of expression has a clearly defined analytic organization. West's rhetorical strategy almost always focuses on an issue and breaks it down into several significant levels of meaning. For example, in the following passage West describes the ways elite America attempted to ignore minority anger in the wake of the police assault on Rodney King in 1991. I've inserted bracketed numerals into his text to highlight the layers of his analysis:

The major American-elite response to [black rage] was to [11 reduce tragic black persons into pathetic black victims and to redirect the channels of black rage in and to black workingclass and poor communities. The reduction was done by making black poor people clients of a welfare system that both sustained and degraded them; by viewing black middleclass people as questionable and stigmatized beneficiaries of affirmative-action programs that fueled their identity crises; [31 and by rendering black working people.] as nearly nonexistent, even as their standard and quality of living significantly declined.

West is basically saying that privileged America intensified black rage by trying to ignore it. While I'm intrigued by his argument, I find his method of analyzing the problem equally interesting.

His mind works like a razor, dividing larger ideas into finer discriminations of meaning. His last three points are really an elaboration of his first point, the different ways tragic black experience is "reduced"-an analysis within an analysis. Even further, his comment that the welfare system "both sustained and degraded" its clients is a deft tertiary analysis of the paradoxical mechanics of social marginalization and the "reduction" of black experience.

In both his speaking and his writing, West usually advertises the major shifts he makes between levels of interpretation with a first, second, third approach, often performing secondary analyses while working with each point, as I've demonstrated. As even a cursory perusal of his published work shows, the major organizational device of his critical expression-either on the level of chapter organization, paragraphing, or sentence structure-is this type of analytic rhetoric.

For example, in The American Evasion of Philosophy, West's first chapter is organized around identifying three premises of Emerson's brand of pragmatism.

Likewise, the narrative fabric of Race Matters is composed almost entirely of critical analysis. His chapters isolate eight problematic issues in U.S. race relations that he wants to further analyse (affirmative action; shared black and Jewish histories of subjugation and diaspora; views of black sexuality, etc).

Within his chapters, West then attacks each issue with several interpretive insights, usually headed with a first, second, third, fourth style of organization. Given his theological training, it is also no coincidence that West advocates prophetic criticism.

Beyond West's interests in moral vision, prophecy describes the cognitive and rhetorical practice of scholars who systematically produce meaning from the events they study.

Because West's vocabulary is heavy going for non-liberal arts majors, I like to use journalism, student writing, and other types of critical non-fiction in my expository writing classes. Written in accessible language, newspaper editorials and magazine columns are good practical demonstrations of prophecying for students with limited reading skills.

Whenever possible I'll assign a descriptive news chapter, paired with a news analysis or editorial about the same event. The contrast helps students see the difference between description and interpretation, a generic distinction which is new to many novice readers and writers.

Andrew Sullivan, well known for his frank treatment of risque social topics, should be better known for his çlassical analytic technique-his articles offer lively demonstrations of how to set up a controversial fact or problem and then systematically derive several interpretations from it.

Critical histories also work well for introducing students to interpretive analysis. History is an excellent overall genre for collegewide expository writing requirements because of its multidisciplinary content and because it features a huge catalogue of useful rhetorical techniques-description, narration, quotation, and analysis.

For example, a text like Howard Zinn's A People's History of the United States, written in lay English, features a variety of analytic passages, particularly toward the end of his chapters.

In contrast to popularly anthologized historical selections like Barbara Tuchman's account of the black plague, which is gorgeously descriptive but not very analytic, Zinn interprets his facts, he doesn't just describe them.

In choosing course readings, I look for passages where an analysis explicitly takes place on a given page, such as, "The response to unionization was significant for two reasons." I like to contrast these obvious examples with sections where the analysis, though present, is not so clearly manifest.

Surprisingly, however, most students have difficulty identifying obviously analytic passages-they simply have little experience paying attention to those sorts of rhetorical announcements. If they can't see it in someone else's writing, then they probably don't know that they should be doing it in their own. My discovery of student blindness to analytic rhetoric has transformed the goals of my teaching over the past few years.

In negotiation with my students at a wealthy private university where I adjuncted, and where the students are already literate members of what Jeff Smith has called the "overclass", I've used West's Race Matters, John Berger's Ways of Seeing, The New Yorker, the yearly Best American Essays, and Lolita as course readings. (The belletristic choices were at their behest, not mine, but I agreed to readings that I thought I could work with.)

At some point in these texts, the authors often provide an analysis of a person, problem, or idea. I ask students to identify these passages in class. I also ask what kinds of social assumptions seem to have generated a writer's approach to the topic in the first place, which asks the students to look for the contexts of meaning that frame the author's analyses.

Teaching advanced exposition at a wealthy school is very rewarding but I'd like to point out that financially privileged students have generally inherited habits of critical analysis as their birthright.

It's part of what their socio-economic class does-their parents are managers, problem-solvers, and thinkers, not instrumental mechanics and clerks. They hear their parents analyse ideas and interpret problems at the dinner table. It's a form of expression spoken everywhere in their lives and an important means of that class's social and economic advancement.

The challenge in my teaching is to get my less privileged students aware of a skill that they all have but which they never thought about enhancing. One reason why we sometimes identify students as under-prepared is because they have simply been socialized away from analysis by community environments that don't encourage that kind of talk as a useful means of professional success.

FRAMES OF MEANING AND DIVERSITY

The direction that interpretative analysis takes is contingent on the backgrounds and on what I call the frames of meaning of its practitioners. Analysis is not necessarily a bourgeois intellectual skill (exegesis is a fairly universal human practice), but a student educated amidst middleclass ideals of possession, independence, and upward mobility might propose different interpretations of a problem than a member of a different class, sex, or nationality.

In Wayne Booth's recent chapter on ethical teaching, he recommends Gerald Graff's philosophy of harnessing the conflicts between texts of differing value systems for a pedagogical purpose. By playing books off each other, and by asking students to weigh the differing ethical systems existing in a single text, Booth argues that students might come to understand themselves better (50-4). I'm sympathetic to his suggestion that the goal of pedagogy is critical exposure to a variety of points of view rather than indoctrination. Similarly, a writer's analyses are enriched by the extent to which different and surprising frameworks are brought to bear on problem solving.

The incorporation of a diversity of points of view into the pedagogy of the classroom is one way to enhance our students' analytic options. Phyllis van Slyck, employing Mary Louise Pratt's notion of the"contact zone," advocates a classroom where"a variety of world literatures, and the cultures they reflect, are discussed, critiqued, and written about in a thematically coherent context". The yield of van Slyck's proposal in terms of our students' critical awareness is an enlargement of their experiential frameworks-the frames of meaning in which analytic interpretation take place. Van Slyck argues that diversity itself is a key part of developing a critical posture toward the world:

I want my students to acquire the analytic skills that will bring about a reflective, dialogic approach to any given text and to the cultural issues it raises, and I want them to feel that we (all of the members of the class, including the instructor) have shared in the construction and execution of this dialogue. This can be achieved only if I identify myself, like everyone else, as an individual speaking from a specific subject position and as someone who does not have all the answers. The repositioning suggested by this model requires a constant vigilance about one's own belief systems; that is, we all need to become decentered subjects.

One needn't be a card-carrying decentered subject to admire van Slyck's pedagogical goals. When van Slyck associates dialogue with analysis, she's basically defending a Socratic tradition of education.

By putting a number of cultural perspectives in dialogue, van Slyck suggests that her students will develop a more critical eye. Although I am skeptical of the idea that the promotion of some innocuous ideal of cultural diversity is the best or only way of enhancing our students' critical capacities (and I don't think van Slyck is saying that), a dialogic classroom environment encourages active learning habits from students and places their own critical consciousness at the centre of their own educations.

One textbook that admirably exploits the critical potential for such cross-reading practices, and which balances analytic writing selections with other genres, is David Bartholomae and Anthony Petrosky's Ways of Reading. (Like Rosenwasser and Stephen's Writing Analytically, however, this text demands a very high initial level of reading and writing proficiency).

For these reasons, creative writing can enhance our student's critical awareness-personal essays, fiction, and other genres of purportedly non-analytic writing can provide students with new frameworks with which to make meaning. Exposure to a variety of cultural and intellectual frameworks is, after all, the rationale behind most composition anthologies from the 1960s to the present.

The key, however, is in teaching habits of analytic exposition in the first place. The problem with the canon of essays by George Orwell, E.B. White, Joan Didion, and Maya Angelou is that they show more than they tell. Or rather, their telling is gracefully covered up, suggested, or implied. As

Peter Elbow has observed, autobiographies and other types of expressive writing are often filled with analysis, but the university curriculum rarely asks students to conduct analysis through these genres of belletristic writing (it's also very hard to do). No wonder our students are puzzled by the disjunction between course readings and academic writing assignments. While I'm fond of the idea that university writing requirements loosen up to allow a variety of expressive genres, I also expect the university system to produce critical thinkers who are able to explain why something is important or dangerous. That's a skill rooted in interpretive explanation, not just the rendering of experience.

ANALYTIC LITERACY AND THE FUTURE

In the preceding section, I've tried to suggest the value of using allegedly non-analytic genres in the classroom and to acknowledge the complex cultural backgrounds that shape the direction that an interpretive analysis takes. Analysis can't be taught without the simultaneous introduction of cultural beliefs and practices that generate the purpose of an interpretation.

For instance, a student unfamiliar with neo-Marxist philosophy probably won't be inclined to grasp the significance of some kinds of class conflicts. Patricia Bizzell, among others, has pointed out basic materials of cultural literacy that create the most rudimentary frameworks for interpretive writing, such as knowledge of Bible stories and commonly recognized patterns in Western history. But multicultural literacy is far from an answer in itself.

Cultural literacy, understood as an archive of facts and beliefs, is relative, and all of our students already have well-developed frames of meaning with which to perform their own analyses. Surely, part of the business of the university system is to expand those frames of meaning, but more importantly, its business should be emphasizing the cognitive practice of interpretation itself. The most important cultural literacy is not the acquisition of facts and beliefs, but rather, the habit of interpreting them.

In reference to my opening comments about religious exegetical practice, I'd like to return to the most commonly understood definition of the word, prophecy. Prophecy, whether it derives from the reading of stars, cat entrails, sacred texts, or court rulings, is an attempt to change the future through compelling interpretation. It's a creative act that explicitly assaults the bounds of knowledge by bringing different frames of meaning to bear on facts. In other words, prophecy is an academic genre that changes the world. As Stanley Aronowitz has recently argued, if we want our colleges to be something other than fancy trade schools to supply yesterday's intellectual machinery, we need to encourage students to think transgressively and to challenge professional authority.

The critical interpretation of authority and fact is how the future is changed. By advocating greater attention to interpretive analysis in our writing classrooms, I'm not suggesting that we train our students to write like clerical pedants. Rather, as my epigraph suggests, I'm asking that we help them"find sermons in the most unpromising texts." After all, it's the very least we expect from each other as public thinkers and writers.

During the 1990s we taught, both singly and together, a place-writing class at Humboldt State University (HSU) that focused either on California's North Coast or on the Trinity Corridor that connects Redding with Arcata and Eureka. Several of our students published revised versions of their papers in the Humboldt Historian; scores more participated in the production of Traveling the Trinity Highway (2000). That 250-page guidebook is a portrait, in pictures and prose, of a trinity of Trinities--the river, the mountains, and the 140-mile road that ties together a dozen small towns divided among three counties. Our decade-long collaboration has convinced us that fieldwork and archival research are equally essential to the perusal and portrayal of place.

This conclusion will leave veteran place writers unsurprised, but many geography departments, including HSU'S, teach the two kinds of methodologies as separate courses, as if they had no common bond. We do not mean to question the validity of such a division, but, based on our experience in preparing a guide to the Trinity National Scenic Byway, we would strongly recommend a place-writing class as a practical medium for integrating the two approaches.

The primary purpose of this chapter is to demonstrate the utility of combining them. At the same time, we draw from a rich fund of Trinity field reflections to illustrate the kinds of methods used to highlight the places portrayed in the book. In trying to make topographers, or place biographers, out of budding topophiles, we wanted students not only to probe a specific locale but also learn how to identify and interpret the quintessential qualities of any small area.

We sought, in other words, to develop place perusal as a skill integral to the art of place portrayal. From the outset we encouraged class members, not all of whom were geography majors, to employ the methods of other disciplines; we also emphasized geography's role as a synthesizer of multiple approaches to fathoming the myriad facets of place.

Students developed a close relationship with their chosen place in a variety of ways. We had them visit the site, walk its streets and trails, probe its plant life and watch its wildlife, locate and interview knowledgeable locals, discover pertinent documents and artifacts, and, in general, try to absorb the site's genius loci and thereby bond with it. We devised no set formula for familiarizing students with a given place, but we did discuss strategies with them and organized at least one exploratory field trip. We also had the class sample the place-writing methods and styles of such prominent American authors as Page and Wallace Stegner.

Eventually we blended the elements of our approach most effectively in a one-day excursion to the Table Bluff area, which embraces a set of historic sites some 20 miles south of the HSU campus. To prepare participants for the trip, we gave them a handout on ways to study place and a packet of maps, photographs, and news clippings of the region. A university bus took us to the locations of two abandoned towns, the remnants of an old port and a defunct railroad, and an aging cemetery. We also stopped at a century-old cider works in Fortuna, a family dairy on the Eel River Bottom at milking time, and a cheese factory in Loleta.

After a lunch stop in Loleta we set the students loose on a "Place Chase." We divided them into teams of two or three and asked them to solve ten riddles, each describing a feature of the community.

For instance, "From what corner bay can you look toward the whey?" and "330 looks mighty handsome gilding which building's transom?" We monitored the progress of the chase and offered hints to help solve the more difficult riddles. After correcting the teams' collective answers, we awarded Jerry's guidebooks to the group with the highest score. Later in the day the dairy treated each of us to a dish of the local Humboldt Creamery's premium ice cream—which rivals any produced by Ben & Jerry's!

The overriding lesson students learned from the chase was that the story of any place is indeed a riddle, a mystery awaiting solution. Such riddles belie passivity, challenging would-be place detectives to involvement—walking, touching, looking, puzzling, talking, and at last, if all goes well, understanding.

All places, even the so-called nondescript ones, are living entities, communities of buildings and beings, plants and perspectives, that can only be apprehended by becoming, for a time, part of them. The written accounts resulting from this experience echo what has resonated with the perceivers, who then present them to the public. When presented clearly, with appropriate visuals and vignettes added to the text, place can become poetry.

We shall illustrate many of the methods used to illuminate the Trinity Highway by roughly following the guidebook's east—west sequence and by quoting freely from it. In our "Bird's-Eye View of a Serpentine Highway" we spotlight the road's history, the region's indigenous inhabitants, its varicolored vegetation, wondrous river, and geologic knots and mining nodes.

Except for the section on fishing the Trinity, which tapped the expertise of a student angler, we relied heavily on jaunts into the pages of aging newspapers, scholarly journals, and old correspondence that brought to life long-silent voices. The ethnographic work of C.

Hart Merriam and John P. Harrington yielded intriguing accounts of the tiny Indian tribes that inhabited the middle reaches of the Trinity River. The little-known Tlohomtahhois' last surviving member, Saxey Kidd, provided Merriam with a few dozen words of his native tongue, all he could recall after not having spoken it for fifty years.

In the chapter covering the Trinity Highway section of Shasta County, we found an excuse to create a Place Chase for our readers. Old Shasta, the first county seat, became a state historic park in 1950 after decades of decline related to the rise of Redding.

Because both the park and the Shasta Historical Society had already produced detailed guides to the area, we saw no reason to prepare yet another one for "Sweet Shasta Town," which so enraptured Joaquin Miller, the young gold seeker who gained later fame, if no greater a fortune, as a poet. Instead, we decided to test park visitors by asking them, for example, "Which of the historic buildings looks most out of place, as if it doesn't belong in Old Shasta?" Or "Which site was most likely operated in 1870 by a German named Simon Maltzer?"

To give readers a sense of what Shasta was like in its prime (1850s-1860s), we compared the data recorded in the 1870 census with the town's first plat map, an 1870 compilation by Colonel Magee. Workers in the diverse occupations that supported mining outnumbered individuals listed as miners. The surveyor's map excluded the "colored" population, even the few Chinese who owned property, just as the whites barred nonwhites from Fourth of July celebrations.

Small towns such as Old Shasta and French Gulch proved much easier to represent than the much larger gateway cities located at either end of the Trinity Highway. Eureka and

Arcata, at the western end, have at least retained well-defined centers in the form of an Old Town and a plaza, respectively. But Redding, with 80,000 residents spread far in every direction, has lost the central focus it once had.

A century ago, as a town founded by the California & Oregon Railroad, the city centered itself squarely on the depot between North, East, South, and West Streets.

Our guidebook included an 1890 map of Redding that shows California and Oregon Streets flanking Centre Street (and the depot) and a series of roads named and ordered, from south to north, after six California counties: Sacramento, Placer, Yuba, Butte, Tehama, and Shasta.

Our "Primer for Reading Redding" explains the town's capitalizing on its situation at the head of the Central Valley to overcome its negative site, eventually transforming itself from "Poverty Flat" into a gateway city.

With the advent of the automobile, it turned away from the depot and adopted distant Mount Shasta as an icon. Redding's logo, boldly displayed both inside and outside the new City Hall, incorporates "imperial" Mount Shasta plus Shasta Lake and Shasta Dam.

The primer also answers the question, "What's in a Place Name?" by pairing two toponyms often confused because they are pronounced identically (as in red): Redding, named after the railroad company's general land agent, and Reading, which honors the pioneer who triggered the 1848 Trinity gold rush. In central but remote Trinity County we ran head-on into the difficulty of sifting fact from fancy. A perceptive student sensed that little Weaverville, the county's still-unincorporated seat, had a surprising density of history buffs, one of whom carried an "I collect facts" business card. Her facts, however, did not always agree with those collected by other local historians. One of the student's sources advised him that "History here is not an exercise in collecting facts. Legends, fanciful tales, and less-than-factual memories embellish much of the oral and written history of this region."

In tilling the Trinity's "tailings" of fact and fancy, we faced the challenge of checking both oral and written histories against documents found in the courthouse and the county historical society's splendid History Centre.

Of the numberless interviews we conducted, a morning-long trip through the little-known but historically important Indian Creek area with Harold Rodgers proved particularly informative. A near-octogenarian member of the region's once substantial Portuguese community, Harold detailed the significance of numerous sites, some of which bore remnants of earlier activities and others of which contained clues evident only in his mind.

He was likely the sole remaining Indian Creeker who could point out the location of the rock-and-corrugated-metal dwelling of "Injun-Chinaman," who suffered the torments of local youngsters only to reward each of them at Christmas with a brightly wrapped gift.

Harold passed away not long after the excursion, but, thanks to the information he provided, some of the region's story survives in our book as a "Backcountry Byway" section.

Since the 1960s the Trinity County Historical Society has created a remarkable museum complex. It also published a guide to Trinity County Historic Sites, Flowers and Trees of the Trinity Alps, and a "Walking Tour of Historic Weaverville" that would exhaust anyone who set out in just one day to see the 116 places listed.

Apart from the Chinese Joss House and a few other sites, most buildings have little architectural distinction, partly because, as a forty-niner pointed out, "The fact is nobody is poor here and nobody very rich....

When a man 'makes a raise' as we call getting from ten to forty thousand dollars..., he takes it and leaves". Almost all of the residents, therefore, built their homes and businesses along simple and similar lines. For our "Weaving across Weaverville" tour, we thus chose sites based mostly on colorful anecdotes related to those who owned or occupied the buildings. For an earlier section of the "Basins Wedged between Mountains" chapter, we featured the "fast feats" of William S. Lowden, Trinity County's best-known road builder and surveyor, who first gained fame as an express rider.

The Weaverville tour includes his home and office, built in the 1890s in a modest vernacular style that characterized much of the town he platted by metes and bounds in 1876.

We inserted an old photograph of his place so that readers could see how much or little the Mill Street site had changed since his time.

A century ago the La Grange Mine, located a few miles west of Highway 299's Oregon Mountain Summit, ranked as the world's largest hydraulic mining operation. Travelers today see little more than a water-powered nozzle and a rock plaque in rusty decay by the roadside.

How, we wondered, could we convert the weathered monument into an essay that might capture the magnitude of la grande La Grange? We feared having to settle for a summary of the geographical extent and historical import of the mine, but serendipity—every writer's indispensable ally—enabled us to enhance our account with From the Known to the Unknown: Memoirs of Baroness de La Grange (2000).

In January 1998 the baroness's grandson donated the memoirs to the Trinity County Historical Society, along with an album of faded photographs of the La Grange Ditch, which brought water 29 miles from the Trinity Alps to Oregon Gulch.

The three nozzles, or "monitors," at the La Grange Mine, the baroness observed in 1894, "sit like big cannons that haven't been loaded yet, aimed at the bedrock." They "are outdoing each other, and the mountain is crumbling and collapsing into a stream of liquid mud that is channeled into the long corridor of the sluice."

She rightly feared that "a little settlement at the bottom of Oregon Gulch runs the risk of being buried when we run our operation full-scale".

Less than a decade later a leading California botanist named Alice Eastwood complained about her party's midsummer climb over Oregon Mountain, which "was hot and dusty beyond any place we had passed" since leaving Redding. They found relief only after reaching "the fresh green trees and shrubs" of Canyon Creek in the nearby Trinity

Alps. En route to the lakes at the head of the canyon, they "passed a lonely cabin in which some old miner lived." To Eastwood, such miners "seemed like the driftwood of humanity left behind on the great tide that swept over the country in the days of '49. They were chatty and liked to talk of olden times".

If only Jerry and his wife, Gisela, could have interviewed such "driftwood" for our Trinity book! Fortunately, they did find Eastwood's account of her plant-finding trip and used it to enliven their own description of mining and botanic sites scattered along the road and trail of ore-rich Canyon Creek.

They were pleased to find her list of more than 100 "rare and lovely flowers" that "ranged through this beautiful canon" remarkably current. Jerry even sighted such elusive specimens as the "step flower" Lewisia cotyledon and the naked broom-rape when Gisela sent him climbing up to a rocky bank above the road.

Where Canyon Creek joins the Trinity, a mining town named Junction City arose to replace, in effect, the nearby Oregon Gulch village buried by debris washed down from the La Grange Mine. With a Compagnie Francaise mine operating on the other side of the Trinity, Junction City became "the liveliest town in the county" by 1895.

The lunar landscape left by the Compagnie Francaise monitors has been transformed during the past decade by a new kind of enterprise. One student spent several days there at the Rigdzin Ling Buddhist conference and meditation centre and then combined the information gleaned from observations and interviews with her reading of the history of the Compagnie Francaise to contrast the present "mindscape" with the past "minescape".

The same student who provided "A New Angle on Fishing the Trinity" also produced a paper about "Raging Times on the Trinity Rapids". Fishing and rafting the river became his passions at an early age, and his HSU—employed parents allowed him to pursue those passions.

Somehow they also nurtured his flair for writing. Alex Fulton's lead sentence (and entire essay) needed little editing on our part: "As our sky-blue river raft floated across the placid green water, I sensed a calm before a storm".

The thirteen maps drafted for Traveling the Trinity Highway by students in KOSMOS, HSU's new computer cartography laboratory, serve to orient readers to each of six regional chapters and to guide them on tours of seven towns. We include historic maps in the book and urge students to use them and other "geographics" as a focus for their writing.

Through perusing maps dating from the 1860s, 1890s, 1920s, and 1950s we managed to reconstruct the series of trails, stagecoach roads, and highways built to traverse the Trinity corridor. Scanning old newspapers, we learned of the U.S. Forest Service's pivotal role in road building.

One official averred in 1913 that "Nothing would create favour for the United States Forest Service as much as this project"—forging a road through the Trinity Gorge. It took a full decade to complete the final stretch of Highway 299, which connected the Trinity's North and South forks. Even then, travel time by automobile from Redding to Arcata approximated tw elve hours, as opposed to three or four today.

We also compared past charts of the corridor with contemporary versions to help fix the locations of vanished or obscured activity, to learn alternative place-names, and to make sense of topographical references in historical records. "Negro Joe Ridge", a grassy, oak-fringed hillside in the Redwood Creek watershed, was finally determined to relate not to anyone named Joe but to an ex-slave named Leroy Watkins, who was attacked in the vicinity by two relatives of his Indian wife. Despite suffering a chest wound, Leroy dispatched the ambushing duo and promptly "divorced" Mrs. Watkins.

A 1902 pictorial map of Eureka seemed a fitting focus, "Up and Down to Old Town." As the map makes clear, the city hosted an array of bustling bayside businesses. Research in the library further revealed that Eureka must have had a lively nightlife, with some sixty-five saloons, an even larger number of "gambling dens," and thirty-two "houses of shame." "Whiskey Specials" transported hundreds of "freshly scrubbed, bear-greased" loggers from surrounding lumber camps every Saturday night. Today's much tamer Victorian Old Town draws a large but quieter nighttime crowd only once a month when it stages "Arts Alive!"

Numerous lunchtime strolls through Old Town Eureka led to the eventual selection of a score of sites for the walking tour that concludes the book. Interesting architecture and artifacts claimed our attention, along with less visible locations that held a more hidden significance. Even after months of preparation, this section underwent a last-hour change when we found archival confirmation that the old Oberon Saloon, its name still proclaimed on the tiled entrance, was indeed the scene of an epic fistfight between the author Jack London and the brother of a local mill owner.

As place detectives, our Trinity team took special pleasure in finding something new about old sites and in describing and explaining them in fresh terms. No place proved more difficult in both respects than the gargantuan, green-hued Carson Mansion at the eastern end of Eureka's "Two Street," which any walking tour of Old Town must include. We described its eclectic style as "Vainglorious Victorian" and pointed out the irony that the mill owner who made his fortune cutting redwoods built his cathedral of "Gothic gloom and Baroque exuberance" out of woods gathered from around the world.

Any success we had in portraying familiar places with fresh perspectives resulted from combining neglected records with careful fieldwork and from presenting our findings in readable and visually appealing fashion. Putting Trinity Highway places in their geographical and historical context has given our students and us the opportunity to apply most of our skills in writing a book for a broad audience of travelers, residents, and scholars.

Chapter 2

From Aesthetics to Liminality

Much has happened in the nearly forty years since Walter Benjamin first published his famous essay known in English as "The Work of Art in the Age of Mechanical Reproduction," in which he argued that techniques of mass production and the new media of photography and the cinema had destroyed the "sacred aura" formerly associated with unique, hand-crafted masterpieces of art.

While subsequent developments such as the proliferation of consumerism and the invention of television have mostly confirmed Benjamin's thesis, the "digital revolution" in information and telecommunications technology, which has reached spectacular (in the Debordian sense) new heights with the popularization of the Internet and the opening up of a "new frontier" in cyberspace, has created a whole new set of challenges for art and literature that go beyond anything Benjamin ever anticipated.

In the wake of this revolution, the boundaries between different media and disciplines have disintegrated; the usual distinctions that are made between the role of the author and that of the spectator/reader no longer apply in the case of mutating works that are electronically "co-produced" (Pierre Moeglin) by a legion of "spectactors" (Rejean Dumouchel); and the basic unit of art, the work/text, has been stretched so thin that it virtually vanishes—or vanishes into virtuality.

Indeed, one could well assert that it is now the work of art's aura of reality that is being destroyed. Since going online, artists have tended to respond to the Internet in three different ways. The most common response has been to exploit the interactive potential and democratic ethos of what is chiefly seen as a new public forum for art. Major examples of this tendency include Douglas Davis's "The World's First Collaborative Sentence" and "Metabody: The World's First Collaborative Visions of Beauty" and the creation of online art collectives such as the now-defunct ada'web.

The second response has been to exploit the technical parameters of the Internet itself for the purpose of creating a new self-referential, web-specific genre of art.

This is the orientation of the growing number of artist-designed Web browsers, which may have practical applications or purely aesthetic ones like Mark Napier's collage producing Website "Shredder" or Entropy Zuper's URL-driven "Eden Garden".

For a smaller number of artists with a long-standing interest in telecommunications, electronic media, and cybernetics, a third response has been to treat the Internet as a new experimental tool at the juncture of art and science, to be used to gauge the effects that such technologies have on the way human beings live and think. Noteworthy examples of this tendency include Roy Ascott, one of the earliest proponents of telematic art; Eduardo Kac, whose protean career has touched upon themes ranging from teleporting to biotelematics; and Stelarc, whose provocative meditations on the relationship between the body and technology have included works such as "ParaSite" and "Evolving URL Body".

One of the clearest statements of the "epistemological" mission of online art is to be found in Forest's 1998 book Pour un art actuel: L'art a l'heure d'Internet:

Artistic practice finds itself taking on an exploratory role that involves a special kind of research touching upon our self-awareness. [...] This evolution leads art to define itself an enterprise of knowledge, albeit one of a different nature that which is specific to the field of science. [...] The artistic approach still attaches primary importance to emotional, symbolic, existential, ethical, and aesthetic issues: the need for meanin. [...] For the sake of clarifying this distinction, we will say t art takes shortcuts designed to place the subject in configurs and situations that lead him to experience alternative forms sensorial and mental adaptation.

In effect, many of Forest's online works take the form of simple experiments designed to get people to gauge the effect that technologies like the Internet have on certain basic parameters of human perception such as time, space, and the body. However, Forest's most original contributions to online art are to be found in a series of elaborate online rituals that reflect a distinctly utopian outlook.

This does not mean that these performances are lyrical glorifications of the Internet. Instead, they are construed as public exercises in "anthropological projection" that are supposed to lead to the conception of alternative modes of relation to time, space, and community in the "hyper-technological" environment.

Such works call to mind the cultural anthropologist Victor Turner's theory of liminality in public performance. Derived from the Latin word for threshold, liminality refers to a shared sense of being on the threshold of a new reality that occurs in certain instances of ritual, festivity, and other forms of public performance predicated on the temporary suspension of existing cultural norms and the state of playful improvisation that ensues.

There is something like a liminal element in many of Forest's works; however, this element is the strongest in Forest's projects for the annual French Internet Festival, or Fete de l'Internet, which is a bona fide nationwide public celebration that takes place both in the city and online. Forest's approach to online art has been shaped by over three decades of work in the field of media and communication art.

After a brief career as an abstract painter and an illustrator for leftist publications in France, Forest "stopped doing art" (i.e., working with plastic media) in 1969 and began experimenting with video and performance.

From that point on, his career was to pass through two major phases. First came a period of Sociological Art in the 1970s that culminated in his collaboration with Herve Fischer and Jean-Paul Thenot in the framework of the Collectif d'Art

Sociologique. Confirming his rejection of the prevailing practices of contemporary art, which he judged a sterile reflection of a materialist society's cult of objects in the case of painting and sculpture, and too elitist to have true social relevance in the case of conceptual art, Forest asserted that Sociological Art was not really art at all but a form of "sociological praxis" that simply used art as a "pretense" or "cover" ("Reflections" 33).

Making regular use of "non-artistic" media such as video, the press, radio, and television, Forest and his partners staged a series of public happenings conceived as direct interventions in the social reality of ordinary people.

The double goal of these "actions," as the happenings were called, was to put people in a position to observe the subtle forces of social control at work in their lives and to offer them opportunities for dialogical communication where it is normally excluded.

One of Forest's own favourite methods of sociological praxis was the introduction of provocative "parasitical messages," or non-messages, designed to disrupt the normal operation of the mass media and to temporarily reverse the one-way flow of information that is the basis of their power. Forest made use of this technique in his 1972 "Space-Media" project.

One component of this multifaceted project involved the publication of a small blank space in the prestigious Parisian daily Le Monde bearing the caption "Titre de l'oeuvre: de papier journal'".

Readers were invited to fill in the space with opinions, creative writing, and artwork of their own and then to cut out and return their contributions to Forest, who later included selections of them in several public exhibitions.

Forest also used the mass media to create "information works," which were designed to expose and ridicule other forms of institutional power, including the art establishment. One such work, created in 1977, began with advertisements in Le Monde and several other publications announcing a public auction at which "artistic square metres" of land—

sections of a small plot Forest had purchased near the Franco-Swiss border—were to be sold.

When authorities made Forest the subject of a real-estate fraud investigation and intervened to stop the sale, he instead auctioned off a "non-artistic" square metre of cloth. This last-minute change of tactics and terminology did not prevent the operation from being a success to the extent that it had already generated a lot of press coverage—indeed, the press coverage was the work—and had allowed Forest to raise questions about prevailing definitions of art, the speculative practices of the art market, and the role that publicity plays in determining a work's worth.

Blank spaces and square metres were to become personal emblems for Forest. This particular emphasis culminated in 1980 when he proclaimed his rural estate in Anserville (near Paris) an "independent state": "Le Territoire du"). The Territory served as the home base of an artistic and political farce in which members of the public were invited to participate.

In particular, they could become "citizens" of the Territory by purchasing a subscription to a square-metre section of the grounds, which entitled them to receive special communiques from the "Artist-President," participate in "public works" projects, and attend events held in the Territory.

Sociological Art was the source of a number of elements that were to become enduring features of Forest's work: his quasi-scientific approach to art in general, his rejection of material artworks in favour of communicational events that are "directly connected" to the social fabric, his playful use of the mass media (an ironic combination of subversion and self-promotion), and his emphasis on reclaiming the abstract space of communication for utopian ventures. Still, major changes in his outlook occurred in the 1980s.

In the first place, he had become more aware of the limitations of the May 68-ish rhetoric of direct action that underpinned the projects of Sociological Art. One could also say that he came to the realization that Sociological Art was in fact the opposite of what it claimed to be: that is, it was really art that used sociological praxis as a pretense.

Perhaps, as a result of this insight, Forest began to reincorporate an explicitly aesthetic dimension in his practice of media art while maintaining his earlier emphasis on social relevance. He also started to shift his attention from the ideological ramifications of the non-interactive mass media to the environmental properties of communications systems that were interactive by nature.

In 1984, Forest and Mario Costa, an Italian academic and critic, founded a new movement of artists and intellectuals with a common interest in the aesthetic ramifications of modern technologies of communication: Le Groupe International de l'Esthetique de la Communication.

The movement saw itself as filling a void in contemporary art, which had dealt with some of the social and cultural ramifications of the modern information and telecommunications revolution (as did Sociological Art), but had largely ignored the effects that the technologies behind this revolution had on sensory experience and perception, which constitute the original (i.e., etymological) preoccupations of "aesthetics," which is derived from the Greek words aisthanesthai, 'to perceive,' and aisthetikos, 'sensitive.' In the Groupe's manifesto ("Manifeste pour une esthetique de la communication" ["For an Aesthetics of Communication"]), which he wrote, Forest described these effects as three-fold.

In the first place, the new technologies vastly extended the range of our dominant senses of sight and sound. In the process, they carried us into "strange new realms of space and time," like ubiquity and real-time, in which our traditional paradigms of perception were contradicted. In the second place, they added a whole new dimension of reality to human experience: a virtual environment of communication that had been "dredged from the void" by technology like so much "reclaimed land from the sea".

A hybrid phenomenon that is partly a mental projection, this environment nonetheless has a sensory reality of its own in the form of various micro-milieus of human interaction with, and through, electronic media that produce a full range of unprecedented sensory stimuli, including many forms that are only accessible to our faculties of proprioception. Finally, these technologies had a profound effect on human sensibility insofar as they contributed to the development of a more holistic and dynamic view of the world as a nexus of data in constant flux.

For Forest and the other members of the Aesthetics of Communication movement, it was clear that a conventional form of art based on physical objects and visual imagery was ill-suited to deal with such a virtual environment, in which everyday experience was dematerialized, sight was superceded by electronic means of "capturing" reality, and electric signals traced "invisible, blazing and magical configurations" in the sky above our heads.

In the manifesto, Forest outlined a new theory of art as a form of "metacommunication" that still forms the basis for his current experiments in online art. Metacommuni-cational art is not necessarily devoid of imagery, but its goal is in no way to provide objects for contemplation or otherwise offer the artist's "vision" of reality.

Working as an "information architect", the artist comes up with the concept of an interactive micro-environment that will enable people to hone their perception of certain salient features of the larger technological milieu but leaves them free to draw their own conclusions.

The "finished" work is ultimately an intangible "intersubjective" event. In other words, it does not reside in some unique combination of matter and form realized by the artist (or the public); it emerges from the self-conscious interaction with the technological milieu, and other people, that takes place in the framework of the experimental environment devised by the artist.

The metacommunicational status of these works of art depends on two additional factors. In the first place, the artist subjects the different means of communication employed in a given work to a process of defamiliarization: media are "deviated" from their normal uses, specific fields of communication are "destabilized," and the signals of the dominant social discourses are "jammed." The goal is to create "plausible states of uncertainty" in the minds of the users, to force them to look beyond what they normally expect to find, and to oblige them to make their own sense out of what they experience in the environment of the work.

This resembles somewhat Forest's practice of Sociological Art; however, whereas Sociological Art used the existing mass media and pointedly left open the possibility of meaningful communication taking place, his practice of the Aesthetics of Communication generally entailed the creation of his own hybrid multimedia configurations having no practical use beyond the temporary context of a given artistic project and attached no more than secondary importance to any messages that might actually be conveyed because, as Marshall McLuhan might put it, the message could distract attention from the medium.

In the second place, the metacommunicational artwork has certain spiritual connotations. In the manifesto, Forest likened the use of new technologies of communication to Zen because of their similar capacity to dissolve our conventional ways of thinking, prolong our senses, heighten our awareness of the present, and renew our relationship to everything that makes up reality: time, space, matter, for example. The artistic, metacommunicational use of these technologies that Forest envisioned in the manifesto is thus meant to accentuate these meditation-like effects. According to Forest, the ultimate goal of the Aesthetics of Communication is to sharpen the vague feeling we are all thought to have of being "part of a global beat made up of an infinite number of distinct little rhythms".

Some of the works created in the spirit of the Aesthetics of Communication have all the apparent simplicity and fascination with gadgetry of high school science fair experiments. A 1992 installation piece called "Le robinet telephonique" ("Telephonic Faucet") provides a good example of this type of work. The premise was to use long-distance telephone calls to fill an empty bucket with water.

By dialing a special number at the "Telephonic Faucet" exhibit in Turin, people as far away as Paris and San Francisco could trigger a switch turning on the faucet, which would automatically spew a small quantity of water into the bucket. It was a simple trick, but one that worked on several different levels—as an ironic illustration of how information "flows" through the telecommunications network, as a gratuitous example of the compression of time and space in the technological environment, and as a subtle reminder of the increased interconnectedness and interdependence of the inhabitants of the global village.

Other works were more like technological versions of the koans, or riddles, used by Zen masters to elicit sudden flashes of insight into the "immanent facts" of our worldly existence. A good example of this type of work is "Intervention immediate," an absurdist media performance in 1983 that played with several registers of space and time and different degrees of presence and absence.

On closed-circuit television monitors installed in the gallery where the event took place, spectators could see a live video of Forest in a nearby telephone booth.

The performance began when Forest called the number of a telephone also placed in view of the public at the gallery. After having chatted with the artist for a few minutes, an assistant placed the receiver next to a tape recorder, which he then turned on.

The tape was a recording of a "phantom" Forest asking a series of questions about mortality that the "live" Forest was to answer. One of the points of the points of the exercise was to break through the trivializing effect of our too-willing acceptance of the reality and naturalness of phenomena like ubiquity and real-time interaction in telecommunicational contexts.

To avoid creating an illusion that would have been too believable, the answers provided were completely out of sync with the questions that preceded them. For example, when asked about his own inevitable death, the "live" Forest answered by giving his favourite cooking recipes.

The most ambitious works from this period in Forest's career involved setting up makeshift communications networks of his own for use in subversive "transmedia events" with broad public participation. A good example of this type of work is his 1984 happening "Apprenez a regarder la television avec votre radio", for which the artist enlisted the help of ten independent FM radio stations, which offered three hours of live broadcasts to accompany the television viewing of the listeners.

Journalists, critics, and other invited guests instructed them to change channels and operate the other controls on their television sets and commented the stream of images on the screen—something the listeners were also invited to do by calling the radio stations. Aside from offering a critical and ironic perspective on the content of the programs and turning a passive medium into an interactive one, the metacommunicational use of radio added a layer of self-conscious immediacy to the aura of "distant presence" associated with television and created a new sense of complicity among individuals otherwise subjected to the personal isolation and social fragmentation inherent to a society of spectacle.

It is easy to see why the Internet would be of such great interest to someone with Forest's background. The many different multimedia combinations to which it lends itself, its association with the quasi-mythical concept of cyberspace, and the challenges it poses to traditional paradigms of perception all contribute to making it an idseal vehicle for testing the methodology of the Aesthetics of Communication; whereas its interactive potential and the speed with which it has become part of the social fabric correspond to the preoccupations of Sociological Art. Indeed, quite a few of Forest's online projects are reminiscent of earlier works in terms of both technique and theme.

One of his earliest online art projects, undertaken in 1996, involved the creation of a Web version of his "Territory." On the project Website, the history of the Territory provided the ironic premise for a series of interwoven texts and images:

private snapshots, archival material from Forest's earlier works, for example.

Visitors to the site could take a self-guided tour of Forest's (e)state/life/career by either clicking on the "forward" and "back" buttons, or by wandering about the labyrinthine Website in haphazard fashion, creating their own personal versions of his (e)state/life/career by clicking on the hypertext links in the texts.

In the end, the second option was perhaps more faithful to the way Forest's own memory probably functions, not to mention how anybody inhabits the virtual space that is his life by weaving an invisible web that ties together various places, events, words, images, people, and possessions. The work also underscores the fact that territorial borders are not natural entities but mental and cultural constructs. Given this fact, it suggests that any challenge to the territorial status quo that the Internet represents, as disorienting as it may be, cannot be taken as a sign of the waning of the real in the face of the rising tide of the virtual; it can only be seen as a further inflection of something that is already virtual.

A whimsical metacommunicational gadget not unlike like "Telephonic Faucet," Forest's 1998 project "La machine a travailler le temps" ("Time Treatment Machine") involved an online chronometric device that visitors could operate by clicking an accelerator or brake button. Each user of the device had to contend with all the others working its controls at any given moment. In the end, the speed of time displayed by the chronometer was the variable average, continuously recalculated in real-time, of all concurrent efforts to speed it up or slow it down. The work thus demonstrated that the effect that technology had on the perception of time and other basic elements of human experience was neither direct nor natural insofar as the use of technology is itself a function of competing social forces.

In 2001, Forest once again used his signature square-metre concept in a work created during his term as artist in residence in the Paris suburb of Fresnes: "Sorties de territoires" ("Territorial Outings"). He placed a grid of "artistic" square metres on the floor just outside the checkout area of a large chain store. A Web camera was installed so that the feet of the shoppers who walked across the grid would appear live on the project's Website.

This work lends itself to a number of different interpretations. Its stated objective was to claim the Internet for ordinary people the way Neil Armstrong had claimed the moon for "mankind," by leaving a symbolic footprint on its surface.

Visitors to the Website could take part in the operation by sending the scanned outlines of their own feet to a special email address. On a subtler level, by combining square metres of cyberspace on the floor of a bricks-and-mortar store with shoppers' feet on the Internet, the work symbolized the yin-and-yang-like interpenetration of cyberspace and the "real" world that is an immanent fact of existence in the age of information.

Finally, the work suggested that there were certain similarities between cyberspace, the drab suburban landscape, and the marketplace in a society of conspicuous consumption: each needed art and other forms of creative trespassing if it was to be more than a postmodern "no man's land."

Forest had these social ramifications in mind when he wrote Pour un art actuel, in which he urges his fellow artists to construe their online works as nonconformist experiments in alternative forms of time, space, and community. For example, he suggests that they could devise events that reverse the tendency to accelerate the speed of exchange, which is how electronic capitalism would have us use the Internet.

Such events would result in temporary, convivial reconfigurations of time that would allow people to fully inhabit the present instead of constantly running themselves ragged in a futile effort to avoid running out of time. He also suggests that they could invent new forms of travel to compensate for the abolition of the "poetry of space" caused by the extensive use of telecommunications and ever faster modes of transportation. Finally, as an antidote to "the machine-like solitude that threatens us", he proposes that artists experiment with procedures designed to bring different types of virtual communities into being.

Forest asserts that Web-based art is ideally suited to these types of utopian projects because it places people in an artificial environment without preconceived models, traditions, or fixed points of reference: "By placing the protagonists outside the bounds of social convention, it gives rise to 'temporary' populations, chains of spectator-actors united by the network". Although virtual communities already proliferate in cyberspace, Forest believes that it is the artist's mission to give them a more ceremonial quality in the form of online "rituals of communion" imbued with a certain sense of "religiosity."

While this position could be considered the endorsement of a limited restitution of the lost sacred aura of art, it has little to do with the fetishistic sacredness of the contemplated masterpiece that Benjamin criticized, and even less to do with organized religion. Forest says himself to be influenced by Pierre Levy's notion of "collective intelligence," which Levy relates to concepts developed by mediaeval Arab religious thinkers and by the twentieth-century Catholic paleontologist-theologian Pierre Teilhard de Chardin; however, Forest's artistic practice owes a more direct debt to Levy's recognition of the importance of ritual than to the theological inspiration for the concept of collective intelligence.

Although Levy considers the emergence of collective intelligence as the "inevitable" result of the dynamic pooling of knowledge he sees taking place in cyberspace, he also stresses that both art and ritual are needed if it is to become a self-conscious reality: "The collective imagination [i.e., collective intelligence] is born out of taking the time to invent the ceremony that is its inauguration". This dictum could well serve as the motto for Forest's most important online works.

Any aura emanating from Forest's works is ultimately more "liminal" than "sacred." Turner borrowed the concept of liminality from Arnold Van Gennep's studies of rites of passage in traditional, small-scale societies.

As used by Van Gennep, the term refers to ritualized forms of play performed by persons on the threshold of acquiring a new social status.

As applied to modern, large-scale societies by Turner, it designates a heightened state of collective consciousness, or "public reflexivity," that is attained in certain instances of collective public performance, particularly in times when a community finds itself on the threshold of a profound change in the social order.

In this type of context, liminality represents a margin for subversive or innovative play with the normative symbols and values of the community, which public performance has loosened from the hold of everyday reality.

For Turner, liminality represents the "subjunctive mood" of socio-cultural process just as more "mundane socio-structural activities" resemble its "indicative mood".

Turner's theory of liminality also makes use of the concepts of flow and communitas. The former is a prerequisite for liminality, whereas the latter is one of its results. For psychologist Mihaly Csikszentmihàlyi, from whom Turner borrows the term, flow designates the experience of "merging action and awareness" whereby individuals engaged in a creative activity become absorbed in what they are doing.

It implies an extreme "centering of attention" and a "loss of ego" that help the participants attain an unusual mastery of their actions in relation to the performance environment. Communitas is a special sense of community formed in the thick of public performance on the basis of the alternative social and cultural norms acted out by the participants, who are in a sense "flowing" together.

It is not to be confused with the more common notion of communion, which also involves an enhanced sense of community that can be attained in public festivities but lacks the critical perspective found in communitas. Indeed, communion sometimes involves a unanimous sense of support for an established order. Given this distinction, it would be more appropriate to speak of "rituals of communitas" in Forest's case.

For Turner, communitas constitutes "an alternative and more 'liberated' way of being socially human". Although it is an ephemeral phenomenon, it may have the lingering effect of inspiring and energizing those who may try to make a different social or cultural model a concrete reality. Liminality and the related concepts of flow and communitas correspond quite well to three of the stated objectives of Forest's practice of online art: the staging of intersubjective events in which a heightened state of awareness of the technological environment is attained (flow), creative forms of "anthropological projection" take place (liminality), and utopian models of community become virtual realities (communitas).

Several of Forest's recent online creations derive a measure of true liminality from their association with the French Fete de l'Internet, which corresponds to Turner's idea of collective performance and playful public reflexivity in a society on the threshold of major changes. This annual nationwide event was created in 1998 by a consortium of nonprofit organizations (with some government support) as a means to promote Internet use in France and to symbolize the idea of a French "exception" in cyberspace—an ambitious objective that Lionel Jospin, the French premier from 1997 to 2002, had explained in terms of fostering "une societe de l'information solidaire".

Another main objective of the Fete de l'Internet was the creation of a democratic interface between cyberspace and urban space to the extent that it involved both live events in public places and purely online ones. Indeed, it can be considered a step in the direction of the "urbanization" of the sprawling "real-time global city" that philosopher Paul Virilio says is necessary if the cultural ideal of the city and its political corollary, democracy, are to be preserved in the age of the Internet.

Urbanity and festivity have been closely associated in French public culture since the Socialist Francois Mitterrand was elected president in 1981. Nothing exemplifies this association better than the event after which the Fete de l'Internet was quite explicitly patterned: the Fete de la Musique.

The brainchild of Mitterrand's flamboyant minister of culture, Jack Lang, and Lang's chief advisor, Christian Dupavillon, an architect, the Fete de la Musique was launched in 1982 as an annual celebration of all things musical oinciding with the summer solstice and culminating in a ıight of free outdoor concerts in cities and towns across ⁻ance. Like Mitterrand's grandiose Parisian architectural projects, or grands travaux, which were originally meant to form the backdrop for a world's fair (a project later aborted) to be held in conjunction with 1989 bicentenary of the French Revolution, the Fete de la Musique reflected the French Socialist vision of the city as a theatre of egalitarian metissage, a transparent mise en scene of "quality" culture in all its varied forms, and an everyday celebration of republican fraternite.

The similarities between the Fete de l'Internet and the Fete de la Musique extend to their timing (the Fete de l'Internet generally coincides with the vernal equinox), their common concern for the democratization and popularization of cultural forms considered to be too limited to an elite ("good" music and the Internet), and the carnival atmosphere each strives to create (a number of the public events organized for the Fete de l'Internet have taken place in the street and some have even included live music).

The liminal nature of Forest's most ambitious online projects is also reinforced by their incorporation of ritualistic elements and themes. On the occasion of the inaugural Fete de l'Internet, which took place on 20 and 21 March 1998, Forest staged a symbolic stoppage of time, "J'arrete le temps" ("I Stop Time"). The action involved placing a Web camera in a major city or some other location in each of the world's twenty-four time zones.

Beginning with a live shot of the Arc de Triomphe in Paris, the camera in each location began transmitting at precisely 12:00 noon in that time zone on 20 March. The instant the clock was about to strike 1:00 p.m., the Webcast switched over to the camera in the next time zone to the west, where it was again 12:00 noon.

This enabled visitors to the project Website to relive the same hour of the day throughout the twenty-four-hour duration of the operation and created an illusion of protracted, globetrotting ubiquity.

Forest explained that his project was designed to give people time out from their busy lives to reflect on what they expected from technology in the new century, which was about to dawn.

The Website offered them a number of thought-provoking ways to make use of their time out of time. For example, they could give their opinions on time and technology in an online poll or peruse the ironic "Chroniques terriennes" ("Earthly Chronicles"), which used hypertext links to combine texts in which Forest mused about the issues his project raised and humorous illustrations.

If they could not afford a vacation, they could send their feet, in the form of a digitally scanned outline, to an email address on a server in Guadeloupe, where they would be kept "warm and comfortable" during the stoppage of time. More frenzied people were given the opportunity to buy time in increments of thirty seconds, one minute, or one hour. (The proceeds were donated to charity.)

Forest tried to attract customers by explaining that the time they purchased could be used whenever and however they desired: "Fight the fearsome pace of modern life: buy time and consume it without moderation!" In this work, the ritual element was provided by the use of time itself, which reproduced the suspension of regular time upon which all instances of liminal flow in public festivity are predicated.

Also designed to instill a sense of being on the threshold of a new age, Forest's time stoppage operation was a rite of initiation within a rite of initiation: the first Fete de l'Internet.

For the second edition of the Fete, Forest and fellow media artist Sophie Lavaud turned their real-life wedding on 18 March 1999 into an online performance. The two main goals of "The Techno-Marriage," as the event was called, were to blur the distinction between the "real" and the "virtual" (or, in other words, to celebrate their union, too) and to show that the Internet, if used with a little imagination, could just as easily enhance acts of communal life as dilute them. There were actually three different versions of the wedding.

There was the official civil ceremony, which was performed according to French statutes in the town hall of Issy-les-Moulineaux in suburban Paris. There was also a simultaneous virtual reality version in which digital clones of the bride, groom, and mayor replicated the actions of their flesh-and-blood counterparts using input provided by sensors worn by the latter.

This version was projected on large screens in the town hall itself and in public venues in Paris, Marseille, and Tokyo. Finally, there was a live video version shown on the project Website.

Was the virtual reality version less real than the other versions? For those who watched it on the large screen at the town hall in close proximity to the physical bride and groom, the question did not make much sense. In this setting, it was not necessarily perceived as a mere representation of the"real" ceremony; it was a part of the"real" ceremony. For those who saw it on the large screens in the three remote locations, the virtual ceremony was certainly farther removed physically from the "real" one and hence more likely to be thought of as its representation; however, the circumstances in which the public viewed the virtual ceremony in the three remote locations were nonetheless closer to the original in feel (i.e., in conviviality) than the Webcast.

Indeed, whatever the setting, the virtual version could be seen as expressing a deeper emotional reality--the wedding in the mind's eye of Forest and Lavaud--and hence as being in this one sense"more real" than the "real" ceremony itself. On the other hand, those who "attended" the marriage online (i.e., the video version) were not limited to passive spectatorship; they could actively participate in the joyous event in a number of different ways: by sending flowers, messages of congratulations, and wedding gifts with the click of a button; or even by serving as long-distance witnesses via Web camera.

"The Techno-Marriage" may have been unusual on account of its extensive use of the Internet in a real-life public ritual, but the secret of its success was that it did this in a way that was consistent with the ultimate objective of any effective ritual, which is, after all, to bring about a symbolic union of the real and the virtual.

Six months after "The Techno-Marriage," Forest created another highly ritualistic work he called"Le centre du monde" ("The Centre of the World").

As presented on the project Website, it was his idea of a response to an urgent existential crisis: the irreversible "disintegration" of the"centre of the world that each one of us carries inside himself."

Unable to withstand the"onslaught" of the dense"magma of fragmented information" in which the modern individual is submerged, this formerly unique and irreplaceable focal point that was "simultaneously geographical, spatial, ideological, and philosophical" in nature and constituted"a vital axis of equilibrium" has been replaced by"the dilated surface of indeterminate dimensions" of a "fuzzy" reality that knowledgeable people call"the global."

With the notion of a stable centre of the world waning more each day and people not yet ready to re-establish it as a purely individual and voluntary creation, Forest decided to pay it a fitting "final homage" by giving it the most explicit representation it had ever had in a temple-like installation at the Espace Pierre Cardin in Paris.

Visitors could gaze at the "centre of the world" by looking down on a holographic image appearing on the surface of an altar. Disoriented cybernauts could visit the temple online thanks to the three different Web cameras that provided continuous live coverage of the installation site throughout the duration of the operation (16-18 September 1999), and they could compose an email message that would be displayed on the large electronic message board that covered the curved rear wall of the installation.

"The Centre of the World" was clearly a parody--as obvious a fake as the great machine in the palace of the Wizard of Oz. Furthermore, Forest subtly deprived visitors to both the installation and the Website of the stable centre for which they yearned to the extent that the holographic holy of holies was not immutable, but changed before their eyes in reaction to the messages sent in over the Internet.

However, the parody was not a cynical one. Forest had created a true sanctuary (i.e., a special haven apart from the profane and mundane), simultaneously virtual and real, where people could go to reflect on the issues of globalization, technology, and the individual's place in cyberspace, joined in their reflection by their fellow pilgrims both in Paris and on the Web, together forming a temporary virtual community. This is perhaps as close to a"sacred centre" as one is likely to find in the age of cyberspace.

Following two less spectacular contributions to the Fete de l'Internet in 2000 (a Web graffiti project based on a famous French children's song) and 2001 (the inauguration of an online retrospective of his life's work at the newly created Web Net Museum), Forest once again created a project with ritualistic connotations for its 2002 edition: "Viande" ("Meat"). On the surface, just the latest in a long line of ironic projects involving the commercialization of artistic non-commodities, it consisted entirely of a Website where one could purchase or rent parts of Forest's body, carved up into sections like the carcass of an animal in a butcher shop.

In "Meat," each parcel of flesh purchased or rented was in reality a small section of a larger interactive image onto which the new titular occupant planted a small flag.

In addition to being an ironic overstatement of the idea that the Internet is little more than a vast electronic marketplace, an apparent assertion of the declining importance of the body in an age of virtual reality, an implicit comparison between the territorial nature of the body and that of the Internet, and an aging artist's fantasy of immortality, the work can also be seen as a sort of virtual human sacrifice. Forest seemed to be putting himself forward as a sacrificial victim whose virtual death and cannibalization might somehow sanctify the Internet.

However, it was also quite apparent that the public was not meant to take these sacrificial connotations seriously. Thus, while Forest's other ritualistic projects combined ironic touches with more serious effects, this virtual sacrifice remained largely an exercise in parody (self-parody, moreover).

One possible explanation for this result is that the artist wanted his public to sense that there were certain limits to "anthropological projection," which is not to be confused with a process of mystification of the Internet or a simple "digitalization" of existing rituals, or archaic ones.

Forest's online art is not the most visually stunning, formalistically innovative, theoretically complex, or politically audacious to be found on the Web; and his Website production values are not particularly sophisticated. The strength of his online work is a function of its place in the overall context of his thirty-year career in media and communication art.

Seen in retrospect, his career appears to have been organized around one general theme—namely, the idea that the overlapping and interconnected networks of mass media, long-distance communication, and computers that are now the source of such a large share of the content of human experience form a unique environment of their own.

The overall objective of Forest's work has always been to get us to see this communicational environment for what it really is, or could be—something that we are not easily able to do because, as Guy Debord would put it, we generally tend to experience this space as a form of spectacle.

Since the environment itself is vast and possesses a varied topography ranging from the flat pages of Le Monde to the labyrinthine pathways of the World Wide Web, the methods Forest has used to help us hone our perception of it have been equally varied, ranging from parasitical messages in the press and gratuitous media hybrids to online rituals. One constant throughout these varied approaches has been his desire to create works for the general public rather than collectors and connoisseurs of contemporary art—works that are accessible, educational, and amusing.

This is another legacy of Forest's Sociological Art and Aesthetics of Communication periods that is well served by his ongoing association with the Fete de l'Internet, which offers him an opportunity to reconcile the "sociological" objective of establishing a direct connection to the experience of ordinary people with the "aesthetic" requirement of an extraordinary framing of attention.

Without question, Forest's Festival works represent his most unique contribution to online art on account of the potential for liminal reflexivity and play that arises from their ritualistic format when combined with the broader festive context; however, these special works can also be seen as the most explicit examples of an anthropological approach to media art that has always been at least implicit in Forest's work. Virtually all of his media works function somewhat like rites of passage to the extent that they offer the public symbolic thresholds to cross between the "real" world and the "virtual" space of communication and information.

In crossing over the threshold, one is forced to abandon many of one's preconceived ideas and traditional paradigms of perception and is thus prepared to be more attentive to the unique features of the virtual space into which one enters, but one is also made to sense that the two spaces are intimately connected (indeed, the threshold is also an interface).

Perhaps, for this reason, his most ritualistic projects make conspicuous use of distinctive physical sites (the locations in the different time zones, the town hall, the temple-like installation) and are reminiscent of more familiar types of modern rituals (the news broadcast with live reports from around the world, the civil marriage ceremony, the pilgrimage to a cherished lieude memoire).

They thus avoid the fallacy that cyberculture could, or should, exist apart from the material world and are more consistent with the process of liminality, which does not invent new cultural forms from scratch, as it were, but begins by inflecting, or troping, existing ones.

This anthropological approach does not exactly lend itself well to leaving behind collectible masterpieces and is unlikely to bring about profound changes in the social and cultural order, but, if it helps break the spell of spectacle that veils one's perception of the space of communication that is such an integral part of the postmodern habitat, then it should surely be considered a worthy path for an "art of the present" to explore.

In an essay written by Brenda Longfellow called 'Love letters to the Mother: the work of Chantal Akerman' she allows an analogous connection between films and letter-writing to surface through an analysis of four of Akerman's films that deal with the mother-daughter relationship, each in different ways.

In grouping these films under the heading of 'love-letters', from a daughter to a mother, an enquiry into a type of correspondence of the feminine emerges out of the site of a film practice. However, only one of the four films deals directly with the mother's writing: her 'love letters' to her daughter. News From Home by Chantal Akerman is the filmic response to those letters, and in corresponding allows a culturally negated maternal 'voice' to emerge within the visible and audible sphere of film.

At a talk given by Chantal Akerman at the Tate Modern Gallery on 8 March 2002, she spoke about the fact that before she became a filmmaker she was 'not interested in visual things [...] I wanted to write'.

If we consider Helene Cixous' phrase: 'woman must write herself [...] bring women to writing' we come closer to seeing how the film, as a 'love-letter' (as writing) appears to take up residence in the place where the Woman/Mother must be brought to live (in writing, in language). The filmmaker in living at the level of the making of the film (having first written it) addresses a co-responding, yet unspeakable, love for the feminine (within patriarchy) as a billetdoux to the mother as self.

The formal structure of the film as it plays with the formal structure of the letter allows a channel of communication to break through conventions of reading and writing: twisting threads of meaning in and out of subjectivity. As I watch this film, however, what comes to greet me is another story; the sight of the foreign city of New York in the film brings with it — as if it were a palimpsest — another journey, one that had occurred in Dresden, where another letter from another mother had been revisited by her own daughter. It was the story of Freud's famous patient 'Dora'.

Freud's treatment of 'Dora' in 1900 formed the basis of his longest case history of a woman. 'Dora's' father, Philip, brought her to Freud as a teenager, while she was suffering from 'tussis nervosa, aphonia, depression, and taedium vitae'. She has long since captured the sympathy of many of Freud's readers, particularly feminists. Helene Cixous saw in 'Dora' 'a very beautiful feminine homosexuality, a love for woman that is astounding'.

In Lisa Appignanesi and John Forrester's book Freud's Women they suggest that this 'homosexuality' was triumphantly kept secret from Freud, as she led him away from her secret love for a woman, allowing him to concentrate his energies and intelligence on a busy masculine network of deceiving and humiliating relationships. Her rapid departure from Freud's treatment [she herself broke off the treatment] is viewed as her triumph, and perhaps her only way out of being recoded back into the normalizing and Oedipal ways with which Freud was unconsciously complicit.

In Freud's case study of 'Dora', called 'A fragment of an analysis of a case of hysteria ('Dora')', consideration of the feminine resides somewhat beyond the analytical scene of writing. With 'Dora's' mother (Kathe), the Madonna, Frau K, and the governess, all appearing in the footnotes of his text, over the fringes of a 'master discourse' (enforcing 'Oedipus', like the Sphinx who waits with her questions outside the city gates). This structure in Freud's writing, in its own way signifies a persistence of the feminine — like a pulse pressing upon the page.

Throughout much of Freud's work his positing of the 'being' understood as the Mother is one that interestingly circumscribes its own negation in his writing — because it is a negation that keeps returning — through a course of 'complicated detours' to the imaginary place and time of the Mother. In idealizing the mother/son relationship, through the 'Oedipal' process, which normalizes the heterosexual, the mother/daughter relationship is made subordinate and thus deeply problematic, unable to be resolved satisfactorily for the girl. The imaginary figure of the Mother as both idealized, and yet psychically castrated, cannot and does not allow for the possibility of her own desires.

Freud's dismissal of 'Dora's' mother Kathe from any consideration in her daughter's case is made explicit, as Freud, in the case history writes:

I never made the mother's acquaintance. From the accounts given me by the girl and her father I was led to imagine her as an uncultivated woman and above all as a foolish one, who had concentrated all her interests upon domestic affairs [...] She presented the picture, in fact, of what might be called the 'housewife's psychosis.'

So, it is here, at an intersection of Freudian dream analysis and feminist counter-cinema that I wish to consider the terms of an unspeakable desire for and of the feminine, by looking through and beyond Akerman's film, to the site of a dream, about a letter written by a mother — dreamt by 'Dora' while under Freud's analysis. This dream is barely veiled beneath the politics of representation, so pressing upon 1970s feminist filmmakers. The film, then, appears as a palimpsest within a complex field of displacement, where letters addressed to 'my dear little girl' privilege the female viewer/listener, as the terms of address call us simultaneously by an/other(s) and our own name.

News From Home is a film that orchestrates a series of fragmentary sounds and gestures (traffic and subway noises: a 'text' belonging to the city of New York) as they interrelate with the 'voice' of the Mother. These city noises, both overlay, and burst upon, the filmmaker's own reading voice as it reads its own text, which is taken from a series of letters (sent from the filmmaker's mother 'back home' in Belgium, to her absent daughter Chantal Akerman in New York). The sounds/'voice' of the city appear to us as a gesture that attempts to smudge itself upon a visible screen, which is made up of a collage of images of New York's streets and subways.

The film avoids a voyeuristic gaze, as static and long-duration camera shots are taken of anonymous people who inhabit the city. At the same time we hear a text that relates to a grieving mother whose domestic concerns appear to us as a re-appropriated text that raises the 'problematic' of feminine subjectivity, as it is spoken by the daughter; the reiteration of the letter's content addresses a sense of absence — the absence of the addressee.

In News From Home, subject and object positions are compounded in a single voice that over'sees' the scenes, and the question of subjectivity is subtly undone within a single voice that 'appears' to move in and out of focus, in and out of silence. The 'I' that constantly moves in variables of the mother and daughter is also our 'I/eye' that is forever burdened with both loss and excess.

As we begin to 'watch' for these sounds — as if they were audible gestures that attempted to mark themselves upon the screen — we hear the noise of the city as it drowns out the words of the mother; this erasure, although full of violent eruptions, does not completely silence the Other. And even though the voice is rubbed out in places — as if it were writing — it remains as silently engraved as a forgotten memory, and we are left as viewers, 'listening' and 'reading' between the lines.

My source of inspiration for this chapter began with an encounter with the work of the Belgium born filmmaker Chantal Akerman, particularly her early films made during the mid 1970s, which seemed to allow a space for articulating what I perceived to be a certain feminine desire, where a so-called 'unalienated feminine language' — which was then demanded and desired by so many feminist theorists and filmmakers alike — was drawn from within a cultural lacuna.

In terms of a meeting between politics and aesthetics this period of filmmaking was ripe for the emergence of a feminist counter-cinema which was to begin to attempt to voice what Laura Mulvey had then called a 'language of desire'.

But I had not seen this film when it was first made but rather as a late viewer, in fact some 25 years late(r). My viewing, and reading of Akerman's films therefore carries with it the freight of another time and space, and yet, without the temporal distance into which I read a certain history, I could not have approached the film (upon which this chapter is focused) without an acknowledgment of its own corresponding position within this filmmaker's ceuvre (an ceuvre which of course did not exist for Akerman when she was making her first films). At that early developmental time, Akerman occupied the position of 'the daughter', a position made most visible in her early films such as News From Home, which was Akerman's tenth film, and was made between what are probably two of her best known films, Jeanne Dielman 23 Quai du commerce, 1080, Bruxelles and Les Rendez-Vous d'Anna.

The chronological site of the emergence of News From Home is of some interest when we consider what is happening, part icularly in the mother/daughter relationship, in these other films. Jeanne Dielman is a beautifully paced meditation that focuses upon the daily domestic rituals carried out by a woman living with her son in Brussels.

Jeanne is the mother who is 'lovingly' gazed at in all of her actions; this film is closest to a 'love-letter to the mother'. As Akerman herself said of the film: 'If you choose to show a woman's gestures so precisely, its because you love them.' It is in the precise observation of gesture and sound that the mother appears to us in the film, allowing for a phenomenological grounding of our own sense of being in the world.

In Les Rendez-Vous d'Anna it is the daughter, whom we as spectators watch, as she herself listens (with us) to others, as they perform their monologues as if they were literally blocks' of speech. We follow Anna's nomadic journey back to the mother, and this meeting provides the occasion for a rarely-seen intimacy between mothers and daughters; as they lie down in bed together, the daughter tells her mother about her first lesbian experience during which she says she had thought about her mother.

In using the Mother as an almost constant point of return in these early films, Akerman defied oppressive cinematic conventions, as well as re-figuring the Mother in terms of something like a 'return of the repressed'. These films force us to read anew, due to her continual breaking of cinematic codes.

'In Chantal Akerman's work, what is most valuable for us is her decoding of oppressive cinematic conventions and her invention of new codes of non-voyeuristic vision; yet these contributions go unnamed.

Akerman's innovative filmmaking approach, which from its inception is born from the dual influences of both European and American avant-garde cinematic practice, begins to open up non-voyeuristic spaces of vision for, and of, women, as both daughters and mothers. We begin to be able to listen to and see the Mother in previously unseeable and unspeakable ways. Adrienne Rich dealt with this issue of invisibility in panel talks at the 1976 and 1977 MLA conference: 'she contended that those things which wo men allow to remain unnamed will, in time, become unspoken, and then unspeakable, and finally end up completely erased, become invisible.

Largely denied the point-of-view shot, the viewer remains more acutely aware of the camera's presence, of a gaze that is always ready to otherwise absorb us in our own viewing. In allowing the Mother to begin to be heard and, somehow, seen to be heard (but not without difficulties), Akerman softly stirs the silent cultural pool, whose ripples begin to break up the oppressive structures within cinema: those structures that work in line with our ideological unconscious, that otherwise binds us in a type of blind viewing.

But let us return to the present day, where Akerman's filial position has somewhat matured — in line with her œuvre — as she can now be regarded as occupying the position of something of a foremother, at least in terms of a feminist cinematic history.

We must, however, be careful to recognize that at the time Akerman saw herself as 'a filmmaker' rather than a 'feminist filmmaker'. She did, however, claim that Jeanne Dielman was a feminist film because of the way in which it considered the Woman/Mother in the film, giving space to that which is rarely, if ever shown.

This cinematic history produced films that were actively engaged with representational politics, and it is to this idea of representation that I now wish to turn, in an analysis of her film News From Home.

Chantal Akerman's film News From Home presents an ever-changing series of shots of New York, both above ground, and underground on the subway, where the sounds of the city are layered with the voice of the filmmaker herself, who reads from a series of letters sent to her from her mother in Belgium.

From the outset the film moves in a non-narrative flow, yet a strong feeling of narrative remains present, albeit disjointed, because of the letters that are studded into the frame of viewing, as if they were themselves somehow punctuating the daughter's film.

With each new letter, however, the narrative turns constantly upon itself. The mother's circular pleading of love and loss 'sounds' like an echo, in the daughter's mouth as she speaks, and in so doing, reiterates her mother's words.

This mother's nagging 'kisses', which are sometimes fuelled with anger, seem to pull at the very edges of the texts in which they appear, while at the same time joining them together — one letter to the next — each one saying th e same thing differently.

Repetition and difference are intensely played out within a disembodied voice that spirals subjectivities as it rhythmically plays with an otherwise culturally neglected syntax — a collection of maternal concerns.

Re-reading 'a letter' ('Dora'/Kathe)

I content myself with what can be written and I dream whatever should be dreamed.

(Marie de Sevigne)

In recalling a dream she had had as part of her analysis, Freud's patient 'Dora' says:

I was walking about in a town which I did not know. I saw streets and squares which were strange to me. Then I came into a house where I lived, went to my room, and found a letter from Mother lying there. She wrote saying that as I had left home without my parents' knowledge she had not wished to write to me to say that father was ill 'now he is dead and if you like you can come.'

The New York of News From Home is like Akerman's very own Dresden. (Dresden refers to the city 'Dora' visited where she had gone alone to the 'picture gallery' and sat before the Sistine Madonna for 'two hours'. Freud connects this experience to the later dream because of reappearing elements, i.e., 'she declined and went alone', and 'two hours'. Akerman also travels the streets of a foreign city alone.

She, too, looks at the 'pictures' that the living city offers her as if staring into her own dream. However, Chantal Akerman does not only dream, but thankfully acts in the real world by creating films which, in their working, act partially, like a dream. By this I mean they re-route our viewing, bypassing the well-trod pathways travelled by the 'manipulated' and 'alienated subjects' caught within the unconscious of a patriarchal society, thereby allowing psychical traces to be felt, as we are touched by the 'dream'/ film in a 'dimension that is beyond appearance.' The result is that we 'strangel y' find ourselves awakened. Whatever has been repressed is allowed temporary release in the dream.

As Freud explains, at the beginning of the case analysis of 'Dora', in metaphorical language that travels upon detours:

the dream is one of the roads along which consciousness can be reached by the psychical material which, on account of the opposition aroused by its content, has been cut off from consciousness and repressed, [...] The dream in short, is one of the detours by which repression can be evaded.

As in 'Dora's' second dream, Chantal Akerman 'had left home without her parents' knowledge'. She had spent seven months in New York before returning to her parents in Belgium; after three months at home she then returned to New York and made the film News From Home. It was midway, while still on the plane between the home of Europe and parents, and her newly chosen home of the United States, that she decided to make News From Home (the title it seems, turns upon a mutually determined axis as the 'news' can be read as travelling in opposite directions simultaneously: that is depending on where you situate 'home').

Akerman said: 'I was in the plane and I thought — my mother is going to send me those letters again [...] That's how I got the idea of the film.' So, in anticipating a new batch of letters from her mother, the idea flew into her head just as she herself flew towards the city that would provide her with the imaginary space of enunciation for her mother's voice.

Akerman, three-quarters of a century after 'Dora' had dismissed Freud, finally allows a space for acknowledging a maternal voice, and at last responds — even if belatedly — to the mother's letter. By valuing the Mother and her own mother's real letters, she inadvertently enables value to be unlocked from an otherwise repressed letter — that is, the 'dream-letter' as represented by 'Dora' to her analyst.

Freud's disavowal of the dream-letter's significance, as a correspondence between mother and daughter, is tied within his repression of the pre-Oedipal Mother herself. But all of this could only ever appear for the 'sick' 'Dora' in a dream, a dream whose structure, like language, was deciphered within a patriarchal paradigm. Although the Mother remains present throughout Freud's writings, she is usually submerged in the text as a resistant voice, hence the unanswered question: 'What does a woman want?' In the 'Dora' case, the mother is the only familial figure who remains outside of Freud's consideration in relation to her daughter's 'illness'.

My analogy between these two oblique forms of communication between mothers and daughters allows us to bear witness to an intervention by Akerman, like a deferred action; her film it seems, steps in at the point of retrieving a possible feminine communication with an-Other. In Freud's written account of the case history, 'Dora's' mother (Kathe) has the capacity to write to her daughter, but only in her daughter's dream.

It is ironically her only letter to the daughter in a case history that is full of letters. In communicating with the daughter she enters the analysis on the level of dream-language, but nevertheless a language which Freud is anxious to interpret. In doing so he bypasses the relevance of a mother/daughter communication (and the missed meeting in the dream) in favour of the actual 'contents of the letter', within which his initial concern is the 'death of the father'.

It is here that Freud's analytical stance on 'Dora's' dream as revealing a 'cruel and sadistic' female punishment of t he father is emptied of relevance, because as the analogous dream touches upon Akerman's film, News From Home, a 'beautiful' feminine homosexual economy comes into force, as it does in so many of her other films.

It is interesting to note how Akerman, like 'Dora' (in interviews at least), presents her mother as 'uncultivated', and 'unsophisticated'. For instance, when Akerman spoke about her mother's letters in an interview for Camera Obscura a few months after making the film, she makes it clear that her mother's words are somehow naively 'her own', originating from a source that takes a direct and deeply personal route to the daughter, rather than manoeuvring through a 'thousand detours'. My mother wrote me love letters, and that was marvellous. With her own words [...I she formulates her feelings in an unsophisticated way, they really reflect her. If she were more sophisticated, she wouldn't have dared to ask me all the time 'When are you coming back? [...]' She wouldn't have dared, she would've said it by way of a thousand 'detours'. But she's not sophisticated, she used the words that she had, [...]

The so-called 'unsophisticated' intimacy contained in the mother's 'own written words' reappear in the film as spoken writing: the text becomes replayed as a performance. A certain lack of sophistication resonates in the monotone reading voice, which acts to re-attune our listening.

The mother's letters appear to be given an/Other material form, as if lifted from the page into blocks of sound. However alienating the effect, traces of intimacy permeate our own hearing and viewing as we listen to a voice, repeating and chanting as if it were a child's voice, learning language, touching upon the mother tongue.

Akerman is generously sharing her mother's words with us, and by allowing her mother's letters to be heard, she follows a tradition of letter sharing that can be traced back to Marie de Sevigne and beyond: 'where letters were not necessarily regarded as private and confidential' — they were passed among friends and relatives who all shared in the 'news'.

WAVES OF VOICES

The city of New York appears in the film as an autonomous series of individual scenes, apparently not directly controlled by the filmmaker. By this I mean the filmmaker observes and then records the city's own visual 'script'. The visual element of the film contains no actors and the people that populate the screen mirror our own movement in the city; this is picked up by a mainly fixed camera position. However, like the letters these segments of city scenes are treated like found objects — meanings are altered because of the filmmaker's decisions, particularly in the way in which sound is used.

As we listen to the noises that appear to us to emanate from the city at that moment of viewing, we assume them to be referential; when traffic passes, the noise of cars sometimes drowns out the speaking voice, and we might imagine that voice to be standing at the roadside at that moment reading aloud the letter, in competition with the noise of the traffic.

However, there are often occasions when traffic passes silently or without making the voice inaudible; this leads us to look closely at those moments of noise intervention. The first time that the reading voice is obliterated by what appears to be diegetical sound, we realise that the mother is writing about her disappointment in the daughter's neglectful behaviour, the fact that she has moved without giving a precise address, and also that she no longer writes as frequently.

But before we know the details contained within the letter, we realise that the opening portion of the letter is being drowned out by the sound of the traffic; beyond the traffic noises we hear only a vague and muffled voice murmuring an unknowable text.

However, this same (traffic) noise has been lifted across from the previous shot, carried from one visual space into the next, in fact belonging to neither. Although the out-of-sync sounds act to interrupt our 'hearing' of the actual letters, we are at that moment placed in a 'strangely' privileged position, as our 'reading', or hearing, moves a cross sounds that begin to speak of the film as a potential site for a struggling maternal voice, and a possible communicative encounter beyond the level of the signifier.

For this scene the camera is set up in a fixed position across the street from four men who sit outside a shop, and one woman who sits in profile, upon a chair beneath a 'Don't Walk' sign. We observe the traffic, which travels along the road directly in front of the group. As the traffic moves into and out of the frame, it is as if each car slices into the letter at specific points. The movement of the traffic is like a type of visual and physical erasure of the letter as it rubs against the grain of the reading voice, which we imagine reading from left to right; the traffic counteracts that imagined act by always bursting across the screen, from right to left.

The 'violent' roar of traffic that makes it impossible to hear the mother's words has been read as a certain type of response to those very words, what Brenda Longfellow has referred to as 'This good humoured resistance'. Yet the different sounds of voice and city maintain themselves within separate spaces, that is, non-threatening.

As the noise of the streets is placed, in a post-production act, like the voice itself, it also belongs to another sphere;

although originating from the street it, too, is lifted out like the letter and re-layered within the film. We begin to sense something like a type of orchestration that occurs as many levels of sound and voice meet (or not) in a rhythmic flow that treats the film as a type of visual music.

By giving the city a voice which is somehow beyond it, and yet seems to respond to the mother's words, a kind of dialogue is created that works through tension, and includes us. As we are continually listening not only to words that revolve in a type of 'skewed autobio graphy', but also to the tone of the voice that reads and is continually burdened with other rhythms and noise, we are caught physically experiencing the thing — edging forward to hear what is perceived as missing.

But no matter how loud or intently we listen, we can never catch an element of the film because that 'escaped' part is the film; it is the experience of loss that reverberates within us as the volume turned up full vibrates a maddening sound that echoes in the real streets beyond our own screens.

Akerman's voice delivers the maternal voice — simultaneously through her own body, and through a body of film. The mother's 'voice' (her maternal concerns as stated in her letters) is placed into an external site, that of the city. However, the voice of the city is itself never placed under threat as it, too, is given an audible voice. A complex auditory dialogue is set in motion as silence, sound(s) and words, prompt us into a relation with the film which requires us to listen, not only to narrative but also to sounds and silence. The materiality of the world is awakened for us as we listen.

It is as if we have been awakened from a 'living' mute and stifling dream, where 'sounds' have become a mutated drone — something like a mother's nagging' voice from which we have switched off. It is as if we are suddenly made aware of the 'everyday' sounds that accompany our very existence, sounds which had paradoxically become 'unheard' by us. In as much as we are made aware, we are equally irritated, because as we veer towards trying to listen to the pockets of 'stories' provided by the letters we are refused entry to this voice as it rubs out before our very ears, never providing us with the 'whole story'.

In 'reading' the film we, too, are positioned, like the letter reader, in a relationship with signs that convey meanings. The mother's 'writing', which transgresses the ground of ink and paper upon which it originates is again read by us in the semiotic space of the film screen; it is re-visioned as sounds and images that dance upon a flickering celluloid.

The flatness of the screen image becomes metonymic of the page of the letter, and as I struggle with the 'meanings' that I am invited as a culturally positioned spectator to create, I find myself moved beyond simply looking and listening. I reach a point where I am also able to read with(in) the sounds and silence of the film an imagined maternal voice, which does not threaten, and is not threatened by the bed of images that are slowly panned across, as if the camera were an eye scanning words upon a page.

In addressing how I hear the relationship of voices in this film, my own distance or proximity to the Other's voice is 'addressed', because as I hear the 'you' addressed in the text of the letter it transmutes into a personal address, which 'I' encounter in viewing/reading.

If, as Chantal Akerman once stated in an interview regarding her previous film Jeanne Dielman: 'this is a love film to my mother', what she then goes on to achieve brilliantly in her next film, News From Home, is a textual space of response for the Mother: for her own mother's letters — as she rightly recognizes — are themselves 'love letters'.

Akerman's recurring use of the letter as a theme in her films reveals a desire for communication — a communication of desire — resonating beyond speech and writing. A long-awaited glimpse of the Mother's voice touches us in the sight and sound of a screen that 'sensually' meets us in its noise, colours and images.

Like an abandoned child we find ourselves gazing into visions of loneliness in this film, as if we were waiting to be found. We observe the text as it performs itself, where a series of memories encounter or miss each other while joining us in unremembered memories that reach beyond the veil of seeing and hearing.

An inscription of memory is revealed in the richly layered 'bonds of reading' that Akerman offers us in her films. The trope of communication becomes embodied in a signifying practice that utilizes silence and absence as Other sites for seeing and hearing. When Chantal Akerman speaks of the last ten minutes of News From Home she says: 'I found it so beautiful there was no reason to stop it, except at the end of the reel!' She thus sums up, in a very concise way, the underlying reason for my watching this film. The waves that ebb and flow in New York harbour (in the final closing shot of the film) provide the perfect closing metaphor for a discordant harmony of voices that struggle to be heard.

Chapter 3

Projecting an Image

What has not been known until now is that he actually projected the images onto canvas and traced from them, incising tick marks in the canvas to guide his brush and then camouflaging these incisions in order to hide what would have seemed to his contemporaries a nonartistic reliance on picture-making technology. This was the headline news of Thomas Eakins: American Realist, the magnificent comprehensive exhibition of work by Eakins that originated at the Philadelphia Museum of Art in the fall of 2001 and went on to the Musee d'Orsay in Paris and the Metropolitan Museum of Art in New York.

The painter's tracing of photographs was indeed news, though hardly attention-grabbing. Even before this latest revelation, Eakins was one of America's most controversial artists. You wouldn't have known it, however, from walking through this exhibition, which downplayed the "human-interest" side of its subject. Darrel Sewell, the museum's Robert L. McNeil Jr. Curator of American Art and a leading authority on Eakins, organized the exhibition in such a way as to steer clear of personal biography. The copious commentary provided by the show in the form of wall texts, introductory video, and punch-in-thenumbers audio guide concentrated mostly on technical matters of artistic process, with only an occasional nod toward biographical milestones.

Such principled discretion had the effect of converting Eakins into a bloodless, sexless creative artist who cerebrally posed various difficult technical challenges to himself and then methodically and mechanically set about solving them.

All the fuss made in the introductory video, the wall texts, and the museum's press materials about the great realist's previously unsuspected reliance on photographic tracing for achieving mimesis only reinforced the exhibition's depersonalization of Eakins. The authentic scandals of sex and social realism that broke during his lifetime and posthumously made him an American icon were displaced into a much milder and more narrowly circumscribed "scandal" about his unorthodox photographic procedure.

What do these paintings have to say about the world in which the artist lived? Why did he make them? What do they reveal about him? What can they tell us about ourselves? These are the questions-the "big" questions, to use the artist's favourite modifier when talking about the art he admired-that Thomas Eakins: American Realist was perhaps too discreet to confront. I wouldn't go so far as to say the show avoided or evaded such questions, only that it turned its gaze away from them and, in so doing, missed a select opportunity to connect the general public with one of the most serious, influential, and intellectually engaging artists the United States has produced.

Big painters, to borrow Eakins's terminology again, have big problems. That is, they set remarkably high standards for themselves and pose difficult challenges. But it would be a mistake to assume that these challenges are limited to technical matters such as, in Eakins's case, how to depict accurately the legs of trotting horses or the cant of a boat under sail. Eakins's problems lay in the personal and professional as well as representational realms, some of them relatively modern (how to make a living by one's mind rather than one's back; how to enjoy leisure; how to adopt a scientific ethos), others ageold (how to supersede one's parents; how to endure agonies of the flesh; how to face the encroachments of mortality).

What proved most fascinating with regard to the exhibition was not its revelation about Eakins's tracing technique but rather the "big" picture it provided of a four-decade-long career repeatedly and often tensely balanced between the artist's unabashedly conservative fealty to the past (be it that of ancient Greek sculpture, Spanish Baroque painting, or the French academic realism of his student years) and his progressive loyalty to the present (as evidenced by his dogged insistence on portraying modern sports, science, and medicine in what seemed at the time a particularly cool, objective, and unsentimental manner).

Laid out through nine rooms in a decadeby-decade sequence, the exhibition at the Philadelphia Museum of Art put on view 68 paintings by Eakins, 128 photographs either by him or by members of his circle, 18 sculptures, 15 drawings, and 8 watercolors. The first four and last four galleries formed two parallel axes with a small connecting gallery in between.

Of the nine rooms, four were large and spacious with creamy white ceilings set high above walls painted subtle shades of gray, beige, or olive green. These displayed some of his largest and most impressive canvases to great visual effect. Three smaller, more intimate chambers, positioned at the midpoint of the viewing itinerary, contained works of the middle years of his career.

The centre of these three exhibited the largest painting Eakins ever attempted, The Agnew Clinic, an appropriate placement in that the work, here the literal turning point in the exhibition, has often been regarded as a turning point in the artist's career.

The first and last galleries, the smallest rooms, felt tight and confining. By the end of the show, the crowd of viewers had thinned, and the constriction of space suited the theme of the artist's autumnal last years.

At the start, however, it created a distinct problem, for two reasons. First, visitors to a large exhibition always cluster at the beginning, so the arrangement of space should alleviate the inevitable initial crowding rather than add to it. Second, the dropped ceiling, drably painted walls, and low lighting of this gallery seemed oddly out of keeping with the works displayed, predominantly of sports and play, failing to match their exuberance.

The dimming of the lights was apparently mandated by the inclusion of a pair of delicate watercolor and wash perspective drawings, but this had the unfortunate effect of starting the tour of the artist's career on a glum note, when brightness and broad vistas were more biographically appropriate. As noted below, darkness did indeed intrude into Eakins's life in these otherwise sunny early years, yet the general tone of his life during this phase was upbeat and hopeful, and the opening gallery of the exhibition should have conveyed these feelings.

Even before reaching the subdued first room, the visitor had to maneuver past the Scylla of a bustling gift shop crammed full of rower refrigerator magnets and horse-and carriage neckties and the Charybdis of a not fully enclosed video projection space, where booming-voiced museum curators and conservators, to the accompaniment of sentimental period music, held forth on their discovery of the master's photographic tracings and the importance of this discovery in appreciating his art. Fortunately, the intrusive sounds of both the didactic video and the Eakins emporium diminished greatly by the second gallery.

This second gallery also proved disappointing. It contained what is surely the most famous object Thomas Eakins ever made, The Gross Clinic. In surveys of world art, this is the one American painting of the 19th century considered indispensable. Yet here it received a throwaway placement on a relatively short wall, flanked by two portraits minor in significance.

Apparently the exhibition designers wished to underplay this obvious candidate for viewer veneration, even as the show as a whole downplayed the personality and life crises of the artist. That's certainly an intellectually justifiable position, but it is one that deprived viewers of the rewards offered by a prime axial view: first glimpsing the painting from afar, then experiencing the mounting excitement of approaching it in stages, its abstract masses of lights and darks cohering at last into a storm of vivid details flashing from the gloom.

Happily, the viewing itinerary improved after this. The dramatic sight line onto the majestic painting of 1880 The Crucifixion created by the tall, narrow archway between galleries two and three provided the high point of the show's misc-en-scene.

Because Eakins has always been regarded as a scientific realist and hard-boiled empiricist with little use for religion until late in his career, when he befriended a small group of Jesuit clerics, the overtly religious imagery of this painting has usually been understood as merely a pretext for an artist wishing to indulge his fascination with the principles of human anatomy (or, from a queer studies perspective, his fascination with naked young male models). Being able to stand before The Gross Clinic in the second gallery and glance through the archway at The Crucifixion close by in the third made me think about these two ostensibly dissimilar works in a new way.

Their juxtaposition suggested that what was repressed in Eakins (or, perhaps more accurately, in Eakins scholarship) was not his sexuality but-I hardly know what else to call it-his spirituality. With the two paintings appearing in direct proximity, one could suddenly see the notorious thrashing fingers of the recoiling female in The Gross Clinic recapitulated in the contorted hands of Christ nailed to the cross.

Does the similarity of tortured hands in the two paintings imply that Eakins viewed Christ-and thus Christianity-with the same disdain he allegedly reserved for squeamish Victorian-era men and women? Or, to the contrary, does this near repetition of involuntary hand gestures intimate that he took seriously the mental agony of the female onlooker in The Gross Clinic and was not, as is commonly thought, invoking it negatively in pointed contrast to the heroic masculinity of the emotionally restrained doctor?

Like the flailing fingers of the female onlooker, the lean, white, bent-at-the-knee flank of the youth on the operating table reappears in the body of the tortured Christ. Other similarities present themselves. The youth's feet are clad in dark gray socks; Christ's feet are "clad" in blood, dirt, and iron nails. A chloroform-infused pillow covers the young patient's head to render him unconscious; a crown of thorns covers Christ's head. His face reposes in shadows, like the face of the anesthetized female patient in The Agnew Clinic in gallery five.

Once I began detecting the theme-and-variation restatement of these shared motifs, I began wondering if instead of seeing The Crucifixion as a piece of scientific naturalism disguised as a religious painting, we might not regard the two clinic paintings as covertly religious tableaux purporting to be documents of scientific naturalism.

Add to The Gross Clinic and The Crucifixion a third large-format oil painting, Salutat of 1898, that also features a white-skinned, seminude young male, and a sort of inadvertent religious triptych spread out over two and a half decades emerges. In the first "panel" of this hypothetical series, the dark passageway to an arena full of spectators (medical students) has issued forth a supine, seminude body in the process of being filleted by a cluster of men.

They happen to be modern surgeons, but in an old master altarpiece they would have been torturers of Christ or some other martyr. In the second of the series, the bloodied, seminude body has been affixed to a cross. In the third, no longer bloodied, supine, or unconscious, the young seminude male, his feet now clad in gray boxer's boots rather than gray socks, has been "resurrected." He raises his arm triumphantly and takes his leave of the onlookers (in this case, cheering sports fans) before departing the arena.

By no means am I insisting that these three paintings literally constitute a triptych, religious or otherwise. Nevertheless, seeing them in succession, I began to sense a through line that made The Crucifixion and the late clerical portraits appear less of an aberration in the Eakins corpus than I had previously thought them to be.

The sequence prompted me to look elsewhere in the work of this presumed atheist and hard-core scientific rationalist for embedded religious themes and motifs. I came away from the exhibition believing that 19th-century America's most acclaimed realist harbored a mystical or transcendental sensibility throughout his entire career, and that these three paintings, when viewed serially, have a story to tell about the mortification of human flesh and its transubstantiation.

If we add one of the early rowing paintings at the beginning of the sequence, the result could almost be considered a four-part narrative cycle such as Thomas Cole's 1840s Voyage of Life. Taken together, they could be understood as betokening four fundamental stages of the Christian body: health, disease, death, and resurrection.

Other well-known works not officially included in the show hung nearby in the American galleries across the hallway. Thus, at its originating venue the exhibition offered an exceptionally comprehensive pulling together of the artist's oeuvre.

As always, one could point to a number of conspicuous omissions. I missed Will Schuster and Blackman Going Shooting for Rail, a painting that, in depicting a white hunter and a black guide precariously balancing one another on opposite sides of a small boat, begs to be interpreted as an allegory about race relations in America at the end of Reconstruction. I also would have liked to have seen Swimming, a genre scene showing a group of naked young men sunning themselves beside a swimming hole, that raises questions today about the nature of male sexuality, be it hetero- or homo-, during the late 19th century.

Perhaps the most disappointing exclusion was that of the stunning late portrait Edith Mahon, which draws on a variety of traditional artistic discourses of defeat and dejection and in so doing appears to deliver an intense psychological study of female subjectivity.

It presents a powerful analogue to the fiction of the period by writers such as Kate Chopin, Charlotte Perkins Gilman, and Edith Wharton. Yet even with these paintings absent from the show, the walls were filled with extraordinarily rich instances of Eakins's engagement with many of the underlying concerns of his time.

In the face of such a complex and diverse body of work, the show's subtitle, "American Realist," seemed misleading. Perhaps "Romantic Realist" or "Neogothic and Neoclassical Realist" would have been more fitting, for these rooms gave the impression of Eakins as an artist who was about much more than recording modern life with hyperrational scientific verisimilitude.

The aforementioned religious motifs aside, The Gross Clinic furnishes a melodrama of life and death, light and darkness, knowledge and despair. With its towering, bloody-fingered Mephistopheles looming out of the black shadows into the stark illumination from above, it combines Mary Shelley with Caravaggio to put forth a scene that might later have been filmed by the German Expressionists. William Rush Carving His Allegorical Figure of the Schuylkill River, far from realism pure and simple, is, in fact, an allegory about realism.

Attempting to establish a reputable precedent for life study, it invites viewers to interpret the primal scene of image production in Federal-era Philadelphia in a manner that draws pointed connections to the Philadelphia of Eakins's own time. Clearly not derived from firsthand observation or even an actual event, this faux-historical painting undermines realism even while offering a brief on its behalf.

The Writing Master, a richly brushed, almost tactile portrait of Benjamin Eakins, an instructor of penmanship, resembles an old master painting not only in its chiaroscuro style and apostolic theme but also in its veneration of the artist's father, his own personal "old master." (Comparing Eakins's study photographs of his father with the oil portrait, we see in a flash the immeasurable distance that the artist traveled, in his finest works, between his source materials and their intensely wrought transformations.)

The most outstanding of the photography derived paintings in the exhibition, Mending the Net, can be identified as a work of realism only by using that term in a narrow and flat-footed way. As Roland Barthes pointed out more than thirty years ago, realism is a mode of representation no more nor less objective than any other; it is the style that goes to the greatest lengths to pretend not to be a style. Even a work as apparently neutral and unemotional as Wending the Net refuses to be understood as simply a snapshot of reality (or, in this case, an artful composite of snapshots).

Poetic and sacramental overtones fill this elegiac frieze of figures on a hillside. Seven adult men wearing hats and suspenders stand or kneel in various postures against the horizon line, green earth below and blue sky above, while they handle the fine filaments of a fish net that, metaphorically, binds them all together. Two small children take their place among them, while, far off to the side, a gentleman in black, wearing a dark hat, sits beneath an expansive, half-living, half-dead tree reading a newspaper or some other piece of writing.

In the lower left portion of the canvas, a gaggle of geese moves about in Brownian motion. Seven geese stationed beneath seven men: Is some sort of religious significance to be discerned in the repetition of the holy number, or perhaps some sort of Aesopian fable, in which men are either likened to geese or contrasted with them?

The painting is cool, austere, and remote, like a Greek funeral stela, yet at the same time Romantic. The huge, solitary tree calls to mind the work of Caspar David Friedrich, as does the figure of the seated man who faces away from the viewer. I'm not source hunting here, simply trying to indicate that while Mending the Net may have been assembled from projected photographs, for all its "realistic" details it comes across primarily as a moody and allegorical evocation of a masculine work community positioned within the all-encompassing vault of nature. To draw on anachronistic movie references, Mending the Net belongs as much to the moral universe of John Ford's How Green Was My Valley and Ingmar Bergman's The Seventh Seal as it does to local-colour realism of the Gilded Age.

Ford's film, showing workmen gathered harmoniously and heroically on the cusp of a Welsh hillside, arouses in the viewer a sense of sadness at the encroachments of industrialism, while Bergman's depicts a linked chain of humanity pulled across the hillside horizon by the black-clad figure of Death. Eakins, too, etches figures of mankind in the middle distance on the crest of the earth and against the sky in a manner that bespeaks innocence, loss, and mortality.

Eakins's oeuvre possesses much more of a night side, a dark, gothic, pre-, post-, or antiEnlightenment dimension, than the exhibition acknowledged either in its accompanying texts or in its steady march forward through his artistic chronology. Committed above all to illustrating in meticulous detail his academic and photographic manner of constructing images, the show treated him as an indisputable Great Artist whose greatness could be safely assumed.

It therefore did not attempt to reassess his body of work for the Eakins faithful or transfigure it for agnostics who were looking for some way into the art, one that would make it resonate for them. Lining up source photographs, perspective studies, and sculptural effigies next to finished paintings may have been, in theory, a good idea.

But this ultimately proved tedious, a musty academic exercise-which, alas, is precisely how Eakins's art itself has too often been seen by nonenthusiasts, who find his brand of realism chilly, contrived, and calculated. The museum's academic approach did not-could not-offer the general viewer any satisfactory explanation as to what in the world is so great or timely or timeless about Eakins and why that art has for so long been so highly esteemed.

EAKINS REINVENTED

At Eakins's first retrospective exhibition in 1917, the year after his death, his work struck Progressive Era viewers as a forceful criticism of the Gilded Age. They appreciated the painter for his obstinate refusal to conform to the strictures of the genteel tradition against which they, too, were in rebellion.

Not only the man himself but also his tightlipped late portraits, such as A. W. Lee, would have resonated with readers of Randolph Bourne's scathing 1917 essay "The

Puritan's Will to Power," which, in the spirit of the new radicalism, condemned puritanical guilt, sexual repression, and pragmatically motivated self-renunciation. The painter's austere images of middle-class isolation, anxiety, possibly even despair, such as The Thinker, Susan Macdowell Eakins (ca. 1899), and Edith Mahon suddenly made sense when seen in the context of Sherwood Anderson's Winesburg Ohio, Willa Cather's My Antonio, and Booth Tarkington's Magnificent Ambersons, all of which appeared within a year or two of the show.

The rediscovery of Eakins roughly coincided with the Herman Melville revival of the 1920s. In 1922, Henry McBride, art critic for the small but influential literary magazine the Dial, drew an explicit connection between the two figures and predicted that now that the long-obscure novelist had finally come into posthumous acclaim, the same would happen to the painter. As the decade closed, Lewis Mumford praised Eakins's "hearty contempt for the hierarchies of caste and office" and compared his mature work to Thorstein Veblen's caustic 1899 masterpiece of social de mystification, The Theory of the Leisure Class.

McBride's prediction of forthcoming public acclaim for the painter proved correct, but only in part. Eakins at last became famous in the 1930s, but with parallels to neither Melville nor Veblen. He was celebrated not as a nonconformist or a mordant critic of American pretentiousness and greed but rather as an artistic embodiment of "Americanism."

Perhaps the stock market crash saw to that, for during the Depression the American public at large, recoiling from over-rapid modernization at home and political turmoil abroad, wanted desperately to feel good about itself and its ancestry. In 1930 the Museum of Modern Art, taking a step back from the avant-garde precipice, mounted a loan exhibition of works by three turn-of-the-century masters, Winslow Homer, Albert Pinkham Ryder, and Eakins, all of them praised for being uniquely American (notwithstanding their European antecedents and, in Eakins's case, formal training).

During the ensuing decade, Eakins's champions hailed him as a microscopically observant local colorist, the forerunner of the Regionalists and other painters of "the American scene." As Henry McBride, ever his advocate, explained: Not being much courted by officialdom [Eakins] had the leisure in which to develop his Americanism. He studied abroad, for in his youth all Americans had the curious idea that they had to study abroad, but on his return he quickly settled down into the business of being himself. It never occurred to him to paint pictures to show how they painted pictures in France. He wished, instead, to show what the people were like who lived in Philadelphia.

When the Philadelphia Museum staged a vast Eakins retrospective for his centennial year, 1944, a feature chapter in Life proclaimed in a headline, "Philadelphians Who Snubbed Him Now Honour Him as an American Old Master." Newsweek, alluding to a story about the artist's gruff manner and preference for working-class apparel, titled its piece on the Philadelphia exhibition "Outlaw in an Undershirt." Thus, at the peak of World War II and befitting the populist rhetoric of the times, Tom Eakins was figured as a regular guy, an ordinary Joe, a man's man, who pictured his world in a muscular, no-frills, no-nonsense sort of way.

Following Life's coverage of the exhibition-including ten colour reproductions of paintings depicting various peacetime activities such as rowing, boxing, fishing, and joyriding in a horse-drawn carriage-an unrelated photo-essay sang the praises of American war production ("OIL, STEEL, GUNS, BOMBS, TANKS, PIAN-FS, LOCOMOTIVES," the captions thundered).

In this context, Eakins stood as a truthful recorder of the venerable American way of life that the war effort sought to defend and as an exemplar of precisely the tough-minded, roll-up-theshirtsleeves masculinity that the war effort required.

Even his sentimental female-sphere pictures such as Singing a Pathetic Song (1881), The Concert Singer (1890-92), Maud Cook (1895), and Tne Old-Fashioned Dress (ca. 1908) would have seemed in that climate to advance the war effort by memorializing the home front and contributing to a widespread nostalgia for America's "good old days." In this way the paintings helped to create a social and political imaginary that was congruent with the one emanating from popular Hollywood films of the war years, such as the 1944 Technicolor musical Meet Me in St. Louis, which lavishly and lovingly re-created a utopian 1904 of Eakins-like parlors, costumes, and family musicales.

In the postwar era, viewers looking for a credible alternative to modernist hegemony championed Eakins as a scientific positivist unflinchingly dedicated to the exploration of his world. Here was a representational artist whose seriousness of purpose, command of the medium, and heroic suffering matched that of the contemporary abstractionists. John Canaday, the conservative New York Times art critic, sniped, "Eakins was twice the rebel that most of the contemporary stable is, and ten times as original as the noisiest of them."

Fairfield Porter, a more temperate observer and himself a skilled representational painter, hastened to show that Eakins's realism was never purely literal or photographic but rather a sophisticated and deliberate construct of elements (although Porter did fault Eakins for sometimes missing the larger picture because of an undue concern with getting all the small local details exactly right).

Clement Greenberg, meanwhile, downplayed Eakins's realism and portrayed the painter as a formalist at heart dedicated to exploring the materiality of his medium. "Eakins seems to try for a hardheaded account of nature that will match the 'hard' mathematical devices he often uses to plot the composition and perspective of his pictures," the critic conceded. "But those devices turn out to be only a framework on which he projects an ideal chiaroscuro. The language of his imagination is revealed as predominantly one of light and dark in which facts are transfigured without being violated."

The meaning of Eakins changed again during the antiwar era of the late 1960s and early 1970s. He was regarded, as on earlier occasions, as a rebel against the stuffy and hypocritical conventions of bourgeois society and admired as a lifelong bohemian who scorned "the establishment" and defiantly snubbed America's "national disease," which William James, back in 1906, had identified as "the exclusive worship of the bitch-goddess succESS." To grasp the 1960s Eakins, think The Graduate, or Catch 22 and Easy Rider.

The most provocative book on Eakins at the time, by a professor of English literature, Sylvan Schendler, depicted the artist and his sitters as victims of an oppressive, coldly impersonal social structure.

A representative passage from Schendler's book describes Portrait of Frank Hamilton Cushing, Eakins's full-length painting of a pioneering ethnologist from Philadelphia who had lived for years among the Zuni of New Mexico. Schendler calls the portrait "a moving image of social failure" and elaborates: "Tragic possibility is written in Cushing's face.... The man exists alone and in the broader experience of the age, expressing his reverence for a civilization being engulfed and destroyed in nineteenth-century America." Eakins shows the gaunt, mustached Cushing dressed and groomed in the manner of the Zuni, with shoulder-length locks tumbling from his headband and his body further adorned by hoop earrings, knee-high leather boots, beads, feathers, and metal studs.

He resembles a white 19th-century Philadelphian playing Indian, but, in an oddly anachronistic fashion, he also looks like a 1960s hippie or biker.

By the end of the 1970s, Eakins, like virtually every other significant cultural producer of the past several centuries, was strapped down onto the table of academic ideological scrutiny. The Death of the Author movement did not bypass Thomas Eakins. My doctoral dissertation, written under the sway of French poststructuralism and feminist film theory, probed, poked, and sliced apart a single Eakins image, The Agnew Clinic, to show that it was hardly the neutral, value-free document of 19th-century surgical dissection that its champions believed it to be. I claimed instead, in a would-be dissection of my own, that it was rife with crisscrossing tensions and hostilities between the doctor and his patient, the artist and his sitter, the instructor and his students, and the male observers in the medical amphitheater and the beautiful barebreasted young woman laid out before their eyes in anesthetized unconsciousness.

Michael Fried ventured into similar territory with The Gross Clinic, dismissing what had become the standard reading of the painting as a heroic testament to the artist's uncompromising realism. With his customary brilliance, Fried unraveled the portrait instead as a brutal manifestation of Oedipal paranoia, homosexual dread, and castration anxiety on the part of a painter obsessed with writing, can-,ing, cutting, and inscribing-the whole panoply of Derridean buzz terms that many of us in academia found chic and daring at a time when Ronald Reagan's "Morning in America" rhetoric lay so heavy on the Cold War horizon.

Viable academic alternatives to the study of Eakins other than deconstruction and new historicism existed at that time. In fact, the latter approaches were relatively marginal compared to the influence of the new social history. Elizabeth Johns's landmark 1983 book about Eakins provided thick description of middle-class daily life in late 19th-century Philadelphia to historicize and contextualize the art in question.

Much fine work on Eakins appearing since then has, in one way or another, added to this descriptive project, amassing a rich body of historical detail mined from a wide array of archival documents, including not only correspondence, diaries, newspaper reviews, and studio account books but also medical journals, rowing manuals, etiquette guides, sheet music, penny fiction, and so forth.

Yet, here, too, Eakins as author was transformed into Eakins as cipher, and those humanistic, transcendent, or social-critical issues that captured the imagination of earlier commentators on the artist received little or no serious attention. Whether deconstructed, Lacanized, new-historicized, or social-historified, Eakins and his art now came to be understood as (or, according to opponents of such methods, reduced to) the outcome of impersonal external or deterministic internal forces.

The autonomous artist of old-fashioned art history who waged romantic or existential war against oppressive social and artistic conventions vanished into the thin, rarefied air of the postmodern academic Zeitgeist. In the late 1980s and through the 1990s, Eakins revisionism grew apace. Martin Berger, Alan Braddock, Whitney Davis, Jennifer Doyle, Judith Fryer, Bridget Goodbody, Randall Griffin, Michael Hatt, Marcia Pointon, and Eric Rosenberg were among those who published essays and, in Berger's case, a book on the various relations of Eakins's work to masculinity, misogyny, sexuality, homoeroticism, representation, and/or race.

Current research on Eakins, including various dissertations in progress, ponders his work's connections to 19th-century ethnography, religion, nationalism, and internationalism. Revisionist scholarship on Eakins has sought to understand how his art came together not technically but ideologically, driven by his own and, more important, his era's collective sexual, psychological, and social-status obsessions.

EAKINS REVEALED

The changes that occurred in Eakins scholarship during the closing two decades of the 20th century can be read in the differences to be found between Thomas Eakins: American Realist and the Philadelphia Museum's previous comprehensive exhibition of the artist's work, Thomas Eakins: Artist of Philadelphia, which appeared in 1982.

The museum's head curator of American art, Darrel Sewell, was the force behind both shows. In his own unassuming way, Sewell has proven to be one of the most important players in modern Eakins studies.

His Eakins exhibitions have availed themselves of the new scholarship, albeit in a relatively selective and conservative fashion, drawing heavily on solid documentation and the latest archival or conservation-lab discoveries while holding at arm's length research that has been speculative, literary, and interpretative in nature. For the hulking, 446-page, double-columned 2001 model, he brought together a team of eleven Eakins specialists (himself among them).

The comparative difference in the size and weight of the catalogues is telling. In 1982, the new Eakins scholarship was only just revving up, having been inspired by three important publications of the late 1970s and one of the early 1980s: the Eakins catalogues from the Hirshhorn and Philadelphia museums, the special issue of Arts magazine devoted to Eakins, and the magisterial two-volume life of Eakins by Lloyd Goodrich, the dean of Eakins scholars, who had published his first book on the painter five decades earlier.

In the two decades since the 1982 exhibition, Eakins scholarship, as mentioned, has burgeoned in numerous directions, deploying discourses of feminism, poststructuralism, and cultural history in a manner that has allowed his work to be examined in fresh new terms. Elizabeth Johns's 1983 book on Eakins and Michael Fried's 1985 essay on The Gross Clinic were two of the three most significant events in Eakins scholarship to follow on the heels of the 1982 exhibition.

The third was the amazing discovery in 1984 of the so-called Bregler Collection, a treasure trove of previously rumored but unexamined Eakins documents and photographs traced by Kathleen Foster, then curator of the Pennyslvania Academy of the Fine Arts, and her assistant, Elizabeth Milroy, in a run-down South Philadelphia townhouse.

Charles Bregler had been a student of Eakins and an acolyte. When the artist's widow, Susan Macdowell Eakins, died without heir in 1938, Bregler managed to salvage from her home stacks of correspondence, clippings, photograph albums, and glass-plate negatives that otherwise would have been committed to the rubbish heap.

After Bregler's death twenty years later, at the age of ninety-three, they passed to his widow, a woman half a century younger than he, who stored them in an assortment of shopping bags and dress boxes in a bedroom of her mother's house, to which she subsequently moved, and where

Foster and Milroy made her acquaintance and began to discuss with her the future of this astounding repository of art historical materials.

The Pennsylvania Academy acquired the collection in 1985 and began its inventory. In 1989 Foster and the academy archivist Cheryl Leibold published a guide to more than one thousand documents in the Bregler Collection. A follow-up guide to the 648 photographic images in the collection appeared in 1994.

Beyond providing a wealth of useful information and documentation about the way Eakins taught, made art, and lived his life at various stages in his career, the Bregler Collection proved to contain materials of a racy, even incendiary nature. These materials, in fact, may be the reason why the reclusive Bregler was so cautious during his lifetime about making his collection available to the public.

In one photograph, a nude Susan Eakins, her face scratched out by someoneprobably either herself or Bregler, apparently in an effort to preserve her anonymity-leans against the artist's horse Billy in a woodland setting, one arm reaching toward the horse's mane, the other cast provocatively back behind her shoulder, giving her breasts an upward tilt.

Many of the collection's photographs show attractive young art students posing nude individually or in pairs, even in small groups. No matter that many of these nude photographs can be correlated to identifiable painting or sculptural projects and were thus an obvious extension of Eakins's dedication to life study as the basis for figurative art. They cannot be viewed today without raising all sorts of questions about intention, propriety, and 19th-century sexuality.

The master himself appears in the nude. In one series of shots, he stands on the studio floor, an unidentified naked young woman (possibly a student, maybe his wife) hoisted aloft in his arms, his genitalia bobbing into the light beneath her rump and his fingers tucking into the flesh beneath her exposed breast. What's going on here? The master appears to be so... so masterful.

Is that a smirk on his face? It's difficult to say for sure, but he seems to be grinning. Are he and she playacting dominance and submission, that is, making theater of the male/female, master/slave dyad in a manner that sets it on its ear? Or is this a straight-up display of sexual prowess and control, the Mermaid in the clutches of the Minotaur?

The wall label of fixed to the one photograph from the series that was used in the exhibition came close to acknowledging the problematic sexual dynamics of the picture, only to brush aside such considerations with a discourse that at once heroized the artist and normalized his behaviour: "Any photograph mixing male and female nudes would have raised eyebrows from all quarters, and Eakins reserved for himself the task of posing for such images and the risk of disapproval."

Eakins was breaking all rules with teaching practices such as these. What we see in this photograph did not constitute normal studio procedure, not in Philadelphia, nor in Paris.

For us today to shrug off such an obvious transgression of the academic, pedagogical, and moral codes of the time by regarding the photograph as one more piece of evidence demonstrating Eakins's disinterested pursuit of scientific and artistic knowledge-and, moreover, his heroism ("reserved for himself... the risk of disapproval")-smacks of either naivete or obtuseness.

The cache of letters and affidavits that Bregler had sequestered from prying eyes turned out to be equally revelatory about Eakins and his circle. It has long been known that Eakins was forced to resign from his position as director of instruction at the Pennyslvania Academy because in the midst of an impromptu lecture on anatomy in a life study class attended by female students he had impulsively stripped away the loincloth of a male model, leaving nothing to the imagination.

The Bregler documents reveal that the loincloth incident precipitated a crisis already in the works; for months, if not longer, a cabal of senior students and junior instructors at the academy had been looking for a way to depose their leader. Rumors, it seems, had been circulating beyond the academy walls that well-bred female art students were posing in the nude for one another (a matter of truth, as it turns out).

In the face of such rumors, certain of these students, and their indignant husbands, boyfriends, or brothers, felt cheapened and humiliated, prompting them to mount a whispering campaign against Eakins for having encouraged the women to remove their clothes in front of one another in the first place.

The most outraged of the assailants was an academy student named Frank Stephens, who was married to Eakins's youngest sister, Caddie. Stephens insinuated that the artist had had incestuous relations with another sister, Maggie Eakins, recently deceased, while she was his pupil. More than a decade later, incest allegations surfaced again when the artist's twenty-four-year-old niece Ella Crowell, who had taken art lessons with her uncle, turned a gun on herself. Her father, another Eakins brother-in-law, William Crowell, blamed Ella's death on the painter, whom he said had corrupted and perhaps even molested his daughter.

All these matters and others, a welter of unproven charges and countercharges, have come to light by way of the documents long stashed beneath Mary Bregler's bed. Such salacious stories, well-founded or otherwise, bear relevance to the art that Eakins produced during this period of his life because they shaped or misshaped the personal context in which he worked.

One of the masterpieces of the show, and one of the most troubling paintings of his career, is The Agnew Clinic, a wall-size picture of a small group of doctors in white coats conducting a surgical operation on a seminude young female patient, while approximately two dozen male medical students in dark street clothes gaze at her with varying degrees of intensity.

The operation in question is a mastectomy. A breast has been or is about to be removed, tissue is sliced open, blood trickles across milky white skin; the patient is anesthetized into sleep; a nurse observer, wedged into a corner, looks on with detachment or professional concern, it's up to the viewer to say which; a student in the upper left corner carves the small phallic penknife clasped between his hands into the wooden back of the bench in front of him in a gesture that echoes, or mimics, or otherwise visually rhymes the surgical act taking place before his eyes; and the elderly physician-teacher for whom the painting is named stands back from the operation in progress as though he were a 17th-century swashbuckling pirate captain gazing on his men as they take their plunder or a 17th-century old master artist, like Eakins's hero Diego Velazquez, leaning away from his easel to size up a work in progress.

The Bregler Collection casts no direct light on The Agnew Clinic, but it does much to bring out into the open the sexual strains of the painting that have for so long been repressed by conventional readings of it as a document of medical realism that illustrates the introduction of modern anesthesia and antisepsis.

With the riches of the Bregler Collection having appeared, as it were, out of nowhere, and with the New Art History having found its way to Eakins scholarship in the years since 1982, the time for a millennial Eakins retrospective was clearly at hand. The catalogue essays cover a variety of topics, among them Eakins's early years, his European training (H. Barbara Weinberg), his relation to the local city parks movement, his long and complex involvement with the Pennsylvania Academy, his writings about art and art instruction (William Innes Homer), and his reputation in the 20th century.

One essay focuses on the branch of his painting devoted to envisioning the past, another on his portraits of teachers and thinkers (Foster), and a third on his relation to the history of photography. Two additional essays (jointly written by Philadelphia Museum conservators Mark Tucker and Nica Gutman) centre on technical matters: the artist's choice of paint pigments and his reliance on photography in making his paintings.

A series of four essays by Marc Simpson, associate director of the graduate programme in the history of art at

Williams College, forms the heart of the catalogue. Covering the life and art of Eakins on a decade-by-decade basis, these thoughtful, sensitive pieces of writing carry the reader through the high and low points of the artist's career with elegantly informative discussions of individual works of art, including their preparation, completion, and reception.

Aside from the photograph-projection revelations, however, nothing particularly new about Eakins or his work emerges from the catalogue as a whole. It primarily weaves together the past two decades of archival discoveries and the previous scholarship of Goodrich and other Eakins specialists. The more adventurous interpretative research of the past twenty years is all but ignored, though at least some of it is acknowledged in the footnotes. Thus, while uniformly excellent on their own terms and filled with impeccable scholarship lucidly expressed, the catalogue essays rarely probe for the metaphoric meaning of Eakins's images or pose questions that do not lend themselves to empirical investigation.

Make no mistake, the copious amount of primary-source research contained in this catalogue is phenomenal and deserves high praise. Still, more cultural synthesizing and speculation, more drawing of connections beyond the immediate and narrow frame of reference, would have been worthwhile. At the same time, more concision on the order of the 1982 Eakins catalogue would have been commendable. That catalogue was lean enough to be picked up and read cover to cover, whereas this leviathan, for all its wealth of offerings, is likely to remain decoratively arranged on coffee tables, an objet more to be admired than read.

EAKINS EXPOSED

It was while Darrel Sewell and his staff were in the process of organizing the new show that the surprising revelations about Eakins's tracing of photographs emerged. Examining Shad Fishing at Gloucester on the Delaware River, a minor oil painting from 1881, two of the museum's paintings conservators, Tucker and Gutman, discovered with infrared reflectography (IRR) the hidden incisions that gave the game away. The bold realist whose candor, even temerity, was legendary turned out to have been hiding a secret.

He was, in effect, a cheater, at least according to the prevailing Romantic tenets of his time. These decreed that, despite occasional help from optical devices and various homegrown drawing machines and other methods of sizing images up or down, true artists relied on their eyes and hands and, above all, their native genius, but never technology, to reproduce the world visually.

The extent to which the Philadelphia painter not only relied on photography but went out of his way to disguise the evidence of doing so suggests a serious concern on his part that such wholesale dependence on mechanical means of reproduction would have been judged prosaic and commercial, and that his contemporaries would have remonstrated against this unseemly devotion to mundane machinery rather than sacred inspiration.

Gutman and Tucker's findings raise more questions than they answer. Why was Eakins, an academic traditionalist in so many ways, and perhaps the finest draftsman that America ever produced, willing to spend so much time and effort on inventing and perfecting this technique? Why, to judge from IRR examination of subsequent canvases, did he cease using the process after 1885? Had he concluded it was an artistic dead-end, of too little payoff to warrant further application?

Did his wife or his closest disciples know anything about his experiments? Why do the papers in the Bregler Collection, which betray no reticence about sexual matters and abundantly detail Eakins's art theory and technique, provide no hint of his fondness for photographic projection and tracing? How can his conscientious commitment to quasiscientific devices and techniques, including the tracing of photographs, be reconciled with his quasipornographic photography of students and other irregular studio practices?

The biggest question of all regarding the new discoveries is: So what? So what if Eakins employed photography in the manner now detected? How does this revelation about the process by which he made a handful of his paintings alter the way that these or other paintings by him generate meanings of a social, aesthetic, or philosophical nature?

These are not questions that the exhibition grappled with, either in its various catalogue essays or in the wall texts, audio guide, and introductory video. Only two of the sixteen catalogue essays-Tucker and Gutman's "Photographs and the Making of Paintings" and Curatorial Assistant W. Douglass Paschall's "The Camera Artist"-even broach the new findings at any length, and, although these both provide skillful expositions of matters relating to Eakins and photography, they do not take up larger and broader issues about the meaning of these findings, or of the photographs and paintings themselves.

Nor do the remaining catalogue essays do so. They concern themselves with other matters, in part, no doubt, because their respective authors wrote them before the projectionand-tracing findings had fallen into place, but also, one suspects, because the findings had little relevance for the topics their essays sought to address.

In other words, to judge from the catalogue, the new findings simply are not all that earthshaking. But at some point along the way, someone at the Philadelphia Museum decided to focus on the photographic disclosures as the selling feature of the exhibition.

The half-hour introductory video explained the "secret" and how the museum staff unlocked it. The audio guide, wall panels, arrangement of source photographs next to paintings, and even the museum's press kit also conveyed the impression that the most important thing to know about Thomas Eakins was that he made an exceptional and innovative use of photography (sometimes together with other, more traditional preparatory tools, such as perspective drawings, oil sketches, and wax models) in order to arrive at his finished oil paintings.

Possibly the decision to give so much emphasis to the photography findings resulted from the Hockney controversy that was making news in the art world at the time the exhibition was being prepared. David Hockney, a prominent British artist living in the United States, claimed to have "discovered" that a large number of old masters had secretly employed optical devices in order to enhance the verisimilitude of their work.

Meanwhile, two high-profile art exhibitions added to public awareness of the connections between photography and painting. These were The Artist and the Canera: Degas to Picasso, at the Dallas Museum of Art, which noted close connections in various artistic oeuvres between source photographs and finished paintings, and the Metropolitan Museum of Art's Vermeer and the De ft School, which popularized the hypothesis that the 17th-century Dutch painter availed himself of the camera obscura and other period optical devices, samples of which were put on display.

This, then, formed the immediate art-world context for Tucker, Gutman, and Paschall's discovery that Eakins traced from photographs. Suddenly, excitingly, Eakins fit into the new paradigm, providing an irresistible hook. Eakins could so easily seem to today's viewers an old-fashioned artist, a conservative, pre-avant-garde, academic bourgeois realist with nothing new or exciting to offer 21st century audiences. With the fortuitous detection of strategically placed tick marks on his canvases, he suddenly seemed up-todate. Not that the paintings themselves looked any more modern or old-fashioned than before the discovery of the tick marks, but the discourse surrounding the painter and his practice of art could be rendered au courant.

Although it didn't do so in an explicit manner, Thomas Eakins: American Realist intervened in the common perception about Eakins by deemphasizing some of the previous characterizations of him as, alternatively, a truculent individualist, a salty realist, a martyr to Victorian prudery, a psychological introvert, or a sexual pervert. Instead, it recast him as a protophotorealist (which, admittedly, has a nice jingle to it), a precursor to Andy Warhol, David Hockney, Chuck Close, Gerhard Richter, and, in his proclivity for manipulating and altering photographic information, current and future generations of digital and video artists. I see two central ideas of our present era lurking beneath or contained within the move to emphasize the Hockneyesque factor in Eakins's art production.

One might be called pragmatic utilitarianism or instrumentalism. The other is technophilia, the love or adoration of technology, in this case, information technology. The Eakins put forward by the Philadelphia show, like the old masters reconstituted by Hockney and his supporters, is a maestro of information technologies, a special-effects magician. Easy Rider with a paintbrush becomes, in this latest perutation, a computer wiz with a cut-and-paste control. The "genius" resides not in what the artist had to say (in his own time) and has to say (in ours) but instead in how he managed to say it. It's not even a question of style over substance, that is, artistic form over philosophical, documentary, or autobiographical content, but rather of technique as content.

In our present age of irony, skepticism, cynicism, and fear of commitment, it's so much safer to talk about how art is produced than to ponder its meanings and, in so doing, appear ponderous.

In addition to our fascination with technology and its workings, we have today a massive and permeating faith in the virtues of pragmatic realism and instrumentalism, that is, professionalism. This, too, was one of the cultural values underlying the show. By stressing Eakins's deliberate, methodical, mathematical, and scientific means of arriving at solutions to representational issues, and by stressing as well his close personal involvement with the "big men" of medicine, science, sports, education, and engineering of his time and place, the exhibition gave us a decidedly non-Romantic artist as its object of admiration.

For all his quirks and departures from sentimental-era norms, his irascibility and impatience with philistine prudery and pretense, the Eakins conjured up by the Philadelphia show was an almost rock-solid, unflappable, two-feet-on-the-ground scientific member in good standing of his local communities of knowledge. This Thomas Eakins was no rebel, with or without a cause, no hippie or dissenter from what Alan Trachtenberg has termed "the incorporation of America." He was a professional who had a job to do-make accurate pictures of the worldand nearly always got it done.

Historians have shown how a "culture of professionalism" sprang up the United States in the aftermath of the Civil War and began to flourish. Eakins belonged to this culture and left us a uniquely detailed visual description of it. His art, however, may have offered an implicit critique of professional culture, as in his intimate late portraiture, with its haunting glimpses of fin de siecle mental and spiritual exhaustion, and even in his earlier, supposedly "heroic" images of celebrity physicians, scientists, and scholars. This is not to say that Eakins ever set out to pillory the eminent Victorian Americans of his era, some of whom were his friends and supporters, or to subvert professional and pragmatic culture rather than avidly take his place within it. Nonetheless, a close look at his art indicates a recurring ambivalence toward that culture.

This ambivalence he shared with many of his contemporaries. I suspect that neither the nature nor the amount of our work is accountable for the frequency and severity of our breakdowns," wrote William James of his and Eakins's generation, "but that their cause lies rather in those absurd feelings of hurry and having no time, in that breathlessness and tension, that anxiety of feature and that solicitude for results, that lack of inner harmony and ease, in short, by which with us the work is so apt to be accompanied."

James, himself a full-fledged member of the professional-managerial middle class who, as a Harvard professor, participated influentially in its perpetuation and extension, was all too aware of the neurasthenic baggage that professionalization carried with it. Eakins's art, like William James's psychological studies, Henry James's fiction, and Henry Adams's historical autobiography, may similarly be understood as a product of the modern civilization of professionalism while also being a finely tuned register of its discontents, as seen in the haggard, melancholy, or emotionally vulnerable expressions of some of his sitters and in the wooden stolidity of others.

This dark side of Eakins's work, this reflexive recoil from the strains of modern wealthand status-seeking, this profoundly mixed response to pragmatic utilitarianism, which led all too many denizens of modernity then, as now, to succumb to what William James called "wear and tear and fatigue," went all but unnoticed by the exhibition. Eakins came across, as he had half a century earlier in the Philadelphia Museum's centennial celebration of its hometown artist, as a can-do man, a brain worker (to use the late 19th-century term for a clerical, managerial, or professional bureaucrat) who set tough but realistic goals and ingeniously devised techniques for achieving them. I'm not faulting the Philadelphia Museum for seeing to it that Eakins reappeared in this manner. I merely wish to reflect that its way of construing him, strongly accenting the positive and the practical, fit him rather seamlessly into the guiding corporate ideology of the United States at the start of the 21st century, when, in politics as well as in business, if not also in arts administration and even the arts themselves, leaders are valued most of all for their clear-eyed, toughminded realism and ability to get the job done.

A more interesting show, if surely one less likely to be corporately funded, would have brought out the dark shades of its subject, his artistic and personal shortcomings, even his most troubling secrets (and I don't mean his furtive projection of photographs), not to pull him down or sensationalize his life but to provide him with the chiaroscuro lighting that he himself often used to such striking effect.

And it would have taken steps, however small and tentative, to indicate that this unusual life steadfastly devoted to the production and teaching of art was nonetheless representative of an era that stretched from the Civil War to World War I and included Reconstruction and its demise, race riots, the rise of the Ku Klux Klan, the birth of the New Negro movement, Indian wars, the Spanish American War, a bloody counterinsurgency operation in the newly acquired

Philippines, financial panics and depressions, labour revolts, anarchist bombings, a march of the unemployed on Washington, feminist activism and suffrage campaigns, civil service reform, the spread of corporate monopoly and the concomitant swelling of citizens' groups opposed to it, and the tidal wave of immigration that forever altered the face of America.

A show organized along such lines might have done a better job of ensuring that viewers connected with Eakins's art in manifold ways and grasped its continuing relevance instead of simply filing past it in dutiful awe.

WHY INSTEAD OF HOW

The Eakins exhibition of 2001, like any other art exhibition, ultimately provided a blank screen onto which viewers projected the times at hand as filtered through their own complex and self-interested perceptions about those times. Planned in the boom years of the mid- to late 1990s, when high-tech information systems spurred the economy and the worldwide American empire reached its zenith, the Eakins show crystallized around the two core ideas mentioned above, technological innovation and hard-edged, toughminded pragmatic realism. The focus of the show fit its cultural moment.

By the time the exhibition opened in October, however, the landscape had radically changed. Tech stocks were tanking, the twintowered architectural symbol of American financial pragmatism and realism had imploded before the horrified gaze of millions of onlookers, and, by late October, disturbing rumors were beginning to gather that one of the nation's most powerful and seemingly unassailable energy conglomerates, Enron Corporation, ranked at no. 7 on the Fortune 500 list of America's largest companies, teetered on the verge of bankruptcy, threatening to leave in its dust billions of dollars in debt and worthless stockholder shares.

To be sure, the relatively swift and resounding success of the United States in its air war in Afghanistan helped offset the drubbing administered to technology and pragmatism that fall. Still, so soon after the appalling calamities of September 11, with the American population grieving, hurt, and insecure about what the future might bring, the way Eakins achieved his artistic effects suddenly seemed less important than what his paintings had to say, in their quiet, nonanecdotal, and nondidactic manner, about big issues such as family, friendship, joy, solitude, and death.

Take, for example, The Pair-Oared Shell, a dark brown, almost grubby painting from 1872 that shows two rowers, the thenfamous racing team of John and Barney Biglin, sculling their shell past the massive stone pier of an unseen bridge. New Yorkers, the Biglins had come to Philadelphia for a race held on the Schuylkill in late May of that year.

One could hardly imagine a more austere or gloomier depiction of champion racers on a river. Cold, lifeless, and static, the picture seems to freeze the two figures in eternal stillness. The Biglins mirror one another in posture and activity-each pulls at his separate oar in a motion synchronized with that of his counterpart-and, as brothers, they mirror one another in body and face as well.

Eakins chose his pigments and applied his paints parsimoniously. This is a painting with no give to it, no elasticity or ampleness. It is spare in all regards but for one: whacked through the image from top to bottom is an immense iron shadow, a vertical slab of impenetrable darkness that cuts preemptively across the horizontal bands of sky, shoreline, and river. The rowers are shown at the moment that they have only barely emerged from the overwhelming blackness of that shadow into the grim fading light of day.

The existence of Eakins's perspective drawings for The Pair-Oared Shell has had the unfortunate effect of leading Eakins scholars to focus on the "how" rather than the "why" of the painting.

Over twenty years ago, Elizabeth Johns made this same point, noting, "The critical obsession with Eakins as a transcriber of reality has been fueled most intensely by the survival of Eakins' detailed perspective studies for his boating paintings of the early 1870s. Somehow these perspective studies have seemed to 'prove' that Eakins' artistic objective was to record precise distance, temperature, and time of day."

Using The PairOared Shell as her example, she cautioned scholars to look beyond its relatively trivial significance as a quasiscientific report of a specific moment and place (determined by scholars to be 7:20 P.M., Eastern Standard Time, on May 28, 1872, beneath Philadelphia's old Columbia Bridge). Instead, she urged interpretation of the painting: "Of rich metaphorical import are the scale relationships, between the small human beings, their fragilely proportioned craft, and the looming bridge pier, and the weight and time relationships, between the heaviness and permanence of the pier and the lightness and transience of the men and their craft."

Johns's astute metaphorical reading of The Pair-Oared Shell, achieved by thoughtfully measuring and contrasting its formal elements, does not resort to biography in order to pull out the meanings she has ascribed to it. Nonetheless, a judicious use of biographical information actually supports and adds to her interpretation of the work's philosophical or existential implications. At the time Eakins was painting The Pair-Oared Shell, his mother died at age fifty-two. The cause of death was recorded as "exhaustion from mania." She had been ailing for a protracted period, and her son, who had resumed living at home after his return from Europe two years earlier, had devoted considerable time to her care.

With her death, the Eakins household consisted of three unmarried sisters, a maiden aunt, Tom, and his widowed father. The two men appear to have been very close to one another, allied by their shared interests in art and sports, and, at that time, by their grief.

Perhaps The Pair-Oared Shell is a metaphorical rendering of shared closeness between two male family members (father and son, in this instance, not brothers) who, literally pulling together, emerge from an extreme period of darkness-the mother's slow and painful demise-into the softer dusk. Time is at a standstill, however: they are poised at the margin between the two realms, fixed at the edge. The painting calls on archetypal Christian, and before that classical, imagery of life, death, and time's passage.

Bridges, shadows, rivers, boats on the water, dwindling daylight-all of these extend far back in Western art and literature as metaphors that provide a means of fathoming-or decrying, or accepting-the mysteries of human existence. Why should such metaphorical elements not carry that same charge here?

This is but one example of how Eakins's art becomes so much richer and more meaningful to viewers when the "why" of it is asked to take precedence over the "how." Eakins himself may well have been a scientific materialist, a pragmatic realist, a committed practitioner of instrumental reason who possessed an abiding faith in mathematical logic and mechanical technology as his means of mastering the visual field and rendering it transparent. He himself may have been opposed to religion, mysticism, and other nonempirical types of knowledge about the world outside and within.

Nevertheless, from the rowing paintings through the medical scenes to the boxing pictures and the parlor musicales and the bleak and haunting late portraits, his art is full of transcendent moments, making him a so much finer and more compelling artist than he would be if his paintings were primarily of value for their ingenious efforts to transcribe external physical reality onto canvas. A strict materialist and empiricist he may have wanted to be, but it is only because he failed at this goal and repeatedly hinted in his work at alternative realities to the one made visible by formulas and photographs that we are continually drawn to his paintings and discover in them noble, and ignoble, ghosts of ourselves.

Chapter 4

The Movement of Vulnerability

Are those who fell to their deaths on September 11, 2001, exploited or honored by the display of images representing their experiences? While the circumstances that led to the actions of the man in Richard Drew's photograph are unprecedented, images of falling are not new to photojournalism or contemporary art. That images of those who fell from the towers became traumatically imprinted in people's minds suggests that they urgently merit not only detailed study but also deeper contextualization within visual culture.

In light of Drew's iconic photograph, an image that, perhaps more than any other, epitomizes the tragedy and the horror of the September 11 catastrophe in Western cultural memory, my questions are as follows: What reinterpretations can be brought to art created prior to September 11 that takes falling as its subject matter? How do artworks made in response to September 11 hold up under critical scrutiny when the photo journalistic images of the actual event are already so aesthetically powerful?

'Further, what challenges do these mostly lens-based images pose for photographic theory, in particular, the substantial contribution made by Roland Barthes, whose work is concerned with the cultural codes of press photography as well as the interrelationship between death and photography?

From the perspective of contemporary art history, my purpose is not to defend whether or not one should look at, display, or circulate such images of falling-ultimately such questions lead to the irresolvable problem of whether or not there is a violation in looking, and then quickly shift to issues of censorship-but to identify what one sees in them, how the perception of movement alters the subjectivity of those falling, and what the stakes are for the subjects involved, namely, those made visible and those who view them.

These questions can be summarized equally as "What is one to make of the image?" and "What does the image make of its subjects?"

When different media capture such fragile subjects, in liminal moments that cannot be adequately named, vulnerability becomes an issue of representation.

This attention to vulnerability is neither prurient nor morbid. Vulnerability is a complex condition centrally tied to agency, to the subject's ability to exert or extend itself in the world and to be recognized by others.

Images of falling make acutely evident the body's simultaneous potential for vulnerability and its capacity for agency. Images of falling challenge codes of representation on two significant levels: visually, in terms of the subject whose body is arrested by the medium; linguistically, in terms of the viewer's ability to respond and identify what is seen.

Vulnerability therefore implicates the subject of representation and the viewer: while the falling subject is left in a state of suspended animation in the image, the viewer is held in a state of speechlessness, unable to name what or whom is seen. I am interested in uncovering how, in subtle and often unintended ways, aesthetic qualities alter the perception of the falling subjects' potential mortality and make it impossible to perceive the vulnerability of the subject in the image.

My hypothesis is that, in the process of identifying moments when vulnerability is or is not apparent in images of falling, formal and ideological problems are revealed to such an extent that an ethical paradigm unfolds.

With its global consideration of the ramifications of September 11 as image and event, a major premise of Retort is that one of the most trenchant results of the terrorist attacks was the exposure of the vulnerability of the state.

The way the attacks made visible a nation wounded with such surgical precision is identified by Retort as the reason they functioned so "well" as spectacle (this is not an endorsement) and why their media visibility had to be immediately suppressed: "Terror can take over the image-machinery for a moment-and a moment, in the timeless echo chamber of the spectacle, may now eternally be all there is-and use it to amplify, reiterate, accumulate the sheer visible happening of defeat."

As the cultural theorist Susan Buck-Morss incisively claims, "What disappeared on September 11 was the apparent invulnerability, not only of US territory, but of US, and, indeed, Western hegemony."

With the destruction (if only temporary) of a financial capital market and a manifestation of modernity's highest architectural aspirations, as well as its working, human subjects, the exposure of the vulnerability of the nation-state was, as Buck-Morss points out, achieved not only at the symbolic level (as image), but also at a concrete, physical level; further, "the photographically mediated experience of the attack was of both the symbol and the real, antagonistically superimposed."

But rather than focusing on the geopolitical implications of September 11, I want to consider representations of vulnerability at the individual level of embodied subjectivity-not without acknowledging, of course, that those individuals represent more encompassing images of nationstate vulnerability.

Because it involves nonfictional subjects, the issue of vulnerability here is profoundly ethical. Subjectivity as I understand it is an ongoing series of effects (involving language, images, cultural and political institutions and their discourses, names and identity categories) that form a subject who must always be assumed to be under construction, a work-in-progress, changing and contingent, less a source of agency than a scene or sight through which the effects of power are materialized. Part of my project is to extend the notion of subjectivity to the dead, to show how they are acutely vulnerable to representational violence. One must keep in mind that subjects are not merely theoretical premises but are as vulnerable to the burdens of the body as they are to the painful effects of discourse and representations.

The dead should be considered implicated in the processes of subjectivity; subjects are vulnerable equally to posthumous distortion, neglect, and dishonor by images and words as to bodily death. How is subjectivity produced for bodies in motion, bodies whose weight and movement led to their deaths, bodies whose deathly trajectories are captured in lens-based representations?

Do some representations contort the process of subjectivity, and if so, how? My focus on vulnerability is also indebted to Judith Butler's 2004 reflections on September 11, in which she develops a cultural theory of intersubjectivity with global reach, an ethics founded on the experience of mourning (national, collective, and individual) in which the self, through the experience of being made acutely aware of the Other's vulnerability to mortal violence, also experiences vulnerability: "Loss and vulnerability seem to follow from our being socially constituted bodies, attached to others, at risk of losing those attachments, exposed to others, at risk of violence by virtue of that exposure."

Imagining an ethics that can be integrated into global politics, Butler proposes that governments base their global policies on a micropolitics of relationality constituted by the awareness of mutual vulnerability, so that a response to terrorism can be developed that doesn't perpetuate violence, isolationism, or unilateralism, or lead to the restriction of personal and intellectual freedoms.

Butler's critical injunction is to be understood in the present global context of war, conflict, and acts of terror that afflict non-Western civilian populations (Palestinians, Afghans, and Iraqis in particular) to a much greater degree man North Americans. Butler acknowledges that although grief is an interior focus, it also directs attention to the ones who are lost. The mourning subject may feel a sense of solitude but not of autonomy: what ensues from mourning is the realization that we are socially constituted subjects, communities, and nations.

According to Buder, the experience of grief is ultimately qualified by the realization that the self is irrevocably transformed, if not also shattered, by the loss of the other, a situation whereby "one finds oneself fallen."

In its affective movement, Butler's description of the mourner as herself having fallen provides an empathetic model for understanding the potential for the present images to reduce the viewer to a state of vulnerability. This is not to prescribe the form that the response to vulnerability viewed should take. It is enough to admit that grief leaves one speechless and unhinged: "My narrative falters, as it must."

Butler's conception of vulnerability as an inarticulate state helps avoid the pitfalls of attempting to establish "appropriate," "good," or "morally acceptable" responses to images of human suffering, a pursuit whose complexity, as Susan Son tag cautions in Regarding the Pain of Others, a book devoted specifically to this issue, leads to other problems and paradoxes (formal, ideological, political, and moral) rather than resolutions.

I introduce this writing about falling with Buder's proposal for an ethics of mutual vulnerability because her premise involves an intersubjective relation conceived as constitutive rather than diminutive or objectifying. If in mourning the living come "undone," the experience of pain when viewing the other's mortality can constitute an ethics of intersubjectivity in which vulnerability is reciprocal.

Can one consider the images in these pages accountable to such an ethical relation? In so doing, can one transform the fallen from two-dimensional figures hovering in a purgatory of the viewer's speculative fascination to multidimensional subjects-embodied individuals whose vulnerability affects the viewer's sense of self, a viewer who becomes therefore shaken from an autonomous position unaffected by others?" In this ethical paradigm, a number of limit points are revealed that are as compelling as they are challenging: embodied subjects at the limits of life, the limits of language to describe them, and the limits of the medium to represent them.

FROM VULNERABILITY TO AGENCY

On September 12, 2001, newspapers around the world such the New York Times and Canada's Globe and Mail published the photograph by Richard Drew of a man falling headfirst from one of the World Trade Centre towers. Letters to the editors of these papers immediately poured in complaining about the image. Drew's photograph became infamous as well as iconic.

In its clarity of detail and striking formal qualities, it not only captured but also amplified the most horrible moments to punctuate the multifaceted tragedy of September 11. The falling people embodied the unfolding of the events themselves, actualizing the disaster with a precise individuation of human loss and giving flesh and form to the falling movements by which the architecture also was destroyed.

This isomorphism between bodies and buildings has been noted by George Lakoff: "Tall buildings are metaphorically people standing erect. As each tower fell, it became a body falling." For some, the images of falling people came to symbolize those friends or loved ones who died, those whose manner of death was never seen, never confirmed, only imagined.

The formal qualities of Drew's photograph are disarming. It was chosen by Drew and his editors for these qualities: "That picture just jumped off the screen because of its verticality and symmetry. It just had that look." The black and silver stripes on one tower facade form a negative mirror image to the white and silver on the other, resulting in a composition whose geometric regularity, materials (steel, glass, and concrete), and monochromatic colors suggest the Minimalism of Donald Judd, Carl Andre, and Sol LeWitt.

Further, the optical illusion created by the inverted striations of light and dark on the facades (a trick of the natural light and the right-hand tower's recession into depth) suggests the optical paintings of Bridget Riley, as well as Frank Stella's early 19605 work in black and metallic paint.

Yet unlike the stark, uninterrupted abstraction of these, Drew's photograph is animated by a man's body; this changes everything. The perfect linearity of the two towers, which meet in the centre of the photograph as if forming the spine of a book, are sliced by the man's torpedolike form. His black and white clothing is complemented by the pattern of the facades, creating a graphic impression that reproduces successfully in print media. Among the dozen images captured by Drew of the man's fall, this particular frame was exceptional because of the chance echo between the missile-position of the man's body and its nemeses, the towers that frame and enfold it.

The aesthetic qualities of Drew's photograph may be emotionally difficult, but they are neither unprecedented nor unmoral. In her discussion and defence of how Americans viewed September 11 as cinematic, as a disaster movie, Wendy Doniger states: "Yet we might ask if there cannot be an ethics of illusion, if the moral and the aesdietic are necessarily disjoint." Nor is the editorial choice to publish this photograph remarkable after Sontag's observation that "To catch a death actually happening and embalm it for all time is something only cameras can do, and pictures taken by photographers out in the field of the moment of (or just before) death are among the most celebrated and often reproduced of war photographs."

While Sontag is correct, she is referring to famous photographs of people being killed by guns (such as Eddie Adams's 1968 photograph of a Vietcong suspect or Robert Capa's 1936 photograph of a Spanish Republican soldier), which are striking for the instantaneous homology between the shot of the gun and the click of the shutter. The controversy caused by Drew's photograph suggests something different: the extreme height of the buildings and the subsequently long trajectories of those who fell brought about a dramatically unfamiliar manner of death and photographic images of it.

The proximity allowed by digital resolution brings personal details into view, such as the man's clothing (a chef's jacket and boots), his facial features (dark short hair and possible goatee), and body type (tall and broad-shouldered). This humanizing, perhaps excessive closeness to the man's position and the unimaginable figuration that disrupts the modernist purity of the composition shocks the viewer out of an aesthetic response and into an emotional one. The traumatic shifts in focus recall Barthes's Camera Lucida, his meditation on the structural and affective qualities of photography.

Famously, Barthes theorizes the punctum as the unintended but emotionally piercing, deeply personal, unassimilable detail in a photograph that is difficult, at times impossible, to focus on or articulate, due to its traumatic content. For Barthes, the punctum haunts one retroactively with a fear of mortality.

Sometimes it is the historically outdated detail that reminds one of the passing of time or indicates the death of the photographic subject; sometimes it is the detail that causes the sudden awareness of one's own impending death. Like many of Barthes's seemingly clear-cut structuralist concepts, the punctum is ultimately evasive, not readily pinned down (due to its traumatic latency), shifting and morphing in memory.

The studium of Drew's photograph would certainly revolve around the smoothness of its formal qualities and the way they stand in stark contradiction to its horrific subject matter. The punctum (despite causing a response that is personal and therefore different for every viewer) would surely involve the man's pose or, at a more fundamental level, the mere fact of his appearance in the photograph. The way the falling man's entire body conveys the jarring punctum that ruptures the elegant compositional aesthetics requires another point of clarification.

What comprises the ultimate punctum (for me at least) is the fact that the falling man in Drew's photograph is not yet dead. Like the others who fell from the towers, he was still alive while his image was being secured on film. This haunting temporality recalls another of Barthes's proposals so significant to Camera Lucida, regarding photography's unique ontology: its noeme, or defining characteristic, is "that-hos-been," the absolute certainty that the object photographed did once exist in front of the lens.

According to Barthes, "This will be and this has been; I observe with horror the anterior future of which death is the stake.... Whether or not the subject is already dead, every photograph is this catastrophe." The photograph is both testament to and index of a past moment and the subject who inhabited it. The temporality associated with photography's noeme is thus complexly associated with death, pointing in its dual movements to the past and the future.

Not only do photographs enact a type of metaphysical death (a petrification, a freezing) of the sitter, but they also, because they often depict people who have died since their likeness was taken, prefigure the sitter's death. Further, they are harbingers for the living, forcing on the viewer the poignant awareness that her or his own looks are taking place in stolen, fleeting time.

These loops through time, into the fact and face of mortality, are most clearly articulated in Barthes's discussion of Alexander Gardner's 1865 Portrait of Lewis Payne, a photograph of the handsome but condemned young would-be assassin in his jail cell, still alive but awaiting his fate of death by hanging.

From Barthes's perspective ("he is dead and he is going to die") the noeme of the photograph is the horrible awareness that, like the man in Drew's photograph, he is both already dead and not yet dead.' The men in these photographs are thus doubly condemned: first to the actual deaths to which these photographs are preludes; second to "live" for eternity in the photographic emulsion. The falling man in Drew's photograph is a transitional figure whose death is more immanent and more prescient than the capital punishment to be endured by Lewis Payne (whose position in Gardner's photograph is posed and composed), but the perceived "future anteriority" (the Barthesian temporal disconnect that always leads to death) is entirely similar.

That the falling deaths of the September 11 victims took time is evidenced in the personal video recordings that have surfaced to track their movements, as well as the eleven additional frames captured by Drew, which follow the man's tragic descent hundreds of feet. This astounding photographic sequence was published in Esquire to accompany the chapter "The Falling Man" by Tom Junod. Knowledge of Drew's full sequence makes one painfully aware of the varying chaotic positions the man assumed as he fell.

The sequence, in which the man's body tumbles against a wind whose force is so powerful that his shirt is torn from his back, is an essay on embodied vulnerability. The fearlessness and courage implied by the headfirst position in the famous seventh frame of the sequence allay some of the trauma of the other panic-stricken ones.

But this involves a paradox. Does the directional, assertive (perhaps even graceful) body position in the seventh frame not also buffer the perceived reality of the event, his actual tumbling, the hard physics of the body's weight confronted by wind and propelled by velocity? Does Drew's photograph not transform the vulnerability of the man whose flailing, cartwheel positions are so clearly conveyed by the other eleven frames? When seen out of context, the aesthetic qualities and symmetry that nuance the seventh frame create a false sense of suspension: a strange buoyancy as if he is floating by a thread.

Is this not a misrepresentation? To ask this question is not to say that if one is to respect, in an ethical manner, the content of the images when they are based on actual events (as photojournalism is), the image should never function by way of visual pleasure and must always retain the trauma of the event. The argument is rather that some aesthetic qualities make it a challenge to know how to speak of these subjects and what their experiences actually were.

In defence and clarification of his work as photojournalism, Drew claimed: "We record history. This was the history of that day. I didn't photograph his death. I photographed part of his life." Drew's attempt to define what he photographed is telling, as it points to the sense of confusion surrounding not only this image (especially as a single frame), but all those that capture falling people. What is one looking at? Or whom? No single word captures their state, their threshold position.

They are hardly dying, because the gesticulation and resistance of their bodies to gravity convey animation, life at its most emphatic.

sIn a way different from the Capa or Adams photographs (involving simultaneity), the falling movements of the individuals of September 11 involve a greater length of time in addition to the temporal disconnect of the Barthesian photographic noeme. What one sees in the photograph (a living body, the exertion of life) and what one now knows to be true (the subsequent death) makes linguistic categorization deeply problematic.

Drew's seventh frame hit a nerve with the public in the sense of agency, perhaps even dignity, conveyed by the position of the man's body, which appeared so directional; this pierced viewers affectively. Junod details how this element-utterly contradictory in the face of such a calamity-was not lost on viewers: "Some people who look at the picture see stoicism, willpower, a portrait of resignation; others see something else-something discordant and therefore terrible: freedom."

Perhaps the force of conviction suggested by the man's position resonates because it describes the unthinkable reality outside the lens: that these were not figures foiling, which implies an accident, but that they jumped, which implies an agency horrific in that it was invoked only to "choose" among dire inevitabilities. The power or courage that graced the man's position is, for some, also that which equates his body's movements with a suicidal "choice" to jump, with despair at its utmost.

That the photograph, as well as the television footage of falling bodies, captured such moments at a mass scale became a challenge because the appropriate terminology for the events and those directly involved was unclear, and there were few precedents offering the news media guidelines on how to proceed.

The falling figures were nameless and relatively faceless, individuals whose biographical specificity had been erased, so there was a sense that showing the images exploited their dignity and privacy (or that of surviving relatives).

On the other hand, the only way television networks could (at least for a short while) show the images was if the proper names or close-ups of those who fell were obscured out of "respect for the families."

Junod's research and other reports bring attention to the many people who may have died this way, a number that no newspaper or public institution wishes to confirm because it suggests that the dead were (unfathomably) suicidal agents during their unthinkable ordeal rather than victims of murderous acts: "And yet if one calls the New York Medical Examiner's Office to learn its own estimate of how many people might have jumped, one does not get an answer but an admonition: 'We don't like to say they jumped. They didn't jump. Nobody jumped. They were forced out, or blown out.'"

Junod describes how the images of the "jumpers" were reduced to a "lemming-like class" to be viewed only on uncensored sites on "the Internet underbelly." That the identities of the dead revolved around this ambivalent notion of agency was a significant factor in proscribing identification of the dead with proper names or depiction of their experiences.

Yet although a coherent linguistic response seems blocked, there were descriptive terms chosen and affixed to these subjects and what they represent that hold much weight, aligning the dead along conflicting sides of agency or accident, heroism or victimization.

These important qualifications had bearing on the identity of the man in Drew's photograph, whose proper name Junod attempted (unsuccessfully) to confirm in order to honour him as a courageous fallen hero (like the unknown soldiers of past wars) rather than an anonymous figure whom some thought had committed the mortal sin of suicide.

One stumbles when trying to address those who died, those whose vulnerability was exposed by the visibility each image allows, to recognize their pain as well as one's own, to find words to call them. What becomes evident is the extent to which vulnerability is the dark side to agency; these conditions are as emotional as they are embodied.

As Butler suggests: "The body implies mortality, vulnerability, agency: the skin and the flesh expose us to the gaze of others, but also to touch, and to violence, and bodies put us at risk of becoming the agency and instrument of these as well." This conception of subjectivity as a double-edged process is a central insight to arise from the controversy of jumping/ falling people and how they are to be respected: their acts, visceral responses to the pain of extreme heat and the anxiety of suffocation by smoke inhalation, show movements where agency and vulnerability are inextricable.

In Butler's view, the effect of naming, conferring existence to a subject, or in the case of censorship, denying subjective existence, confirms that names are not merely "descriptive" but also "inaugurative."

This is a strange concept in relation to the dead, but of serious consequence. Butler's theorization is here useful to account for the painful effects of being named, not only with proper names but also with descriptive terms (falling or jumping), effects to which Drew's falling man becomes subject, despite his apparent anonymity.

The corporatization of language reflects a particular vulnerability in the discursive field, so that language appears to act in a physical way: "linguistic agency" can quickly descend into "linguistic vulnerability" when the name one is called is wounding. Could die use of the name "jumper" subject the dead to an act of naming that carries as much lethal weight as the falling body?

Butler describes the directions taken by the interpellative process as a movement that can be arrested momentarily by the sedimenting, fixative power of the name. This process is mimicked by the photograph, whose structure arrests, develops, and transforms the movement of the body dirough processes bodi chemical and connotative. This effect is exaggerated with representations of the dead because they are not in a position to claim or refuse names for themselves but entirely vulnerable to this posthumous activity.

FROM TRANSCENDENCE TO IMMANENCE

The ambivalence that arises in so many ways from Drew's photograph, revolving around the pull of aesthetics in tension with or perhaps due to the impossible indeterminacy of the man's position, shows parallels with lens-based artworks made before September 11. A consideration of these will lead to a better identification of the stakes involved for the subjects of representation in terms of embodiment and ethics.

The contradictions put into motion by Yves Klein's Leap into the Void reveal characteristics that make images of falling so compelling, metaphysically, existentially, and representationally. A pivotal gesture situated between artistic generations (modern and postmodern) and geographic traditions (European, American, and Asian), Klein's performance also hovers between material realms: it exists as a nascent example of body art by an accomplished judo practitioner and as a photograph by Harry Shunk, who documented the event.

The body position in Klein's Leap into the Void shows a contingency between agency and vulnerability that similarly haunts Drew's photograph, but because Klein's work is a staged performance, the stakes are entirely different (in particular, not fatal). The artist is shown rising upwards, his chest and head arced heavenward, attempting to throw off the body's weight. On one hand, Klein expresses modernism's Utopian aspirations, unbridled sense of freedom, and championing of the powers of the individual (which, as Amelia Jones has argued, are predicated on a masculinist, white, and Western subject position).

On the other hand, an incipient postmodern skepticism is built right into the work: Klein's jump is not as perilous as it looks (due to the pile of mattresses excluded from the frame), and the circulation of a faked version in which a cyclist in the background has been doctored out makes the very documentary status of the photograph a sham. Weight and embodiment are the inescapable and necessary facilitators of Klein's dematerialization of art into a mystical, transcendental realm (accomplished ironically, as Thierry De Duve points out, by cementing its commodification through sign value).

The contingency of conditions usually held in opposition (transcendence and immanence, agency and vulnerability, the spirit and the body) informs Klein's Leap into the Void and makes it relevant for September 11. Klein's display of his desire to soar into the air despite the limitations of his body results in an ambivalent, struggling position within the photograph. The performance works intentionally in tandem with the stillness and instantaneity of the photographic medium. Klein's body remains "safe" in the photograph, hovering in a sovereign Cartesian situation of (masculinist) transcendence and subverting the immanence of his burdensome body, all the while deploying it as a creative vehicle. Klein's photograph is itself a mischievous performance where magic and religiosity still seem possible.

In 1962-63, most certainly with Klein's Leap into the Void in mind, Andy Warhol created a series of silkscreen works using tabloid news photos of people jumping or having jumped from buildings in urban environments. These Suicides are part of his larger Death and Disasters series produced at the same time, which include the better-known Car Crashes, Race Riots, Electric Chairs, and Jackie images. Suicide (1962) is striking among Warhol's Death and Disaster series because it doesn't rely on his novel serial technique but offers the mid-air jump of a man just once, a unique instance in which Warhol accepts this singular focus as enough.

The man hangs in the air adjacent to a brick apartment building, the geometric regularity of which is at odds with the spectral bubbles and creases caused by the application of the silkscreen ink. The terrifying figure, whose face and body are obscured (set off crisply as a silhouette, but lacking any surface detail to articulate the figure as an individual), is caught in an emphatic, Ninja-style crouching position from an oblique angle, as if ready to pounce on the spectator.

Warhol's appropriation of photojournalistic images should not be considered disengaged, nor part of a so-called deadpan aesthetic (mechanically reproduced, lacking in respect for the original image, without emotive touches or statements clarifying his intent). Scholarship suggests that his choices in subject matter and formal qualities revolve around affect and trauma, and may imply a critique of contemporary American life and state politics.

These works of Warhol's, which exemplify the parabolic scope of his imagination and certainly contribute to the emerging tenets of postmodern visual culture (in which images are equalized into an economy of sameness), also function by way of a resistance to that economy (while mirroring it), reflecting the horror attendant to the vulnerability in the subjects of representation as much as those who view them.

In 1979-80, the New York-based artist Sarah Charlesworth created a series of seven works based on newspaper photographs of people depicted in mid-air, all jumping or falling from buildings, enlarged to a massive six by four feet and then printed as unique stills. Charlesworth's work recalls Warhol's Suicides but excises the "artistic" manipulations of his silkscreen process (e.g., image repetitions or acceptance of accidents in the printing). Unidentified Woman, hotel Corona de Aragón, Madrid shows a woman falling in front of a smoky high-rise.

By appropriating an image from one context and exhibiting it in another, Charlesworth continues Warhol's legacy of mixing genres (high art and photojournalism) and their functions, as well as their traditional hierarchy. Charlesworth's decontextualization takes a critical stance toward notions of artistic genius and authenticity, and exposes the seeming naturalness of the signifying frameworks through which photographic meaning arises.

In Unidentified Woman, hotel Corona de Aragon, Madrid, the woman's stocking-clad legs are exposed as her dress billows up above her torso to cover her head and face. The graininess of the enlargement adds to the mystery of the image, in which the dense black of the bottom of the photograph gives way to lightness at the top, suggesting an underwater environment.

Charlesworth has emphasized her attraction to the momentary beauty of falling figures captured by photography, as if they were floating or swimming in an ether-world apart from gravity. The feeling that the figure is held up by a pool of water removes a good deal of urgency concerning the woman's possibly impending death.

The curator Susan Fisher Sterling notes the way that photography, in its ability to capture an image of a body in motion, dilutes the viewer's perception of its impending impact on the ground: "Having made sure that the violence is only potential here-contradicted by the stillness or arrested motion of the figure-Charlesworth also placed the viewer in metaphysical limbo, somewhere between fascination and dread."

While the transgressive repetitions in Warhol's work result in compositions of panic or shock, with Charlesworth's approach the tone has shifted to a cooler interrogation of signs and semiotics.

While Warhol gives much information to confirm the manner of death, in either the titles or images, Charlesworth holds back, perhaps allowing one to hope otherwise, but ultimately establishing a situation whose most provocative aspect is its indeterminacy. "This information as well as the outcome of the jump are not disclosed (in part to explore the narrative capacity of the photograph)."

This intentional occlusion also leaves the nominal identity of most figures a challenge. Did some survive? What should one call them if their status (as either dead or alive) is unknown? The "unidentified" element in Charlesworth's tide (like the others in this series, which all begin with the same word) is interesting because despite its almost archival neutrality, a meaning emerges that has consequences for the deceased.

Barthes suggests the ethical importance that captions and titles hold for fixing meaning (precisely what Charlesworth is trying to avoid) when he writes: "The text is indeed the creator's (and hence society's) right of inspection over the image; anchorage is control, bearing a responsibility -in the face of the projective power of pictures-for the use of the message." Did Charlesworth make the choice to keep the proper name unknown, did the original journalists fail to ascertain it, or did the families of the deceased fail to identify them, suggesting they were unclaimed or unmourned? By withholding the specificity of the proper name, "unidentified" also implicitly codes her identity with a derogation.

The cipher could be seen to grant privacy to the dead, imposing an objective distance, or alternatively, as a blunt renunciation of responsibility. It may also be significant that there is no reference to the embodied experience of the subjects in the titles: the titles are almost clinical in their exclusion of the fact that the women and men are falling-a recognition that would at least encourage a reading of the work as a document of an embodied life, rather than an instance of an anonymous, weightless figure, suspended by aesthetics, perhaps transcending fate.

INDETERMINACY AND SUSPENDED ANIMATION

In September 2002, Eric Fischl's over-life-scale bronze sculpture Tumbling Woman was installed at Rockefeller Centre and after only one week was covered up with a tarpaulin and then removed due to the public outcry against it. The naked female figure was depicted in a free-fall position and stood a few feet above the ground so that, like those falling in Charlesworth's and Drew's photographs, it would appear perpetually suspended. Fischl's stated goal was a personal tribute to a close friend who worked on the 106th floor of one of the towers.

Fischl, a New York-based artist known since the late 19705 for figurative work in painting and sculpture, also wanted to create a universalizing statement, a monument that would allow mourners to grieve not by "sanitiz[ing]" the loss or covering up the brutal "narrative" of the day, but by forming "an appropriate expression for tragedy" that in his mind would convey a sense of the reality of the victims' experiences.

Rather than using abstraction, Fischl's neo-Rodin/ Maillol strategy was to represent a sense of the body in its mass, presence, and weighted movement, to counter the disappearance and disintegration of the bodies of those who perished, many of whose remains were never recovered. In this regard, Fischl's descriptions of the contrasting reactions a viewer could have is telling, as they speak to the way figurative realism exaggerates as well as dulls the imagined reality of the event: "One might see a moment of impact in a kind of way that implies brains splattering, a graphic moment there.... So somebody else looking at it might say, 'God, it reminds me of falling in a dream right before I wake up.'"

The ungainly position of Fischl's Tumbling Woman, involving flipped-over limbs, seemed excessive to some viewers, who "interpreted this body twisting in freefall as a piece of grim, plastic photojournalism." Despite its three dimensions, Fischl's depiction is close to Drew's and Charlesworth's in at least one important way: the body is shown in a relatively elusive moment before it makes contact with the ground-a moment of suspended animation that is compelling in its indeterminacy.

This appears to have motivated Fischl in the formal choices he made with Tumbling Woman, which he describes as follows: "It feels like a dream in which somebody is floating. There's no weight there that is sending this crushing, rippling current back through the body as it hits a solid mass." But the overtly memorializing response Fischl was trying to achieve, predicated on representing the vulnerability of the body, backfired, despite the fact that his chosen medium (unlike photography) bears no causal relationship to a particular dead individual, only to the private memory of his friend.

The New York-based performance and multimedia artist Carolee Schneemann's Terminal Velocity consists of a series of black-and-white computer scans of newspaper photographs, including Richard Drew's, of bodies falling from the towers on September 11, greatly enlarged and then collaged onto an imposing grid of eight by seven feet. The repetitions and symmetry of the grid pattern, as well as the imposing scale, recall Warhol's serial work, in particular Suicide [One Woman's Suicide], which depicts a nightgown-clad woman, arms and legs akimbo like a rag-doll, falling in mid-air in front of a brick apartment building.

Warhol repeats her image an excessive thirty-five times (a gesture both comic and obscene) and allows a great deal of variation in print quality from one frame to the next, with lacunae and doublings of the image in the silkscreen application of ink. Unlike Warhol's and Charlesworth's approach, Schneemann's purpose, like Fischl's, was public eulogy. For Schneemann, the process of creating the work was an attempt to individuate those who fell, a "consecration" due to the "ultimate" process of scanning and enlarging the images, allowing her to get "closer" with each successive frame.

Schneemann's desire to "personalize nine people" with the enlargements, making the "fleeting visual attributes of nine lives become clearer," may have transpired in her studio relationship with them, but this was not perceived by the New Yorkers whose violent disapproval of the work when it was exhibited in 2001 was expressed by defacing gallery signage and writing obscenities in the guest book. By Schneemann's account, "People went crazy," and her comments in this regard are significant: "Interesting: that presenting this degree of vulnerability was seen as exploitative and shameful."

The emotional charge was so intense that despite the artist's explicit attempt to acknowledge the suffering of those she represents, her means was not considered adequate. Why not? The negative public reaction may have been partly due to the bombastic scale of the work, which oppressively confronts the viewer. The scale of the bodies in the work is another element that, although it first appears to be a formal problem, might actually pose an ethical one.

The increase in size from one frame to the next bears an inverse (and perhaps also perverse) relationship to the tragic lack of agency that is incorporated by people falling to their deaths. Enlarging their size only belittles their vulnerability rather than paying tribute to it. Moreover, the grid format Schneemann uses in Terminal Velocity, repeating the same images in vertical columns, should be classified as serial rather than sequential; the distinction is important.

A sequence implies change in the image from one frame to the next and the unfolding of movement, much the way Eadweard Muybridge's or Etienne-Jules Marey's chronophotographs of human and animal locomotion did in the 1870s. Barthes also makes note of the emotions that can be conveyed by a sequence of photographs so that a narrative arises from the movement perceived within the "repetition and variation of the attitudes." Schneemann's repetitions are complex because she uses many different figures in the composition rather than just one, yet the image of each of these figures is identical, despite becoming successively larger moving down the panel, so that the stripes created by the photographs parallel those of the towers.

The grid format and seriality used by Schneemann involve a sense of movement in the rhythm of the overall composition, but not in the falling bodies themselves, whose movements do not change. While Schneemann works in a serial rather than sequential format, the enlargements result not in a more dimensional perception of vulnerability, but in its simplistic magnification.

As the tide Terminal Velocity indicates, Schneemann stops and makes still bodies that in actuality were in the throes of motion. Rather than fostering identifications with those who are falling by narrating their trajectories to a greater degree, the sense of embodiment is spectacularized.

While the structural capacity of photography is "complemented" by a dead body but in tension with a transitional figure like a falling body, movement, according to the film theorist Christian Metz, is the key feature to differentiate film from photography. Because motion is stopped by the still photographic image, the body is cut out of the space-time gravitational pull of the world.

A single news photograph is therefore a limited view of a catastrophic, encompassing event that involved time, movement, and the weight of the body, as well as sound. In a short film created in response to the events of September 11, the Mexican filmmaker Alejandro Gonzalez Iñárritu-the director of Amores Perros (2001), 21 Grams (2003), and Babel (2006)-focuses attention on two of the movements that defined that day: the bodies falling from the towers and the implosive fall of the towers themselves, the former represented visually, the latter aurally. Iñárritu s unique montage of documentary elements was made for a feature-length compilation of short films entitled 11'09"01 (2002) and produced by Alain Brigand, who commissioned eleven different works (of eleven minutes, nine seconds plus one frame each) by international directors to offer a global perspective.

Inarritu's contribution to 11'09'01 is largely an anxiety-provoking sound experience as, during his eleven minutes, he projects mostly blank film stock. While one sees nothing but a dark screen, one's attention focuses on the various discordant, clipped sounds of emergency calls and radio broadcasts, as well as cell-phone calls from those trapped in the towers and recordings of witnesses on the ground whose hysteria is broken by the distinctive sounds of bodies hitting the pavement.

These sounds soon give way to several minutes of ponderous orchestral music (by Gustavo Santaolalla and Osvaldo GoIijov) at increasing volume to form an encompassing auditory shroud, only to give way to the sound of the towers collapsing, interwoven with Chiapas Indians chanting healing prayers and an irate American radio host calling for retribution and revenge.

Rather than offering a steady stream of visual pleasure, the cinematic experience is one of visual deprivation, interrupted only by the intermittent glimpses of bodies falling from the towers, flashed on the darkened screen for seconds at a time. What Inarritu achieves with the film medium is emphasis on the traumatic reality of the falling bodies, projected long enough to get a sense of their speed and motion, but not long enough that the viewer's look can ever rest comfortably on them.

The way the image is offered only as a momentary break from the anxious darkness inverts the structure of dominant cinema: normally, editing techniques are hidden, and the seamless projection of light dominates. The flash effect burned in the viewer's mind becomes a retinal experience as painful emotionally as it is physiologically. It is the viewer who now waits, almost perilously in a state of suspension in the cinema's darkness, while the normally desired image is withheld, only for it to appear like a shot at any moment, a sliver of brightness in which bodies register but never come into focus.

Iñárritu's inversion is twofold. The normally passive, receptive spectator is immobilized, plunged into extended darkness and a state of vulnerability. The dominance of darkness over light is also a metaphor for the speed with which the falling bodies, engulfed by their materiality, disappear from the world-sparks of light that cannot be touched, arrested, or protected, only witnessed.

With Inarritu "s film there is a painful realization that the medium ultimately cannot suspend disbelief, break the victim's fall, or offer some sort of psychological, apotropaic mechanism. Only the rhythmic chanting of the Chiapas Indians offers holistic relief, but this too is intangible.

If the sense of motion that film carries is usually thought essential to convey a sense of life, the reality effect reaches its limit point when the motion conveyed is fatal, as in falling bodies, so that the medium holds a capacity opposite to what Metz describes-not the appeal of animation, but shock. The heightened realism of film, especially when the footage is "live," therefore holds a greater "projective power" to convey a traumatic event. Inarritu's searing moments present a phenomenology of shocks whereby visual blows and soul-crushing sounds are accompanied by the viewer's body flinching and heart palpitating.

High stakes are involved, especially in the affective use of sound (in particular, the cell-phone recordings of a man's plaintive screams, "Oh my God, Oh my God!" and a message from a trapped woman telling family members, "I love you"). These voices function as means of identification through which the viewer experiences his own pain as a secondary witness to trauma-yet Inarritu's short film is so difficult to experience that any response may remain trapped in a chokehold of emotion.

In conclusion, we are faced with a series of representational issues in which every representational approach holds its own set of violations, either in relation to the collective historical memory of the event or to the posthumous subjectivity of those who died in it. When works are oriented to aesthetic interests, certain embodied aspects of the falling individual's experience-her or his vulnerability-are glossed over or misrepresented.

The subjects were not only vulnerable to the effects of bodily harm, but are now posthumously vulnerable to certain linguistic or representational "deaths," to the forms of distortion inherent to each medium, no matter how neutral it appears. When works represent or even augment the visibility of suffering with such unflinching eyes, the viewer is reduced to a state of excessive or solipsistic vulnerability, made blind or speechless to the vulnerability of the Other.

The visualization of falling, after September 11, is an ethical concern because it comprises a paradigm of vulnerability. In this paradigm, three forms of vulnerability are revealed. First is the corporeal vulnerability of the subjects conveyed by the images of falling. Are the experiences endured by them recognized as having been fatal rather than merely serving as visual curiosities for the living? This is not the simple proposal (disputed by many) that aesthetic values in representations of human suffering preclude an ethical engagement with them. The goal is not to impose prohibitions on certain aesthetic or formal gestures but to identify what they do to embodied subjects in this unique genre at the limits of life, language, and the medium.

Second is posthumous vulnerability to a subjectivity slandered by representations or names the dead can neither refuse nor negotiate. The fact that subjectivity is produced posthumously (and how) is not often enough considered in cultural theory, but even in death, subjects continue to be vulnerable to representations and to the names one calls them (e.g., "falling," "jumper," "suicides," "unidentified").

Third, I am concerned with the extent to which the viewer's relationship with the images is one in which an openness to the state of vulnerability is maintained-but not necessarily prescribed. After Butler's insight that in mourning the living come "undone," the experience of pain when viewing the Other's mortality constitutes an ethics in which vulnerability can be conceived as a reciprocal possibility.

Despite the obvious, radical imbalances inherent to the situation (in which the living view images of people about to die), a paradigm of vulnerability might offer an enabling point rather than a weakened state, a humbling manner of approach whose result is ultimately the dignification of the experiences of all the subjects involved.

Chapter 5

Social Constructions and Aesthetic Achievements

Raising aesthetic questions about ethnic writing has been opposed by those who associate aesthetic concerns with an elitist betrayal of the social roots of ethnic art and by postmodern critics who deny the claims of heritage on individuals. Both attitudes have obscured how the clash between old worlds of origin and new American lives evident in current ethnic writing can operate to create an innovative, socially relevant aesthetic.

Yet it is possible to formulate a conception of the relationship between the historical and formal properties of recent Italian American writing that can serve as the basis for an understanding of an innovative and even revolutionary aesthetic that it may share with other ethnic writing. Italian American writing helps return history to centre stage after postmodern denials of its lasting and ongoing effects. Ethnic heritage is history in action; it subjects the fact of immigration to a scrutiny of its ongoing effects. It not only exposes historical episodes of conflict between margin and mainstream, but also reveals the lasting impact of immigration on individuals who may be second or third generation.

Its aesthetic experiment returns a new combination of realism and symbolism to current writing and explores the interactions between public and private worlds. It constitutes a revolt against the devaluation of the past, of heritage, history, and the individual in postmodern critical discourse. Italian Americans are heirs to two diaspora: the first from

Italy (predominantly from the South) from 1880 to the 1920s and the second from post-World-War-II urban Little Italys throughout America.

The first transposed Italian lives into the new world; the second preserved Italianita by a process of appropriation or reinterpretation.

Both journeys produced narratives of cultural collision and change. Recent writing constitutes an emerging ethnic aesthetic which both draws on and gets beyond the conventions of postmodernism that have guided critical discussion in the past decades.

This aesthetic revolutionizes our thinking about current art with a powerful return to realism about the continuities of history, and to symbolism in dealing with the complexity of individual experience. It introduces new approaches to the interaction between America and its ethnics.

The innovative aesthetic of contemporary Italian American writing challenges many tenets of postmodern theory and, by doing so, acts as a corrective and even revolutionary force.

The excesses of much postmodern theory include its denial of the force of class, economics, and history as felt effects preserved in individual consciousness, its outsized affirmations of universal unreality and simulacra, its repudiation of the individual subject, its failure to deal with affect, and its de facto relegation of the ethnic "other" to the static role of victim forever without a public voice.

An important first step in challenging such excesses is to restore to our awareness the longtime role ethnic art has itself played as an avant-garde in the canon of modern literature. Doing so helps underscore how the empirical energies of ethnic writing encompass concern for those at the margins and incorporate social concerns in the practice of art.

The formal energies of Italian American art cannot be separated from its democratic embrace of the consciousness of individuals as valuable in its own right and as a barometer of the pressures on character and culture. The stature of the ethnic self has been devalued in a general postmodern mistrust of the individual as hegemon: "Enlightenment epistemology... produced as its most common and worst effect the sense of unity and privilege in the observing self".

The ethnic self is ruled out by such absolute definitions of the self as simply imperialistic or narcissistic, a view Levi-Strauss may have had in mind when he referred to the self as "the spoiled brat" of philosophy.

In their extremism, these absolute views are questionable and have little to do with the actual practice of ethnic writing or the current use of the ethnic self as a site for the intersection of cultural and personal complexities. Not all selves are alike; the concept "self" should not be monolithic nor should selfhood be denied in theory to the ethnic immigrant any more than it is in fact.

The ethnic self is multidimensional, a living measure of the breakup of the power of historical traditions as part of creating something new and, particularly, new narratives about the relationship between past and future. Marie Hall Ets' Rosa: The Life of an Italian Immigrant documents how self-fashioning and cultural history intersect in an ethnic life.

It reveals Rosa'ss instinctive mastery of dramatic folk narrative and the role it plays in her evolution. A penniless orphan raised in Italy on grudging charity, Rosa had been taught to obey her exploitative boss, the cruel nuns, and the indifferent guardians who sent her to America to marry a stranger, and to bow to the authority of her Italian priest in Chicago who tells her to accept her husband's outrageous abuse as her lot. Rosa's life is a complex folktale in its own right. Her social and self-reconstruction emerge through both the American emphasis on individualism and the Italian religious humanism she has been taught but never received.

As Fred Gardaphe notes, Rosa emerges in "the literate tradition of Ets, who recorded only the story of Rosa's self and its struggle to survive in a new world". But Rosa brings to her own life story her Italian storytelling gifts and a folk emphasis on the tale of the poor outwitting or exposing the machinations and hypocrisy of the rich. Fred Gardaphe points out the centrality of fear and overcoming it in the process of social and self-fashioning: "Rosa's fear in Italy is generated by the Italian class system, which demands that the poor never look into the eyes of the rich" and by mores which make women the property of their husbands and sinners against God's will if they try to escape.

Rosa leaves her husband and overcomes oppressions of class and dogma. For her, that does not involve a postmodern break with the past, or a desire to control others, but an ongoing reintegration of humanistic folk and religious values with democratic ideals.

Rosa simply wants to speak for justice and against hypocrisy. She wants to go back to Italy and actually "talk to the bosses in the silk factory" and confront the nuns who were cruel to her: "'You threw out that poor girl whose heart was so kind toward you? You think you'll go to heaven like that?' I'd scold them like that now. I wouldn't be afraid.... Me, that's why I love America.

That's what I learned in America: not to be afraid". Rosa's "lesson" is, in part, that a historical change like immigration is as much a reinterpretation of the past as it is a new vision of the future. It is felt in deeply personal ways and registered in transformations of the self.

The Italian American self discloses not only the energies and effects of immigration but also the shaping impact of American ethnic diversity.

Mary Bush, in "Planting," writes of relationships between Italian immigrants and African Americans in the American South in 1905 which transform the visions each has of the "other." In Tina DeRosa's Paper Fish a young woman in contemporary Chicago experiences a revelation of the uses of her heritage for the future as she realizes that her grandmother's Italian wisdom, conveyed in stories of her own experience of hardship in Italy and America, will help her imagine a new life for herself beyond Chicago's Little Italy.

The Italian American self that emerges in contemporary fiction incorporates and uses histories of economic deprivation and experiences of injustice to develop new sources of cultural strength and consolation.

Such dynamism can establish aesthetic and historical concerns as both formative and revolutionary relationships. Interaction between an ethnic past and an American present was once recognized as a key aspect of both critical theory and ethnic narratives, particularly before World War II.

In "Avant-Garde Ethnics" Thomas Ferraro pointed out the role ethnic poverty has played in bringing about innovations in form, content, or acceptance by mainstream readers and reminded us that, in his critical and autobiographical book, Starting Out in the Thirties, Alfred Kazin wrote: "What young writers of the Thirties wanted was to prove the literary value of our experience, to recognize the possibility of art in our own lives, to feel that we have moved the streets, stockyards, the hiring halls into literature—to show that our radical strength could carry on the experimental impulse of modern literature".

The experimental impulse of ethnic writing was grounded in hard knocks realism, but carried with it an innovative use of language charged with emotion and self-report. Alfred Kazin commented that the "grandiloquence of William Saroyan in his breakthrough story, "The Daring Young Man on the Flying Trapeze," "expressed perfectly... the young writer... conscious of being a nobody, a greaseball, an outlander, but who delivered himself every time he sat down at the typewriter."

Saroyan, Kazin noted, saw writing as his "escape from meaninglessness, uselessness, unimportance, insignificance, poverty, enslavement, ill health, despair, madness".

Selfhood and language work together as escapes from a combat zone of internalized social conflicts. They shape the development of Italian American writing in Maria Mazziotti Gillan's poem of the writer as an Italian-speaking child driven into a tormented silence in "Public School No. 18: Paterson, New Jersey":

Without words, they tell me
to be ashamed.
I am.
I... want to be still

and untouchable
as these women
who teach me to hate myself.
I am proud of my mother,
dressed all in black,
proud of my father
with his broken tongue
proud of the laughter
and noise of our house
Remember me, ladies,
the silent one?
I have found my voice
and my rage will blow
your house down (320-21).

Gillan's poetry, like Saroyan's own experiences and voice as a writer, document a crucial mixture: the power of social experience, the role of the writer as a representative ethnic self, and the emancipatory power of the ethnic voice in both imaginative art and self-fashioning.

Inclusion of a proletarian subculture is at the heart of much Italian American writing and achieves remarkable effects from combining both ethnic and economic marginality with an acute rendering of individual sensibility.

The innovative forms produced accordingly juxtapose social realism with an inventive symbolism and language that capture a dramatic struggle against the fixed identities both old world families and new world exploitation impose on the first generation child.

For example, Pietro Di Donato's Christ in Concrete combined realism about urban poverty with a prose laden with religious symbolism that transposed and reinterpreted Italian expressive styles in a multivocal form that captured the clash of two cultures, each of which had its own ways to suppress the self. A bricklayer by trade obliged by the death of his father to begin backbreaking construction work at the age of twelve, Di Donato created Paul, a child-protagonist burdened by family and work. Paul is caught between a heritage of religious fatalism that idealizes self-sacrifice on the altar of family devotion and a crude capitalism that exploits his labour on its own altar of greed.

Social realism and aesthetic innovation meet in Paul's attempt to carve his own selfhood as a verbal synthesis of the forces arrayed against him. That effort is captured in the novel in Paul's ability to utilize both the charged, figurative, Italianate language of Christian fatalism to describe Christ as the model for all men, and a stripped, harsh New York style to convey his emerging secular and political outrage at his situation. Both meet in Paul's all-consuming rejection of Christ as only a "plaster man".

A dynamic relationship between aesthetic and cultural concerns was once a key factor in aesthetic theory. In "Historical Truth in Fiction," Georg Lukacs defined a Marxist aesthetic by simply affirming that "the development of mankind does not and cannot finally lead to nothing and nowhere". Lukacs described Marxism as "a signpost pointing the direction in which history moves forward," deriving from a "proletarian humanism" that determines its "central aesthetic problems". For him, Marxism's "central aesthetic problem" is "the adequate presentation of the complete human personality".

Aesthetics in Lukacs' conception are deeply intertwined with both collective social reality and individualism. Lukacs called for a synthesis of social and psychological forces which "organically binds together the general and the particular both in characters and situations".

Individual characters reveal the operations of social and psychological reality. He considered the ideal historical novel one in which personal crises interweave within the determining context of an historical crisis emphasizing "the organic, indissoluble connection between man as a private individual and man as a social being". This means that individual characters can provide the crossroads between the psychological and social. Italian American fiction and other ethnic fiction achieve such a synthesis.

An updated aesthetic model for current ethnic fiction that is comparably inclusive has not been developed, even though there are abundant examples in Italian American fiction of the power of personal crisis and individual consciousness to express social concerns.

For example, Anthony Julian Tamburri's theoretical work has drawn on Charles Sanders Peirce's Principles of Philosophy to use cognitive psychology as a basis for conceptualizing relationships between social and religious consciousness and styles of ethnic writing.

His reading of Tony Ardizzone's "Nonna," in A Semiotic of Ethnicity: In (Re)cognition of the Italian/American Writer, explores how the mind of an old Italian woman is transformed by exposure to the Mexican immigrants who have moved into her formerly Italian neighborhood. Changes in her views of guilt and absolution are marked by the changing symbolic meanings she attaches to the Mexican and Italian breads that reverberate in her consciousness as she encounters the forms of nourishment that fill the stores her new neighbors have built. Economic and social forces can find expression in the changing self-images of women.

Mario Puzo's The Fortunate Pilgrim and Marion Benasutti's No Steady Job for Papa provided powerful portraits of the price paid by Italian American daughters in transformed body-images or visions of motherhood when their impoverished families need them as wage-earners. Poverty pins them between traditional ideals of Italian womanhood and the claims of urban workplaces. Postmodern, post-Marxist critical models have not only rejected such expressions along with Lukacs' sense of the profound interaction among socioeconomic crisis, individual character, and the novel, but have also disdained historically rich fiction.

For example, Frederic Jameson exemplifies both tendencies. He has condemned the historical novel as only escapist, as recording fragments filled with nostalgia. The clash of premodern folk culture and bureaucratized modern cities apparent in much ethnic reality has little relevance in Jameson's rejection in Postmodernism or the Cultural Logic of Late Capitalism:

What was once, in the historical novel as Lukacs defines it, the organic genealogy of the bourgeois collective project... has meanwhile itself become a vast collection of images, a multitudinous photographic simulacrum. Guy Debord's powerful slogan [the society of the spectacle] is now even more apt for the "prehistory" of a society bereft of all historicity, one whose own putative past is little more than a set of dusty spectacles.

Such a vision simply ignores the power of ethnic experience, writing, and the ethnic self to continuously engage the past in the process of creating a future and, very simply, to "feel real," by conveying the raw power of lived experience. It rejects in extreme terms the real, the historic and the ongoing vitalisty of the interaction between Italian heritage and American mores.

It completely ignores the role of the writer as a representative ethnic engaged in self-formulation and self-creation. Jameson claims postmodernism mainly theorizes about change, but "change" appears defined as what he calls "the telltale instant" when a corner is turned and the power of the past disappears. Jameson writes as though the resulting new "inaugural" narrative is largely the story of the triumph of capitalism.

The rich depiction of felt ethnic difference and concern for variations in language that are characteristic of ethnic fiction now are not well served by that vision of culture as little more than advertisements for capitalism. The ethnic individual struggling with the often competing interests of cultural preservation and self-definition is obscured or denied by theoretic affirmations of the death of the individual subject and the impact of heritage in favour of DeBordian or Baudrillardian "simulation." Nor does that vision take seriously the power of Italian—or bilingualism itself—to serve as the competing force that undermines or at least challenges the primacy of the social establishments that codify language.

New ethnic fiction restores historical realism, the past as an active presence in felt experience, and the importance of the individual to centre stage. An innovative ethnic aesthetic can incorporate the past in new narratives that exhibit original syntheses of ethnic identity, narrative strategies, modes of realism, and symbolism. The means of that synthesis is language, which mirrors cultural interactions most explicitly in bilingualism, incorporates multiple linguistic and storytelling styles, and focuses on the individual as the site for crises of culture as well as character.

That one language can reveal the hidden densities of another is enabled by the capacity of American English to serve as a medium which sustains and even adopts phrases, concepts, attitudes, and cadences of other languages, a fact exploited in the past by writers ranging from Bernard Malamud to Don DeLillo, from Mari Tomasi in the lyrical Like Lesser Gods to Dorothy Bryant's spare realism in Miss Giardino. The raw power of the ethnic voice can only benefit from the development of a theoretic basis for articulating its aesthetic values and practices.

Can an aesthetic of current ethnic fiction be developed which avoids both the excesses of prevailing postmodern approaches and a retrogression that simply returns to an earlier model that may lack a sense of contemporary fragmentation and multiplicity? Ethnic fiction not only explodes the excesses of postmodernism but also extends and appropriates its insights for new uses. The processes of meaning, interpretation, and storytelling can provide the key to formulating an aesthetic for Italian American and other ethnic writing that avoids the pitfalls of postmodern excesses or a return to an outmoded Marxist model.

The innovative aesthetic of current Italian American writing draws on aspects of postmodern theory that recognize the persistence of continuities of meaning and value while acknowledging that both are open to change and revision.

In the context of a critique of the postmodern tendency to see history, "family.... Class Struggle" as only outmoded essentialist categories, Peter Brooker opens up the inconsistencies and distortions in the postmodern vision of both Marxism and language contained in a too complete advocacy of DeBord's formulation of society as a "spectacle" or Baudrillard's faith that "reality" has been replaced by "simulacra." He calls instead for a focus on the processes of meaning and interpretation found in "deconstruction" which, he argues, "does not countenance absolute rejection any more than absolute affirmation; it talks not of turning the page (of philosophy), but of reading in a new way, of setting the concepts that underlie a metaphysics of presence 'under erasure': that is to say, of simultaneously writing and unwriting but not simply and absolutely of canceling these concepts. Deconstruction, in short, is a method of critique".

An affirmation of the Italian American self is crucial to understanding the process of continuity and change at work in interpretation. Although the excesses of postmodern theory generally regard the claims of the self as part of an outmoded humanism, Jacques Derrida has argued otherwise. In "Spectres of Marx," he wrote: "A deconstructive thinking... has always pointed out the irreducibility of affirmation... and thus of the promise, as well as the undeconstructability of a certain idea of justice" that Derrida affirms he himself would never repudiate.

Derrida stresses continuity as much as change in the process of interpretation. Derrida not only sees deconstruction as "a radicalization of Marxism," as Brooker has noted, but one that could bring the critique of culture to bear on language. Derrida recognizes that the tools used to "radicalize" are precisely the tools that once crafted the concepts undergoing change. As Derrida wrote: "the deconstruction... of logocentrism, linguisticism, phonologism, the demystification or the de-sedimentation of the autonomic hegemony of language... would have been impossible... in a pre-Marxist space. Deconstruction is... an attempted radicalization of Marxism".

How can this approach to stirring up the settled "sedimentation" of language be related to ethnic fiction? The use of Italian in English, the verbal constructions and configurations of narrative evident in contemporary Italian American and other ethnic writing, the manipulation of plot sequences through fragmenting and cutting narrative, and the inclusion of multiple discourses drawn from personal and public experience are all possibilities enabled by the Marxist notion that despite its many bumps, inconsistencies, and facets, human life is purposeful as an ongoing narrative. The Italian folk practice of conveying truths through storytelling may be part of that persistence.

As an issue of craft, the continuity of the human story surfaces in the incorporation of the folktale form in contemporary writing. Fidelity to traditional form can stress cultural continuity as it does in Gioia Timpanelli's lyrical Sometimes the Soul: Two Novellas of Sicily which incorporates the miraculous in the telling of emotional truths.

Exploitation and revision of the form can underscore cultural change, as it does in Josephine Gattuso Hendin's novel, The Right Thing to Do, in which a father tells his daughter a story in folk style, but deliberately fragments his conclusion into multiple possibilities as a way of conveying her freedom to develop her own life story. Italian American fiction both sustains and alters folk narratives to achieve a spectrum of meanings based on calling attention to the collision or interaction of past and present forms. The mixture of continuity and change can also be seen as "a method of critique" applied to both Italian traditions and American practices. As such, one aspect of deconstruction seems to me to provide a particularly apt theoretic tool for interpreting meaning.

Derrida's theory of supplementarity is useful in understanding the extent to which ethnic art explodes postmodern theory in unexpected and unexplored new directions. It underscores the extent to which history, the self, and the dynamic processes of synthesis that ethnic writing illustrates can be seen as contributions to a new aesthetic. In "Structure, Sign and Play in the Discourse of the Human Sciences," Derrida describes his theory of supplementarity in a way that enables connections among the innovative aesthetic of Italian American writing with both history and the individual.

To paraphrase: Derrida's theory of supplementarity holds that we use the language we inherit as a ready-made system, with its own history and practice built in. In expressing ourselves, whether in opposition or agreement, our language expresses that past system, and carries it into different and new expressions.

The absolute opposition between such binaries as nature and culture, essentialism and subjectivity, the real and the textual, is thus questioned. In effect, "supplementarity" operates according to its own double meaning:

- A supplement provides something that is missing and fills a gap and, as Derrida suggests,
- Adds something new, a "surplus".

Both steps are equally part of producing a new meaning by drawing on the past as part of an ongoing process of continuous change. Implying that even provisionally completed meanings contain something old and something new, Derrida, in effect, describes the process by which historical understanding is both contained in and changed by the use of language and interpretation.

It is possible to extend this reading of supplementarity to encompass some of the ongoing dramas, usually dismissed as outmoded "essentialism," that flow from the collisions between heritage and present and that result in transforming interpretations of both.

"Supplementarity" is a way of describing change. In Italian American writing, it can be applied to a variety of themes: the clash of cultures in John Fante's Wait Until Spring, Bandini, of generations in Octavia Waldo's A Cup of the Sun, or as a cri de coeur in Diane di Prima's striking poem, "To My Father—2," in which a young woman drawn to pleasure rages at her depressed father: "You were dying of grief from the moment I saw you," and stirs herself to revolt.

Violent change or "catastrophe" is how Derrida describes supplementarity in "Of Grammatology." By that he means an encounter between the "absence" or gap to be repaired and the "presence" of the new structure or meaning that must replace it. He cites Levi-Strauss's ethnographic project as focused on "origins" which are seen [by Saussure] as missing in language.

Derrida believes that the very "catastrophe" of change implies that origins are actually not missing in language, claiming: "Usurpation necessarily refers us to a profound possibility of essence. This is without a doubt inscribed within speech itself and he [Saussure] should have questioned it, perhaps even started from it".

Thus Derrida acknowledges both continuity and change, the survival of origins and the possibility of "essence" which seems to be defined dynamically as the past endlessly reconstituting itself in altered form in the present. Just as Di Prima's "I will not die/yr death" inevitably preserves her father's grimness as a spur to finding joy, so the alternation between heritage and present provides a spectrum along which both a sense of origin and a sense of newness are located.

Cultures of origin and of the present can be linked theoretically by an expansive view of Derrida's concept of supplementarity. Derrida sees the entire ethnographic effort of Levi-Strauss as a search for lost or absent "origins," a search for "natural innocence, purity of presence and self-presence in speech".

But the project of literary ethnicity can be far more than an effort at recovery. Ethnic writing can be said to illustrate how processes of continuity, change, and newness can use the ethnic self as a both a bearer of a larger cultural past and an originator of something new that affects both personal and social life. That potential within the concept of supplementarity is implied in the phrase "the Outside Is the Inside" in "Of Grammatology" and emphasized in a meditation on the identical sound in French of "is" [est] and "and" [et], a sound-effect Gayatri C.

Spivak underscores as meaningful to Derrida in her translator's note. As a concept, supplementarity contains the idea that the "is" of being and the "and" of connection, or the states of existence and conjunction, or even, perhaps "otherness" and commonality, are not opposites but part of a continuous spectrum of individual consciousness and speech.

A spectrum of relationships connects insiders and outsiders in current Italian American fiction which effectively reinterprets Italian traditions when confronted by change. For example, traditional family cohesiveness is based on the centrality of the mother and fixed gender roles that emphasize marriage and motherhood for women and authority and physical strength for men. Italian American fiction which deals with gay and lesbian characters reflects the challenge posed by nontraditional lives.

Rachel Guido deVries's Tender Warriors records the surviving pull of the Italian family on both an authoritarian father and his adult children who return home after the death of a protective mother despite the father's difficulty in facing either his daughter's life with another woman or his son's weakness from illness. Neither child has fulfilled his father's traditional expectations; nor does the father entirely meet their hopes for acceptance.

Nevertheless, the importance of family ties remains vital even as the concepts of family, sexual identity, and gender roles are altered by every moment of the interaction between the father and the younger generation. "Otherness" and commonality are not fixed opposites but part of a continuous spectrum of experience, consciousness, and expression.

The effects of heritage and American lives collide, interact, and perpetually upset the fixed terms "Italian" and "American" as opposites. Ishmael Reed provides an earthy expression of such dynamism while describing his own heritage: "I'm not going to abandon Western values. I want to mix things up a little. We salute the postmodernists and we have a coalition with them".

Narratives of Italian American experience mix things up in interesting ways by using the multiplicity and openness of the ethnic voice to tell the American story in new ways. That voice speaks in an innovative aesthetic mixture of forms that open heritage and newness as well as public and private experience to each other.

One of the major achievements of Don DeLillo's Underworld is its use of narrative form to configure an intersection of personal and public experience over the long span of the second Italian American diaspora. In scrambled time sequences over the period from 1951 to 1998, this encyclopedic epic opens the traditional American master narrative of conquest and optimism to multiple discourses of politics, sports, media, art, work, religion, and science.

It links this abundance to the ethnic individual who must create himself within and through American multiplicity. Underworld uses the ethnic passage of Nick Costanza Shay from a Bronx Little Italy in the nineteen fifties, through the upscale suburbs of the Southwest, towards global prospects, to describe the course of all American experience over the past fifty years. Reversing the mainstream's dictation of the American story, DeLillo uses an Italian American voice to tell a fuller story.

American triumph at the end of World War II could reaffirm the master narrative of American conquest. The ethnic voice of Underworld places the American story of triumph and optimism against competing and even global narratives.

The symbolic use of the "national pastime" as part of the great game of global competition opens the novel. DeLillo sets his prologue in the climactic game between the Dodgers and Giants in the pennant race for the World Series of 1951. The symbolic use of this "world" series emphasizes its universality by focusing on multiethnic teams, fans composed of all races and classes, and announcers broadcasting what happens worldwide. Official history, ethnic diversity, and the "people's history" are brought together as J. Edgar Hoover, watching the game, receives notification that the Soviet Union has detonated its first atomic bomb and American nuclear hegemony is challenged.

In the game, Ralph Branca, on the verge of winning the series for the Dodgers who appear set for victory, pitches the ball to Bobby Thomson who hits it into the stands for the home run that wins the series for the Giants. The reversal of fortune reverberates throughout the novel in the mind of the ethnic protagonist, Nick Costanza Shay. That unexpected reversal in a ballgame that DeBord or Jameson might see only as a "spectacle" has richly symbolic importance throughout the novel.

Nick, a teenager at the time, like others in his Little Italy, is fascinated by the linkage between Branca's pitch and Thomson's hit, called "the shot heard round the world," on the front page along with the news of the Soviet atomic bomb, another "shot heard round the world." The phrase, from Emerson's poem of the revolutionary war, "Concord Hymn," does not reinforce the old master narrative of conquest, but a new one that reveals the shadow cast on American triumphalism by the Soviet bomb. Nick judges the ballgame from the dual perspective of winner and loser and begins to weave a new, more meditative narrative with political and personal dimensions.

The implications and interpretations of Branca's pitch and Thomson's hit and the atomic arms race frame the novel. Will both contests come to symbolize victory snatched from defeat or defeat from victory? What matters in the novel is how both the winners and losers are bound together by the unintended consequences of the contest. The official male discourses of victory in war and politics interlock with the "people's history" of sports. Setting up a set of oscillating connections between winning and losing, Nick's meditations interweave his own personal memory with public history and misgivings about the meaning of victory and loss.

"Bad luck Branca luck. From him to me. The moment that makes the life.... I have to have that moment in my hand when Branca turned and watched the ball go into the stands—from him to me," Nick thinks. The ball itself in its progress through the novel acquires symbolic weight. The moment sparks meditations on the bond created between winners and losers and the difficulty of determining the longterm effects of either victory or loss: "Branca... appeared with Thomson, at sports dinners. They form a bond—they sing songs and tell jokes. They're the longest running act in show business".

Their bond is even acknowledged at the beginning of the Nineties by "official" culture: they are photographed "on the

White House lawn with President Bush between them, holding an aluminum bat". By 1998, the Soviet Union is in disarray and American military and economic power seem secure, but both modern Russia and the United States are victims of borderless threats posed by the radioactive and toxic wastes produced by nuclear and industrial power at places like Three Mile Island or Chernobyl, the effluvia of success that brings contamination. The blowback of radiation poisoning symbolizes the "underworld" of indeterminate, unexpected, and unintended consequences, and raises questions of private, public, and global connections.

Italian is the language that provides an ethnic voice for unexpected, changing interpretations of the American master narrative from unqualified certitudes to recognition of the mystery of unknown effects. DeLillo's Nick notes: "There's a word in Italian—dietrologia, for the science of what is behind an event... the science of dark forces... the 'imaginary' sciences opposed to... the 'hard sciences'". Italian American experience not only provides a perspective on the larger public world, but interweaves one of its own "master narratives" with it.

The master narrative of Italian American family life is the story of the authority of the father and the cohesion of the family. Nick tells that story through its unexpected disruption in an America grown familiar with single mothers and high divorce rates. Nick's father "did the unthinkable Italian crime. He walked out on his family. They don't even have a name for this". Nick wants to believe his father, a numbers runner, did not run away, but was murdered. Although his mother insists he use her own Irish maiden name, Shay, Nick's identity is bound up with the sudden loss of his father who went out for a pack of Lucky Strikes and never came back. The modernist search for a father is turned into a complex meditation that raises the personal question—whether the disappearance of the father was or wasn't his choice—and the public one involving questioning the survival of "the patriarchy" and perhaps its institutions.

The male-dominated street corner culture and pool hall are anchors of the teen patriarchy in a nineteen fifties Little

Italy. A dropout from school, Nick is one of the macho guys on the block.

He works delivering heavy appliances to admired older Italian American men who, despite their poverty, find in their families and food-laden kitchen tables reasons for saying, "Who's better than me!" the mantra of DeLillo's immigrants who find fulfillment in physical satisfaction and the emotional support of family life. In George the Waiter, who is "the loneliest man" he's ever met, Nick seems to find a father surrogate who proves you can live without a family. But when he visits George to play an Italian card game, briscola, he discovers that the man he cast in the role of father has cast him in the role of executioner.

The purposes of the "father" and needs of the "son" have diverged as George gives Nick an old shotgun he says he found and reassures him that the gun is not loaded when Nick, predictably and playfully, points it at him:

In the extended interval of the trigger pull, the long quarter second, with the action of the trigger sluggish and rough, Nick saw into the smile on the other man's face.

Then the thing went off and the noise busted through the room and even with the chair and body flying he had the thumbmark of George's face furrowed in his mind.

Dietrologia, that science of hidden forces, reveals an Oedipal drama as a suicidal complicity against the certitude and confidence once associated with "patriarchy." Here George abdicates both fatherhood and direct aggression. Nick is revealed as a perpetrator who is also a victim, and George as the victim who is also a perpetrator. The stereotype of Italian American male violence that dictates that, given a gun, Nick will shoot, is demolished by opening up ambiguities of intention and commission and questioning their long-term effects. Nick's accidental murder calls into question who had power in the shooting and what its long range implications will be for him. It turns out to be Nick's "lucky strike," the "shot" that will send him around the world.

Sent to a Jesuit-run reformatory in Minnesota, Nick receives an education that wins him upward mobility and world travel as an expert. His success is anchored by the weight of his past, for the Jesuits teach him to search for hidden meanings, to understand symbolism and dietrologia. His life is an oscillation between a Thomson-Branca role, a win that binds him to unforgettable loss and culpability. He reconciles both in his expertise as an executive in waste management.

His job combines the science of toxic waste disposal with its symbolic affinities for recycling and transformative reclamation as wider human missions that call into question issues of politics and male power. The purpose of postmodern art was said to be to expose the destructive work of power. The new ethnic avant-garde could be said to treat doing only that as the "danced out plot—the crush the weak plot" that has been displaced by new possibilities.

These apply to the political and personal meanings that associate power with the nature of men and the culture of patriarchy. Just as the dialectic of ideologies collapses in the end of the Cold War, enabling an emphasis on the globalization of effects, so does the opposition between nature and culture emphasized in the excesses of postmodern theory. In Underworld, the effects of fallout and toxins produce genetic mutations in boys and girls across national borders. These override differences in gender.

Moreover, differences between "nature" and "culture" are blurred by the industrial economies whose radioactive wastes have literally caused physical mutations and, in effect, destroyed the opposition between "culture" and "nature." In addition, culture and nature blur in the effort of even afflicted children to continue children's "universal" culture by playing, as well as they can, the same games children have played for centuries.

DeLillo's meditations on the world's uniformities encompass its interconnectedness in both its tragedies and its affirmations, blurring distinctions of power in a scrutiny of universalized effects and practices. This tragic humanism is the product of dietrologia that finds mutuality in differences and emphasizes complicities of completion.

Postmodern theory retained its own master narrative of gender that inadvertently reified the patriarchies it claimed to attack. Its excesses substituted rigid linguistic coding to define authority as masculine or phallic.

It saw "otherness" as feminine and relegated minorities of race, class, or sexual orientation to the "feminine" position, rendering gender classifications functions of dominance or subordination. The ethnic aesthetic may use gender differences as supplemental or mutually transformative. "When my mother died I felt expanded, slowly, durably, over time. I felt suffused with her truth, I thought she'd entered the deepest place I could provide, the animating entity. She is part of me now," Nick thinks.

This transformation by incorporation underscores gender hybridity. By accepting the opposite, a new configuration that stresses commonality is created. It reflects the recycling, reconciliation, and incorporation of two Italian traditions—clearly differentiated sexual roles and the son's attachment to the mother—in one ethnic consciousness.

Italian American art may serve as an inclusive discourse that reveals the impulse to reclaim and recycle as a primary creative drive and a major part of its innovative aesthetic. The poor immigrant's hatred of waste is a first step: "Mannaggia l'America," complains a traditional Bronx man of American waste: "This goddam country [has] garbage you can furnish your house and feed your kids". In DeLillo's novel, fictional artist Klara Sax and actual artist Sabato Rodia each create art out of discards.

Gender reversals surface in Klara Sax's exploitation and recycling of the masculine discourses of war. She creates a vast installation in the desert of discarded World War II B52s, repainting the drab planes in bright colors, restoring the nose art of the flight crews, recycling warplanes refitted to carry atomic bombs as art.

Sabato Rodia created the Watts Towers out of broken "7-Up" and "Milk of Magnesia bottles," building them out of domestic products associated with the female space of the home and working at his art for thirty years. Engaged in a labour of love, Rodia donates his finished towers to the Watts community.

This Neapolitan worker turned artist reminds Nick of his father whom he once saw helping masons in the neighborhood with masterful brickwork: "I could imagine him rising this high, soaring out of himself to produce a rambling art that has no category, with cement and chicken wire. My own ghost father was living in the wall".

Neither a silenced victim nor an iconic Christ figure in concrete, Nick's imagined father lives in an art that affirms the surviving value of the waste products of commerce and consumption. In doing so he claims what was trashed as a basis for new creativity and affirms imaginative recycling, with its combination of preservation and newness, as the process of art.

Discourses of politics, patriarchy as personal memory, and art all interweave with the traditional American master narrative of triumphalism, sharing its affirmative energies, but coloring it with a nuanced and complex humanistic vision. The vast encyclopedic breadth of Underworld is unified by Nick's striving, wary, but loving intelligence, large in its energies, but tempered by skepticism about perfect triumphs. Its compassion for the discarded and the failed and its recognition that no win is forever are often conveyed through Italian.

Language interpenetration is an important mechanism used in Italian American narrative to synthesize cultural myths and legends from the past with present experience. Bilingualism underscores the role of language effects in creating an ethnic aesthetic. In Helen Barolini's novel, Umbertina, four generations of Italian American women define the changing landscape of economic and gender concerns partly through their relation to the Italian language.

Underworld uses accented American English as a medium that sustains multiple discourses and suffuses the American present with an Italian heritage: "The men spoke mostly English but used the dialect when an idea needed a push or shove into a more familiar place... the dropped vowels, the vulgate... so that English was the sound of the present". This weaves aesthetic styles out of a spectrum of language-effects. From bilingualism to a use of the narrative form of the folktale told in English to achieve linkages between Italian and English, such practices convey the survival of one language through and within another.

Similar effects can be found in contemporary writing concerned with a variety of ethnic groups (Dreaming in Cuban by Cristina Garcia comes to mind). Bilingual or multilingual effects are having a profound effect on mainstream American writing as well. For example, Cormac McCarthy's The Border Trilogy contains alternating paragraphs in Spanish and English and features a bilingual Anglo protagonist raised by a Mexican woman. Here the bilingualism of the modern hero connects him to multiple traditions as McCarthy draws on Hollywood's mythic cowboys and the heroic Mexican corrida to encompass the interaction of two inseparable national histories in the modern legend he weaves.

Writing by Italian American women focuses on the close interaction among language, gender, and innovation. Mary Jo Bona's landmark study, Claiming a Tradition: Italian American Women Writers, uses the traditional rules of the Italian family as a baseline against which larger social changes can be measured. Bona's work confronts the innovative effects of women revising their roles by speaking out. Breaking the code of silence, (omerta, that Bona notes, forbids women to tell family secrets) makes language and speech a primary concern.

Bona discusses Carole Maso's comments on Ghost Dance, a novel that interweaves multilingual and multiethnic practices: "The way to resist [silence], to speak against silence, is very much what the book is about. To live next to silence, but to speak". Layering Italian as her voice of self-containment and English as a voice of self-expression, Maso's writer-heroine uses bilingualism to capture her creative struggle.

Multiplicity in point of view joins bilingualism as a frequent technique of Italian American writing. Montages of points of view providing different perspectives on the same events are often marked by switching between first and third person narratives. Doing so helps integrate a realism of observation conveyed in describing setting and circumstance with the suggestive possibilities of symbolism used to underscore the different, subjective meanings of the event for its participants.

A montage of multiple points of view also conveys the affective and psychological continuity of the ethnic self, as it does in Underworld. Shifts in narrative from first to third person can also provide interesting relationships between protagonist and ethnic author.

In some fiction, the author is self-implicated in the protagonist's process of self-examination, a process often signaled by the intrusions of the confessional form. In this process, the ethnic author who may use historical or descriptive realism to set forth a field of events and the ethnic protagonist who experiences those events may express the return of the author as an active linking mechanism within the novel. In Underworld the shifts between the voices of Nick Costanza Shay and Don DeLillo illustrate that practice.

Just as bilingualism and multiple points of view inscribe the interactions between ethnics and America in the form of fiction, so the use of Italian traditions of storytelling contributes to innovations in craft.

The uses of folktales as a means of conveying both the invasion of ordinary life by the strange, unjust, or miraculous, and of the cleveness of the poor who outwit the designs of the rich are strong Italian traditions.

In memoirs such as Jerre Mangione's Mount Allegro, such tales play a role in developing a cosmopolitan world view grounded and nourished within a traditional, Sicilian family.

In current fiction, the invocation of legendary premodern female figures may frame a modern narrative or play a crucial role in the efforts of women to use their mythic heritage to create their future as weavers of their own life stories. The Sisters Mallone: Una Storia di Famiglia by Louisa Ermelino demonstrates in its very bilingual title how sisterhood in

America can be affected by the Italian past and its exploitation of stories.

The Mallone sisters are raised by their Italian grandmother in a house without male authority in a novel that extends from 1929 to 1953. The only Italians in an Irish neighborhood, this household of women is open to the ethnic diversity around them which underscores the multiple ways women can prevail.

The novel provides a mixture of realism and folk forms: Grandmother invokes premodern myths of female power, saying she will be "like a wolf, like the Mother of Rome". She nourishes the sisters, Italian style, through telling stories illustrating the need to be strong and fend for themselves and to resist entrapment in docile obedience to men. Her granddaughters reinterpret her tales, finding in the folk wisdom of the Italian past all the energies of self-invention for the future.

The innovative aesthetic of Italian American literature is part of a larger concern for more fluid, cosmopolitan models of ethnicity and for ways to correct the excesses of postmodern theory. It can be seen in the context of the developmental, ethnographic approach of Fred Gardaphe's magisterial work, Italian Signs, American Streets: The Evolution of Italian American Narrative, Anthony Julian Tamburri's illumination of the critical uses of the psychology of consciousness in A Semiotic of Ethnicity: In (Re)cognition of the Italian/American Writer, and Mary Jo Bona's analysis of family and gender in Claiming a Tradition: Italian American Women Writers.

Such approaches make it possible to interpret the optimism of the American story not in terms of a rejection of otherness, but, in part, as a reconciliation.

Experience as art is a concept that helps characterize the aesthetic of Italian American writing and extends earlier progressive definitions of art that stress both multiplicity and subjectivity. John Dewey, in Art as Experience, developed a definition of art as celebrating American ideals by defining human nature dynamically as an interaction between active and passive forces that Dewey describes as "doing" and "undergoing". New Italian American writing is driven by comparable energies but may extend them into every dimension of public and private life.

Crafting multiplicity is a goal in an experiential aesthetic that restores both realism and symbolism to a postmodern ethos that had disavowed both. The use of multiple narratives enables a theoretic grounding for an aesthetic that appropriates the concept of supplementarity—with its dependence of the new on the old, the present on the past, its emphasis on change, and its fluid conception of repairing or completing missing meaning—for use in Italian American writing. The novel's ability to bring together political and cultural discourses that originate in historical crises, ranging from immigration, to the crises of the Cold War, and the ways in which social forces reverberate in consciousness and affect sensibility all serve to reconstitute meaning as a dynamic relationship among culture, character, and language.

In the process, realism and symbolism each complete and advance the meaning of the other. The supplementarity of the ideas of fragmentation and continuity is evident in the role both play in self-fashioning, political dissent, and inquiry.

As "supplements," the mainstream and ethnic "other" are in dynamic, interactive relationships. That mixture performs a complex function: it can both support a critique of economic or cultural exploitation and escape the trap of political ideology.

In linking the ethnic "other" and the powerful across a range of oscillating social and personal meanings and discourse relationships, this experiential aesthetic also links and opens to each other the thematic, linguistic, and narrative functions shared by both realism and symbolism. Its integrations constitute an attack on the excessive postmodern insistence on the fixed, subordinate status of the "other," and rewrite the traditional master narratives of American dominance from an ethnic perspective.

Those revisions vary and include the joy in democratic empowerment found in Marie Hall Ets' Rosa, anger at injustice like Pietro Di Donato's in Christ in Concrete, and a compassionate embrace of human commonality in our universal susceptibility to those global effects symbolized by nuclear fallout in DeLillo's Underworld.

The formal construction of current Italian American writing is typically rich in a montage of time sequences that open chronologies in public and private experiences to each other. In order to capture change, multiple chronologies may reveal the different ways people experience the same historical moment. This technique is used in Jerry Mangione's memoir, Mount Allegro, to contrast the unchanging ritual time in which his parents celebrate Sunday feasts with his own gently impatient desire to leave for college.

Time sequences are scrambled in Underworld for multiple effects including the simultaneity of the past and present in consciousness. Italian and its traditional storytelling devices may be employed in greater proportion to convey either the past, or periods of cultural crisis or personal drama, or to convey specific time frames.

Narrative styles that encompass bilingualism, or Italian folk and storytelling traditions, also help form aesthetic effects that capture the multiple languages, perspectives, and themes that persist over time in Italian American experience.

The individual returns to aesthetic centrality as an ethnic. An empirical impulse drives the use of the Italian American self as both instrument and measure of change after postmodern disdain had declared the individual obsolete. Redefining the self in terms of expansive, fragmented, or multifaceted experience and competing loyalties, the novel often uses the individual as its meditative centre. In the crossroads of consciousness, multiple discourses and perspectives find a home.

The ongoing force of heritage preserved in consciousness may be defined by styles of thinking or speaking, by expressive cultural practices, or by psychological disposition. All permit a return of symbolism as the play of memory, perception, and the continuity of changing impressions.

Emerging through the meditations and consciousness of characters thinking through their own immigrant heritage, interacting with American culture and its optimisms, the ethnic consciousness reveals the reverberations of events postmodern excesses might dismiss as simply "spectacles."

Unlike the "schizophrenic" discontinuity or "the rush" Jameson has described as the characteristic "emotional groundtone" of postmodern art, the affective as well as the meditative qualities of ethnic characters are varied and often subtle. What the excesses of postmodernism might dismiss as disconnected fragments, this Italian American aesthetic connects through processes of reinterpretation.

The author may return as a representative ethnic rather than an omnipotent narrator. Declared despised, dead, or obsolete by much postmodern criticism, the author may return in Italian American writing as a survivor who has journeyed through slums and suburbs and has felt the pressures of heritage, adaptation, and self-creation.

In other terms, the ethnic author/persona embodies the hybridity of character, one who incorporates multiple affiliations and can combine as a speaking subject both the symbolic code that governs the public self and the language of "otherness," that emotive self once considered silenced in the public world. In this sense, the concept of supplementarity may serve as a chain that links author and protagonist, individual and group, analytic intelligence and emotion.

The innovative aesthetic of Italian American writing subjects abstractions of multiplicity and diversity to a scrutiny of their emotional, intellectual, and dramatic effects.

It redefines both mainstream and ethnic in terms of interaction rather than opposition. It aligns realism about immigrant hardship or social mobility with symbolism, folklore, and myth on the axis of individual experience.

The self-fashioning of ethnic protagonists offers a demonstration of continuities of heritage, of the transformations that flow from understanding the multiple discourses and perspectives Americans share, and of the democratic value of the individual. In the force and importance it grants to the raw power of experience, the innovative aesthetic of Italian American writing reminds us of life lived face to face. All funding sources require an application or proposal with similar requirements. Good project ideas have to be well-expressed and must fit into the sponsor's high priority areas for funding.

Proposal writing fits into the metaphor of the Diving Contest. First, just like great divers who must be ready to perform according to the rules, well-practiced and informed in their field, and with a strong desire to win, so too must proposal writers' principal investigator (PI) be well-prepared. It is essential to know which project ideas get the best marks, that is part of knowing the rules and recognizing what the reviewers' value.

Which of the state-of-the art project ideas is the one that will generate the most enthusiasm? What are the reviewers looking for? Who are the reviewers? And where, strategically, should the most important material be placed? Should it be up-front or should it appear later? The strategic submission of a proposal to a runding agency and the strategic placement of essential information within a proposal are essential parts of creating a competitive proposal.

Not all agencies require the same types of applications. For example, proposals to some Canadian agencies are only six pages long. That is the good news. The bad news is that the six pages must describe the entire project, including methods, significance, references, and what die investigators have done in the past. Canadian proposals must be succinct to get the point across.

The shorter Canadian applications have the advantage of increasing the feasibility of getting good reviewers because even busy people can read six pages. Reviewers find that the shorter proposals also result in better reviewing because the information in the proposal is more focused and authors do not have space to digress.

But shorter proposals also place a lot of trust in the reviewers to determine whether the PI has the skills to be able to do the research since many of the details normally included in a proposal are simply not there. Although proposals to U.S. funding agencies are typically longer than six pages, the principle of writing a focused, well-organized and succinct proposal that follows the agency guidelines is a sound one.

THE ABSTRACT-IDEA IN A NUTSHELL

A proposal's central idea must connect with the agency and the reviewers. The proposal must represent a novel idea, a new approach, method or tool, or must address a critical issue that has not been well-studied in the past. There must also be a compelling reason to fund it.

The importance of the project must be captured throughout the proposal but is especially critical in the abstract. Reviewers who are assigned as first, second, or third reviewers will read the entire proposal but other reviewers may read only the abstract.

Therefore, the abstract needs to be carefully crafted. The abstract as well as the body of the proposal must hook the reader with an interesting and well-articulated idea and a feasible plan of study so that all the reviewers on the panel will be able to understand the merits of the proposal.

PROJECT DESIGN-A SLIPPERY SLOPE

Reviewers often single out the quality of the project design as the main reason a proposal makes or misses the funding cut.

Many proposal writers focus on the literature review and seem to attend less to the quality of the project design. The design must fit the project goals and be methodologically sound. Regardless of the type of proposal, the methods, measurements, procedures for evaluating the project's goals, hypotheses or research questions, and the time line for completing the project must be complete and carefully described.

The reviewers, many of whom are experts in their areas, spend much of their time examining the project's design. Reviewers also examine the expertise of the investigators for executing the methods and the promise of the approach for revealing new information.

For U.S. agencies in general, but particularly for Canadian funding agencies, a great deal of emphasis is placed on the investigator's research record.

Past publications count a great deal, so it is essential to include details on findings from past research projects that are relevant to the project.

This information shows that the investigator has the capability to conduct the proposed research and assures the reviewer that findings will be translated into peerreviewed publications. This is, of course, a disadvantage for new investigators or those switching to a new field but often special consideration or special grant competitions are available to new investigators.

Because the research design is so important, proposal writers need to get all the help they can in writing this section. For this reason, we suggest that proposal writers have their protocols reviewed by appropriate individuals or local committees before submission.

This way, proposals may get helpful feedback for strengthening the methodology, avoiding a critical oversight that makes a project impossible to execute. Pre-submission reviews need to be timely and constructive and applicants should submit their proposal sufficiently before the deadline for the pre-proposal review.

Reviewers are busy people and are often faced with a large number of proposals to review in a short period of time. The review duties come on top of the other work reviewers have as part of their daily jobs. Therefore, efforts directed at making the review process easier are worthwhile. Several problem areas follow.

NON-PROFESSIONAL APPEARANCE

One of us (TM) reviewed a proposal with a handwritten cover sheet and budget pages. This proposal did not look professional. Appearances are influenced by different font styles and sizes but in the end the reviewers must be able to easily read and understand the text. Many reviewers are at the age where they have to wear glasses to read; tiny letters serve to remind reviewers of their age. Making the proposal text easy to read is critical.

DISORGANIZED PROPOSALS

Reviewers are not sympathetic toward proposals that do not follow the agency's format. Reviewers are looking for certain key sections or proposal elements, either because they are going to have to write a review that critiques those sections, or because they are key pieces of the proposal. For these reasons, headings and subheadings are very important. Page numbers and accurate references to pages in the Table of Contents, and references to figures and tables within the text are important. Finally, if you say it actually should be there. Sometimes proposal writers get so rushed at the end of the proposal process that they can forget to change the text. Reviewers expect accurate information.

INCOMPLETE PROPOSALS

It is hard for proposal writers to attend to every detail but reviewers do expect proposals to be complete. If the agency asks for a dissemination plan, one must be described beyond "I'll publish an chapter." Reviewers tend to be compulsive and they look for things such as whether all the references are included, especially if they read a section with an interesting citation. They note incomplete text, especially when the text notes "Bill, put something important in there." Reviewers examine the proposal in detail to determine that all information required is there.

SPARSE JUSTIFICATION

The entire proposal must be reasonable and logical. Reviewers are not impressed when:

- Important details are omitted or only vaguely specified,
- The PI devotes little time to the project,
- The budget is not realistic because it reflects plans to completely equip a lab for the project,
- Funds are not well-justified.

Missing material, such as letters of support from consultants, collaborators, or other cooperating agencies is also noted by reviewers because it substantiates the project's feasibility.

UNTESTED MEASURES

A classic non-starter for reviewers is a lengthy list of measures to be developed or identified after the project is funded. Developing a valid and reliable instrument or implementing a complicated technique is difficult and time-consuming. Projects relying on complex techniques or critical measures are jeopardized when techniques and measures are unknown and the PI Jacks expertise in their use. Reviewers are not trusting about uncertainties in these areas.

No alternative approach as backup. Reviewers usually are looking for leading-edge approaches but they may also worry that the leading-edge approach will not work as proposed. If the proposal does not work out as planned, then what? Reviewers can be reassured when investigators combine their approach with a more standard approach so there is a fall-back position.

In general, reviewers are overworked, Type A but caring individuals, although they can also be malicious, vindictive, and self-serving. Thinking about the reviewers as individuals may help the process of successful proposal writing. Find out, if possible, which panel, study section, or subcommittee is likely to review the proposal and who the members are. Ideally, none of the members will be the intellectual or personal enemy of the investigators.

The composition of the review committee may influence how the proposal is prepared. For example, if mathematicians will be included on the review panel, the proposal should be written from their perspective.

The word math is an abbreviation and it irritates mathematicians, so the word mathematics should be used throughout. The reviewers also are likely to be prominent in their fields and chosen for a review panel because their expertise is relevant to the proposals under review.

Their work should be cited in the proposal where appropriate because they will look for citations to their work. Finally there may be differences of opinion between experts about theory, methods, and interpretations of findings. Knowing this, proposals should be written to explicitly consider these differences and to use evidence to justify the proposed approach. The reviewers may not change their opinions but at least they can not fault the proposal for ignoring opposing views.

Research administrators play an important role in the development of successful proposal writers. Few people are born with excellent proposal writing skills, but all people can learn to write successful proposals.

Research administrators can be helpful in communicating information about the proposal review process, such as the information in this chapter, to proposal writers. Research administrators can identify proposal elements that are needed to support the proposed project.

For example, ideas about budget elements (costs to include and exclude), reasonable bases for justification of budget elements, inclusion of a time line for the proposed work, and seemingly naïve but helpful questions such as, "Does this work differ from that of others in the field?" "How does this project address the agency's funding priorities?" "What will we really learn if this project is successful?" Finally, research administrators can encourage proposal writers to resubmit an unsuccessful proposal using information contained in the review.

Reviewers spend a lot of time on and give a lot of thought to their reviews. The intention of the reviewer is to provide a critique of the proposal and to also offer suggestions for improvements.

Research administrators should encourage proposal writers to share their reviews and to continue working together to develop the proposal in light of the reviews. Many ultimately successful proposals were initially rejected by agencies. But when rewritten with consideration of the reviewers' comments, these proposals can result in grants.

Furthermore, comments from reviewers even on proposals that are funded can be critical for future funding.

Projects submitted for renewal are sometimes re-reviewed by the same people who reviewed the initial application. These reviewers remember what was suggested to improve the project during the initial review and if these suggestions are not followed, the renewal application could be jeopardized. Therefore, it is important for research administrators to help proposal writers to understand the importance and helpfulness of the reviewers' comments.

Chapter 6

The Basic News Reporting Classroom

Basic news reporting classes offer us an excellent opportunity to alert future journalists to important aspects of human perception such as those studied in the field of general semantics. Reporting required identifying and discovering enormously complex events and responsibly representing them in summary form.

Even the most energetic and capable reporter, however, cannot discover all the complexity and detail available in a single observation of a single event, and describe it while still meeting deadlines. Scholars in the field of general semantics have made the study of perception central to their discipline, and acquainting novice reporting students with some of their findings can help students understand the role perception plays in reporting.

Journalism scholarship includes perception among its many areas of investigation, but the articles that focuc on perception tend to primarily identify examples of differences in the way people perceive and how these differences contribute to interpretation of events.

Eberhard demonstrates that "news value" treatments differ among newswriting texts; Van Ommeren shows that knowing reporters' backgrounds changed student views about published stories; McAdams examines relationships between psycholinguistics and perception; Allen shows that journalists often do not explain how disparate pieces of information fit together; Stocking and Gross establish that people make errors in assessing risks; and Abbott and Slattery explore topics like "intuitive goods ears." Journalism scholarship does not appear to have directly focused on examining and explaining human perception as it relates to observing and interpreting human behaviors and world events.

Allen perhaps comes closer to recognizing a need for specific focus on perception than most scholars when she observes that we need to be "...more aware of culture as a blueprint for perception..." and suggests "But neither anthropologists nor journalists nor educators nor anyone else is assuming the responsibility for sharing the contextual framewordk necessary for interpreting this morass of data..."

Stocking and Gross suggest we may be "unknowingly failing our students and profession" not only in failing to point out common perception errors, but also in not developing exercises that "...will provide opportunities for learning about cognitive distortions without sacrificing the basics." We propose the field of general semantics and specific focus on human perception as one contribution to meeting Stocking and Gross' requesting.

If you ask basic news reporting students (or even experienced reporters for that matter) if their stories accurately represent what actually happened in a given instance, they are likely to say yes.

They are used to relying on the fact that as humans they have sophisticated powers of observation and are able to quickly process large amounts of stimuli. They might readily accept the analogy that they record events much like a camera.

Korzybski, the founder of the general semantics movement, suggested even the mosot careful observer is unable to observe all stimuli within range. Bois offered an extension of Korzybski's work in a somewhat more understandable form. Both authors offered models that explained how perception necessarily differs from a given stimulus field. The models also show how perception may even result in reports that add up to more, or in some cases less, than the sum of the stimuli observed. Russell has adapted these earlier perception models and added to their range. This modified model may help basic news writing students understand that, much like a camera, their perception is limited and subject to distortion.

Available Stimuli

This human perception model illustrates how perception is incomplete and how it always differs from the observed stimulus field.

The open-sided box on the left represents the infinite stimulus field containing all individual stimuli potentially observable (dots). Some of the stimuli are in free space and others are within contained areas labeled Remembered Past, Attended to Present and Anticipated Future.

The Remembered Past box represents our ability to recall some, but not all, of the events from our past. We can recall events in varying degrees of completeness, but never completely.

Our recall of these events can serve as a filter of present and future events. For example, previous deception by an assumed reputable source can influence belief in a present source. The Attended to Present box represents stimuli available for detection in the present. Again, these stimuli are not all of the stimuli available.

Fewer stimuli are attended to than are available. Psychological experiments show only a few of any available stimuli may be attended to by the senses and consciously registered at any one time. Magicians and three-card monte players know this principle well, as do sources who mislead by answering with an avalanche of irrelevant facts instead of those few facts which would answer a question.

The Anticipated Future box represents stimuli thought to be probable in the future. Those things, which are inconceivable to the subject simply do not exist in this perceptual frame. But items in an anticipated future can filter both present and remembered stimuli. For example, suddenly realizing that a source, caught in a compromising position, plans to lie to protect his reputation, could contribute to reconsideration of his previous comments and also the conclusion that his present comments may be untrue. The model presumes a balanced individual in whom the Attended to Present is larger than the other two areas. Healthy observers pay more attention to the present than to their Remembered Past or Anticipated Future.

The most important feature of the figure on the left of the model is that it has more dots than can possibly be observed. No individual can ever be expected to discover all stimuli available or even exactly the same stimuli as another observer.

To next box represents human observers as limited in the sense that cameras are limited. Cameras, in fact, do not record everything in front of them. They are mechanical devices limited by their physical nature and outside factors such as lighting and film type. Inadequate lens power and shutter speed, for example, may distort of fail to record certain images, and objects that otherwise exhibit a wide range of colour, will be recorded as monochromatic if shot with black and white film or under the wrong lighting conditions.

The limits of human perception may be compared to the limitations of a camera. Limits in a reporter's perception prevent her from perceiving some stimuli. Stimuli that are merely available are less important than those an individual actually can discover. For example, a reporter who did not see a source wink his eye after responding "Of course all members of the opposition party also believe the earth is flat," might not be aware the source was answering ironically.

A significant reduction in the number of stimuli occurs between the first and second boxes. Reduction of simplification is the first act of human perception. This happens because perception does not take place primarily, but is mediated by the individual. Heil, for instance, suggests perception is actually a two stage process that begins with direct perception. After this initial stage, however, cognition begins and language starts to play a role, so the perception then becomes indirect.

In the direct perception stage, for example, someone might observe the physical characteristics of a rock — its weight, its shape, colour, etc. But in the second, indirect stage, that person may perceive it as a paperweight or a weapon. Direct and indirect perception can be expected to be subject to a number of influences. Beginning news reporting students might be infromed of the following influences that could affect each or both of these stages.

EXPERIENCE

And individual's private experiences can influence perception. Some reporters, for example, may have experienced government officials withholding vital information in the name of national security. Discovering later that the information was, in fact, withheld to save the officials from embarrassment, may affect how those reporters view such withholding of information in the future.

Formal Education. In school we are literally taught how to perceive our world. Education in the scientific method, for example, would enable reporters to better perceive what is going on in experiments in physics, medicine, and chemistry, and better evaluate claims made in those fields.

Value System: Things believed to be important can change reporter's perception of a situation. Reporters who believe in fairness, for example, are likely to perceive there may be another side to a story even though they hear a version of it they accept as true. They may perceive the first version as more tentative, than those who do noto hold such a value.

Role or Profession. Reporters are taught it is part of their professional duty to protect the right of the public to know how their public institutions are functioning. A public official who attempts to withhold public records may therefore be perceived very differently by reporters than others who have no such professional mandate.

Language: Language can serve as an additional filter for perceived stimuli. Military spokespersons who use "protective incursion" rather than "military invasion," or "collateral damage" rather than "civilian deaths," show an understanding of the power of language to alter perceptions. Lutz (1989) offers students an excellent reference on doublespeak and its power to influence. Other influences, such as physical condition and competing stimuli can also serve to filter perceptions, of course, but the five offered above can begin to help students in recognizing human perception is more complex than a simple stimulus-response act.

Classify: This box only has only one dot in it which represents the tendency in human perception to think in terms of classes and thereby reduce something complex into something overly simple. Classification encourage equating the characteristics of new members of a class, with characteristics of established members of the class. Perhaps, the intent is to help understand the world, but the outcome is more often to ignore important differences among members of the class.

Making the comparison with known members of the class can contribute to assuming the new member is "exactly like" the known members. For example, knowing that a source is a Catholic could contribute to assuming she is opposed to abortion "because Catholics oppose abortion."

Name: The box also only has one dot in it to represent yet an additional reduction of stimuli that are attended to. In naming, something complex is overly simplified. For example, a complex and unique individual can be reduced to "politician," or a thousand separate activities can become "war." Names represent on enormous reduction of available and observed stimuli.

Meaning: This box represents an expansion of the reduction process that has occurred in the first three boxes. At this stage of perception, individuals begin to determine the meaning of their experiences.

Scholars in the field of general semantics hold that meaning is something created by an interaction between the individual and stimuli. The increased number of dots in the meaning box represents the capacity of expand what was previously reduced. The additional dots in the box do not mean the available stimuli, or only those attended to have been faithfully reproduced. For example, a police officer could primarily attend to the reflection of light in a suspect's hand,

and conclude the reflecting object is a gun. The officer may then assign this perceived stimuli to mean danger and that he must therefore protect himself.

Meaning is a very private construct and the meanings of stimuli are not necessarily universally shared. Assuming they are may lead to misunderstanding. Determining that a public official is acting out of caution or weakness can be as much the consequence o the observer's assigning meaning as the official's actions.

What We Can Share

The final box represents an additional reduction inthe perception process. The fewer dots in this box compared to the meaning box suggests we are unable to share all of our private meanings. This is particularly important for reporters since time and space constraints alone will always limit their ability to offer all that they know.

The lines going out of the What We Can Share box enter the available stimuli for others. This area is represented by a question mark because we have no way to be sure what others do with our stimuli. The number and nature of dots in their perceptual field is subject to their control and limits, not to the journalist's.

As a result of long experience in assigning meaning in particular situations, a reporter may understand the implications in a political candidate's refusing to debate an oppenent. Merely reporting the action, however, does not mean the reader will automatically grasp these implications. Exposing news reporting students to the models of human perception suggested by general semanticists may help students appreciate what Harrison Salisbury recognized after many years of reporting.

The war in Vietnam was the first of the separating images which, as time went on, showed me that in war, as in the simplest things in life, truth is multifaceted, a crystal that refracts light in many forms and many shapes, the quicksilver of the mind. Basic news reporting students who can understand and appreciate that human preception is not a simple stimulus-response act, and is always incomplete can perhaps begin to demonstrate what has been called maturity and good news judgement. If they can be taught their observations are by definition incomplete, perhaps they will learn to ask even more questions and search for more sources and vantage points before concluding they have observed and reported everything.

As fewer young Americans attend to newspapers and television newscasts, their levels of political participation have declined, along with their trust in political institutions and in the mass media. U.S. television news has lost half of its young adult viewers since the 1960s and newspapers have lost an even larger share as part of a longer trend in declining readership that began in the 1920s. In surveys political participation does coincide with attention to news, especially newspapers, and young citizens have voted in declining numbers as their readership levels have fallen. These trends cannot sound heartening to the major U.S. news organizations or to those concerned with the informed citizenry of U.S. democracy.

The trends have also been confirmed by field studies. One study based on life histories recounting experiences with newspapers found that young U.S. citizens attending college did report difficulty with becoming committed newspaper readers, just as the survey data suggest. Among the many reasons they had a hard time committing to being newspaper readers, one seems the most important: They found the stories did not touch on the areas of civic activity they encountered in their daily lives.

Although the newspaper retains its meaning as a symbol of adulthood, the young adults often failed to sustain the family ritual experienced in childhood. A second study on television news found that college students who turned away from newspapers did not appear to substitute another news medium to inform themselves as citizens. Although they held television news in minimal regard, they still credited the first major news story they remembered from television with making them feel part of the larger national community. In spite of this fairly strong generation effect from watching news, many of the young adult participants considered newscasts primarily a form of entertainment, and only a few mentioned any other source far news, such as radio or the Internet.

Surveys and field work confirm that, although some older Americans may experience a strong need for news, the younger generation does not share that appetite. A growing minority of young Americans get along without what the major news organizations serve up daily, and those who do pay attention, especially to television news, do so without attaching great significance to the news as the Fourth Estate in U.S. political life. The view of the news arena as a space where the public sphere operates is declining among the young citizenry.

Because of the clear impact on the civic role for news businesses, with the potential to weaken political participation, the trends among young Americans have aroused debate about the future of democracy. Carried on without reference to other countries, the debate raised questions requiring comparative research abroad. Are the increasingly negative experiences with news among young citizens peculiar to the United States? Or do the changes pertain as well to young adults in other contemporary societies? To search for answers, this monograph presents the results of two qualitative studies abroad that closely replicate the U.S. research, examining newspaper and then television news experiences that college students recount in life history narratives.

Spain was selected as a comparative case for several reasons. The most compelling comes from data on the young audience for news: Among Western democracies, only in Spain is news viewership reaching an almost universal national audience and newspaper circulation growing among young citizens. Spain provides a setting within another advanced country that differs from the United States in most particulars: Spain's development came recently, as did its return to democracy.

Besides their differing language and parliamentary monarchy, young Spaniards grew up in close-knit extended families and attended highly structured schools that emphasized rote learning. More important, the Spanish media arena diverges greatly from that typical in the United States. Where local newspapers and commercial broadcasting dominate the U.S. press, national newspapers and public television predominate in Spain. In such a contrasting political and media settings, young citizens will likely report distinct ways of informing themselves as citizens.

The decisions of young adults in another country present opportunities to build grounded theory. By looking at groups that contrast strongly with those previously studied, field work can seek cases that break the rule, clarifying the contours of the new relationship to news emerging among the young. The process may also generate concepts useful to understanding subjective experiences of the news arena.

Comparing groups reared under a greatly differing news arena permits a search for common patterns. Any strong similarities found to cross cultural or national boundaries would contribute to the general understanding of subjective experience. The comparison could yield insights into the structure of generations as the news media globalize. Expected differences might indicate alternative policy choices for news organizations and their role in informing citizens.

The idea of comparing nations has long been employed to build theories of politics and society. Since Durkheim and Weber, "the father of crossnational research", tried to understand modern society by holding it up against historical and primitive groups, scholars have used examples from different nations as a way to illustrate their ideas, from the social Darwinism of Spencer and the functionalism of Radcliffe-Brown, to the structuralism of Levi-Strauss. Herbert Blumer criticized these comparisons to remote societies as an exercise in nostalgia.

Comparative studies of contemporary nations, on the other hand, give observers a vantage point closer to home, reducing the danger of romanticizing a traditional or historical society. Interest in comparative research was surging, principally at the intersection between sociology and political science, when Seymour Martin Lipset wrote his classic studies. The new field, political sociology, took on several topics that cross the borders of the two fields, such as the fate of democracy, the role of the media, and the participation of individual citizens as part of different generations.

Defining and measuring "the political culture of democracy" and "the social structures and processes that sustain it" inspired the pioneer study of comparative political attitudes in the United States, United Kingdom, Germany, Italy, and Mexico. The news media clearly took part in these structures and processes. To illustrate the patterns found in survey questions about media use and political interest, the authors also conducted life history interviews.

During the early 1960s Americans facing the cold war, fearing a domino effect if small nations fell to Communism, wanted to know how to encourage the broadest democracy without causing instability. "How can the apathetic peripheral man become the aspiring participant man without a deep seachange in the psychic weather?" asked Daniel Lerner.

The answer was found in Lipset's three requirements for political democracy; a regular means to change officials, a loyal opposition, and (important for this study) a mechanism for the largest possible share of society to participate. Communication seemed to provide one of the most likely mechanisms. "In the world today - whether you like it or not, whether it is advisable or not, whether it is good policy planning or not - tremendous developments in communication," Lerner went on, "are occurring in every country". These changes at mid-century began to shrink the global community, and several contemporary studies identify communications (including newspaper consumption) as a strong indicator of political development.

Subsequent studies have paid most attention to voting, but the news media also provide a key to citizens' involvement in democratic governments. As mass communication grows, clusters of older social, economic, and psychological commitments end, and citizens become more open to new patterns of action.

The commitment to participate in politics can clash with the roles the media play in generating economic profits, and this contradiction may limit their legitimacy and effectiveness in the political system. News media can block as well as encourage change, because "the construction of political reality is essentially a 'mediated' process". Young adulthood, when political reality takes firm shape in personal commitments, is rarely studied. Socialization research emphasizes childhood and adolescence and pays little attention to the media, although media research shows that television often provides the earliest encounters with politics in the United States. Cross-national research on media and politics usually focuses on media content, not audiences, and mass media researchers have called for more comparative study of public communication.

This monograph on young citizens and the media has two theoretical aims. One is to describe and delineate elements in the structure of subjective experience. In his suggestions for studying the media, Blumer proposed that they do not operate within clearly demarcated and distinct outlets and forms, such as newspapers and television, but instead act within a larger zone that he called an arena. Viewed from the perspective of citizens' symbolic interactions, subjective experiences with the news arena have been little studied. To extend understanding of the political sociology of news, this monograph employs a descriptive strategy to discover grounded theory.

After identifying other groups for comparison, a principal task is to describe subjective experience in detail, thus adding to the store of empirical observations of responses to the media arena. To build theory, groups are chosen as negative cases, selected to delimit the news arena and clarify its role in young citizens' experience. That Americans increasingly reject news invites the search for cases where a different news arena holds sway. Cross-national research looks for similarities between nations because "if the same factor produces the same effects in two very different situations, its influence tends to be confirmed".

National distinctiveness makes finding the same processes less likely in more than one country, and so similarities are not only unexpected but also valuable to add to the general understanding of the media arena. Differences contribute as well, and the most important source of contrast, of course, is national history. As they confront problems, the citizens of various countries find alternatives and reach different decisions. Their contrasting responses can be used to suggest policy options.

Another theoretical aim is to examine generational change. Generations are produced only in modern societies, where rapid changes produce longterm shifts in ideology. Events give each new group of children a different set of experiences that tie them strongly to others their age.

What people know about politics is influenced by their position in a generation, and studies of generations suggest that their collective memories emerge not only from massive traumatic events such as wars and large scale demographic shifts but also from mass exposure to events shown in the media. Karl Mannheim noted that an actual generation, whose coming of age coincides with a set of common experiences, does not necessarily interpret those shared events uniformly. The conflicting meanings they assign events divide them into what Mannheim called generational units.

Maurice Halbwachs agreed that collective memories play a central role in distinguishing different social groups and classes. Mannheim further suggested that, although their life spans may overlap, different age groups experience the same moments of history differently, each generation living in its own subjective era, as he called it.

This has been borne out in subsequent research. Finally, Mannheim proposed that national differences effectively separate people of the same chronological age: citizens in Germany and China in 1800 could not form part of the same actual generation because they could share no formative experiences.

The growth of news organizations that extend beyond national borders, the consolidation of media ownership globally, and the resulting international spread of political reporting styles raise the question whether citizens of nations separated by geography and language had begun to share sufficient media experience by the end of the 20th century to form a generation in effect.

These theoretical considerations guide the study: the search for commonalities that indicate new social and political meanings for news crossing national boundaries, the observation of differences with an eye to discover alternate policies for American news organizations as they inform citizens, and the testing of boundaries of subjective experience between a political generation and its units in the United States and Spain.

As a practical matter, choosing countries is the first task in any crossnational comparison. For the greatest detail and depth, a binary analysis comparing only one country to another -works best. Because it "leaves out neither the specific nor the general," binary study can contribute "to an understanding of general phenomena". The choice of countries requires a balance. The two should share enough to make reasonable comparisons but also have enough differences to make for robust results.

The United States shares with Europe many cultural, political, and economic traditions, including the modern phenomenon of youth culture. Within Europe, Spain differs from the United States perhaps more than any other nation. The United States and Spain stood as complete opposites in the early 1960s. Among developed American and European nations, Spain had the lowest newspaper circulation (70 per thousand population) and the penultimate rate for televisions (13.1 per thousand population) - only the Portuguese owned fewer sets.

During the Franco era, Spain also had no meaningful gauge of voting. By contrast, the United States had newspaper circulation in the middle of the range (326 per thousand population, compared to the United Kingdom, 506 per thousand population) and the highest number of television sets (306.4 per thousand population). The percentage of U.S. citizens who actually voted, while not high (64.4 per cent in 1960), ranked with those nations lacking mandatory voting laws. The United States also had the highest level of college enrollment (1,983 per hundred thousand population) and Spain (258 per hundred thousand population) the lowest (Britain had 460 per hundred thousand population, but a larger share of enrollees graduated). Perhaps because of these differences, most Americans know little of Spain beyond the tourist cliches of bullfights and flamenco, necessitating a brief overview of recent political, media, and generational history.

Unlike the United States, Spain experienced an extended pause from democracy during the Franco regime, which had a profound impact on the country. The "executions, the imprisonments, the torture, the lives destroyed by political exile and forced economic migration point to the exorbitant price paid by Spain for Franco's `triumphs'. Despite these depredations, Spanish citizens remained committed to the ideal of civic culture. Under Franco, citizens in the different regions of Spain preferred democratic rule by "all of us" rather than by one caudillo, even in the most conservative strongholds. The commitment to democracy was based on the culture of Spain, rather than springing from economic factors or social structure.

In Franco's later years, Spain underwent a "Prussian-type economic development... beginning in the mid-1950s and promoted by national ruling classes". Preston characterized the 1960s as a period of robust economic growth resulting in broad social changes. Business and professional people became independent-minded in increasing numbers, and unrest from the worker movements applied growing pressure for change.

The Franco regime did institute some liberalizing policies, such as the Press Law enacted in 1966. Liberalization took firm root in such places as the universities, where Marxist publications became widely available and prominent intellectuals criticized the regime, calling for reform, and where "tolerance at the ideological level was unquestionable". Spain also experienced greater contact with the outside world, through flows of migration from Europe and increases in tourism primarily from the western hemisphere.

The assassination in 1973 of Carrero Blanco, the ultraconservative head of Franco's government, "was a factor of overwhelming importance". He was replaced by Carlos Arias Navarro, who, although not progressive, did support limited reforms. In his most important act, televised on February 12,1974, he announced that "the national consensus in support of the regime must in the future be expressed in the form of participation". Arias Navarro's speech opened the door for Francoist institutions to reflect more political pluralism, although that aim faced repeated setbacks. The regime then enacted a Statute of Associations, which allowed groups to register, although few did (and opposition political parties remained prohibited).

The hopes for reform in the early 1970s clashed with economic frustration over Franco's "paternalistic regulation of the labour market", as well as his policy of keeping Spain out of the European Economic Community. The energy crisis put a break on increases in the standard of living for the working class, which lacked political rights and became increasingly militant. By 1975, "it had become clear that socioeconomic and institutional change as well as modifications in political beliefs at both the mass and elite level of Spanish society had eroded away the underpinnings of the authoritarian regime".

Franco himself became ill, and the media kept a vigil outside the palace. The extreme measures to postpone his death, the machinations to extend the regime, and the hope of installing a new head of the Cortes (Parliament) who would resist change - these things came to light only later. At the time, Spaniards witnessed only the head of government in tears, announcing Franco's death on TVE1, the state channel.

TRANSITION

Franco left behind a constitution that envisioned Prince

Juan Carlos becoming king. This went as planned. The king would have ruled only as the successor to Franco, without full dynastic legitimacy, but then his father Don Juan de Borbon renounced his right to the throne. Arias Navarro continued as head of the government from November 1975 until the king replaced him in July 1976 with Adolfo Suarez, who followed a strategy of seeking pacts with the right and the left. He got the approval of the military and Cortes for a Law on Political Reform, ratified in 1976.

The process secured the right to form political parties, granted political amnesty, dissolved the state labour unions and the single Francoist Movimiento party, and then set free elections for the Constituent Assembly.

The consensus completely rejected Franco's plan: "trade unions were legalized, political parties, including the hated Partido Comunista de Espana [PCE], were permitted". Extremists of the right wing began a violent backlash, which reached a nadir in Madrid, January 23 to 28, 1977, during the semana negra or "black week" that left student activists and lawyers, as well as policemen, murdered. The fate of Spanish democracy seemed uncertain.

In May 1977, during preparations leading up to the first general, multiparty elections, the Union Centro Democratico (UCD) formed a centre-right coalition of political forces. The communists (PCE) "played a major role in the transition and... gained 20 per cent of the vote in the 1977 election", and the socialists (PSOE) won more than a quarter of the vote (28 per cent and 118 seats). The centre coalition (UCD) received one-third of the votes (165 seats) and began a period leading a minority government that lasted until 1982 (in the 1979 general election, the UCD won 34 per cent and 168 seats, and the PSOE won 30 per cent and 121 seats).

The country put its economy on abetter footing with the Moncloa Pacts in October 1977. The accords imposed austerity, with budgetary control, tax reform, limits on wage increases, and a devalued peseta.

As a result, inflation decreased (from 29 per cent) and exports went up, but unemployment also increased. The accords caused discontent when many of the promised reforms failed to materialize.

"Inevitably," Preston wrote, "the most dramatic difficulties encountered by Spain's newborn democracy were the direct legacy of Franco's rule". One of these, the Basque separatist movement (ETA), enjoyed some popular support through the 1970s.

The rigid centralist policies of the Franco regime had left such regional movements stronger, especially those in the zasque country and Catalunya. Although the new constitution adopted in 1978 recognized regional autonomy, the separatist movements still presented a violent threat.

A military trained to distrust democracy presented another difficulty. This bore fruit when Lieutenant Colonel Antonio Tejero led a group of senior military officers in an attempted coup d'etat on February 23, 1981. The king went on state television to denounce the failed attempt, and the public responded with mass demonstrations.

From 1977 to 1982, the socialists remained the principal opposition party. Then the socialist era arrived: "Felipe Gonzalez became prime minister in 1982, after his party's crushing victory in the elections that year.

His second administration saw Spain enjoy dramatic levels of economic growth. His third administration was marked by internal party strife, exacerbated by growing evidence of corruption". Following an unexpected victory in 1993, the government became increasingly mired in charges of corruption and was defeated in 1996 by the Partido Popular (PP), which formed a minority government with Catalan support. The 1996 elections marked the end of the transition from the Franco era.

Since the transition, Spain appears to have entered a period of stability, similar to the quiescence characteristic of the mature U.S. democracy.

At a time when the left-leaning socialist party controlled Spanish government, the United States by contrast had a series of conservative administrations. A decline of trust in the U.S. government and its institutions marked the period. Surveys of opinions and attitudes since the transition to democracy indicate a Spanish citizenry consistently moderate in ideology and supportive of democratic principles.

They also have low levels of political interest and information. From the late 1970s through the late 1980s, a consistent share (about three-quarters) said they knew little or nothing about politics. When asked their general response to politics, a majority expressed boredom or indifference, while one-third expressed interest and enthusiasm and one-fifth expressed annoyance and disgust.

These survey results lead researchers to identify an "outstanding feature in the political attitudes of Spanish people, namely, their political passivity".

In a study in the 1960s, the United States and United Kingdom plotted high and near the regression line correlating communications (an index computed from newspaper consumption, newsprint used, telephones installed, and mail volumes) and political development.

Spain stood near the middle in communications development and the low-middle in political development, well below the average. This combination suggested a country poised, because of its communications development, to experience a spurt in political development - an accurate prediction, as it turned out.

Under the Franco regime, changes in the laws governing the press took a first step toward liberalization (although an extremely small one by U.S. standards). The 1966 reform changed the process (but not the fact) of censorship, ending it before publication but imposing "post hoc suspension or closure", so that editors had to guess what might get censored.

"Franco, the Falange, the Army and the principles of the regime could not be criticized, but for all the limitations, the law constituted a real change, and the most reactionary elements in the regime were furious at the implications".

The policy change "gave rise to hopes of more substantial political change". Under the new law, periodicals such as the newspapers Informaciones, Ya, and Madrid and the magazine Diario 16 published criticism of the government and called for reform, working within the constraints of the regime. (The newspaper Madrid came under censure in 1971 and then closed.) Publications also sprang up in regional languages such as Catalan.

Spanish television was founded as a state monopoly in the 1950s. "Under the Franco regime, television held the key to reading the eyes and ears of the Spanish population" because, unlike newspapers in the country, "television commands massive audiences". After Franco's death, government control continued over what were by then two state channels, TVE1 (also called La Primera) and TVE2 (La Dos). Newspapers gained much more freedom, and the transition saw several newspapers start up.

The most important national paper to emerge, EI Pais, established a left-leaning socialist editorial line, in contrast to the right-leaning monarchist position of the newspaper ABC. The strong political agendas of Spanish newspapers did not come as a novelty. Much earlier, for example, "Franco spoke of the monarchist daily ABC as an `enemy'".

During the period of socialist rule, two important shifts occurred in the Spanish news media, bringing them closer to their U.S. counterparts. On one hand, the government revised (by some accounts timidly) the broadcasting laws.

"In the 1980s, Spanish television evolved from a public monopoly, with only two state channels, into a competitive multi-channel system". Two new channels began free broadcasting, Antena 3 and TeleS, and a third emerged based on subscription, Canal Plus.

On the other hand, Pedro J. Ramirez founded in the late 1980s a national newspaper, EI Mundo. Ramirez, who worked as a young intern in the Washington Post newsroom the day Nixon resigned, introduced investigative journalism at EI Mundo. The paper took a strongly anti-socialist line against Felipe Gonzalez and his government.

Ramirez made himself a household name in Spain by pushing the stories of corruption in government to the forefront of the political agenda. The national newspapers in Spain circulate throughout the country, alongside (and in competition with) the local and regional press, and both continue growing in circulation. By the 1990s, all the older Spanish newspapers had reformatted themselves as smaller tabloids.

The press has adopted an aggressive pattern of redesigns and received a number of awards, particularly El Mundo for reporting and EI Pais for design. U.S.-based journalism associations have named both of these among the best newspapers in the world. The changes in newspapers accompanied an erosion of press partisanship, with an increase in claims to professionalism among reporters and in market orientation among publishers.

Television news also has a history of partisanship in Spain, although less overt than the printed press. A study of the 1993 election, for example, shows that the state-controlled TVE1's favorable coverage of Gonzalez and the socialist government became especially pronounced in the pre-campaign period. In that election the private channels, Antena 3, Tele5, and Canal Plus, first covered the campaign in full. The entry of commercial broadcasters "has created a new audience map, and all the networks and stations are increasingly guided by ratings". As a result, public broadcasting, although still dominant, has seen a continual erosion of its audience and income.

Despite some growth, newspapers still do not receive wide readership in Spain, and total circulation reaches only one in ten of the population.

The press has been expanding, however, with the number of newspapers published increasing since the 1980s. At the same time, the trends have been toward greater concentration of ownership, including the growth of newspaper chains and cross-ownership of television and radio stations and magazines. These trends have parallels in the United States.

Electioneering in the news media of various countries has begun to follow a pattern as elections become Americanized. That trend makes a clear picture of U.S. news essential for understanding the Spanish media. Historically, the U.S. news media have operated under market competition with only limited government regulation. Public broadcasting arrived late and has played a very small role. The press remains predominantly local, with competition at that level declining as newspapers have closed or consolidated.

Coverage of politics has changed substantially since the 1960s, when newspaper reporters and television correspondents gave a largely descriptive chronicle of the candidates' words and movements during election campaigns.

Studies show that U.S. journalists have increasingly described presidential campaigns using the metaphors of conflict or the horse race, positioning themselves as political interpreters for the public. As a result, media organizations may have largely supplanted political parties as the principal power brokers in the selection of U.S. leaders.

Competition for readers and viewers has imposed entertainment values on U.S. news. Since the 1960s, television journalists have greatly shortened politicians' sound bites and increased the relative share of time and emphasis given to their own judgments about campaigns. Newscasts became dramatically more visual in the 1970s, at the time when they reached a pinnacle of audience share and advertising revenues. Seeing themselves in competition with television, newspapers followed suit, updating their designs at a rate that accelerated in the early 1980s.

Both television and newspapers began to face audience declines in the mid-1980s, as cable expanded the alternatives for news (including CNN and C-SPAN). Newspaper executives identified and attempted to slow the erosion of readership among young adults. By the early 1990s, news executives viewed computer networks as a potential competitor.

Unlike the ideological competition among Spanish newspapers, the U.S. press sees itself as part of a news market, where television broadcast news competes with cable and radio and where newspapers - most of them local monopolies - compete with broadcasters. Driven by market considerations, the U.S. news media aim for the greatest visual and emotional impact within the constraints of the widest possible audience appeal.

YOUNG ADULTS

A persistent puzzle of Spain since Franco has been the political culture that survey researchers characterize as passive, with low rates of participation, weak party allegiance, and limited social capital, as measured by memberships in civic associations and neighborliness. Despite low participation, the levels of cynicism and efficacy in Spain during the transition were no worse than those in the United Kingdom and the United States, and in general the "political culture in Spain did not differ too greatly from the political cultures of stable democracies".

The period of rapid change in Spain did, however, produce clear differences between generations. Those in young adulthood during the late 1970s belong to what has been called the transition generation, born after 1951 and reaching adulthood after Franco. In 1980, 21to 25-year-olds had the highest feelings of political efficacy and lowest cynicism of any group. On the whole, the young voiced more support for democracy, had more interest and confidence in politics, participated more, and had greater party allegiance, while they indicated less trust in the actions of authorities and in their country as a whole than did older Spaniards.

General levels of participation ranked lower, but the young were among the most likely to participate in politics. The idea "of a generalized lack of interest in politics among the youngest age group is not borne out" at that time. They culminated a trend in which each succeeding generation, in response to the dictatorship, identified more strongly with the left in Spain.

Young adults of the post-transition generation are even less the product of their country's period under Franco than were their parents. Born near the time he died, they are reaching adulthood with Spain fully integrated into the European Community.

They appear to be moving away from the left. Recent surveys show that they have levels of political interest similar to those found in 1980. The highest level of interest appears among those recently of voting age, and the level and growth of their interest corresponds to the availability and access to information such as news about politics.

Their most common modes of political participation include voting, informing themselves, joining associations, and discussing politics. They report being most influenced by the media and by friends, followed by their families and by schools. They overwhelmingly support democracy as a political system, although they tend to judge their own country's system harshly in comparison to others in Europe. The survey data tend to contradict popular wisdom among the transition generation that their heirs in the posttransition era are less interested in and knowledgeable about politics, and more disengaged from and cynical about public life. No previous field work has examined this contradiction.

In the young generation's media experience, the newspaper landscape has had regular growth in circulation and in the number of newspapers published. Unlike their parents, they see EI Pais as a fixture and, of course, the anti-socialist, crusading EI Mundo as a novelty. Despite growth, newspapers form a small part of the media environment, but they offer a range of competing ideologies (contrary to the rule in the United States or in Spain under Franco).

Newspapers during the young adults' lives have been constantly changing - not only growing but redesigning and altering formats requiring regular adaptation and adjustment by the audience. Television, however, remained under state control through most of their formative years. Public broadcasting provided the only news on television through the 1989 campaign, when the post-transition generation entered its teenage years. The addition of private channels occurred in the political calendar during the next two elections, just as the young generation reached voting age.

In other ways, the new generation of Spanish citizens presents a particularly interesting case. The country saw a baby boom immediately after Franco's death. Upon reaching an all-time high, the birthrate then dropped in subsequent years to reach the lowest level in the world. As a result, the group reaching young adulthood in the mid-1990s is the largest in Spain's history. Their demographics create a case study in contrasts. On the up side, they have experienced the expansion of education and stabilization of democracy.

The number of Spaniards completing college doubled between 1973 and 1992, and successive elections since the transition to democracy have produced rising levels of voting and other participation among the young. On the down side, the large size of the generation has caused problems. With general unemployment high (22 per cent at the time of the 1996 election), discontent among young voters became a factor cited in the defeat of the socialist party. The counterpart cohort of young Americans are also part of a bulge generation, the children of America's earlier baby boom, and they have suffered similar economic consequences, with the attendant levels of discouragement.

INDICATORS TODAY

By the 1990s, the political and social gap between the United States and Spain had closed substantially (Miguel,1995). The share of Spanish workers employed in white collar jobs had grown dramatically (from 30 to 44 per cent, 1960 to 1981). Television had reached close to saturation in 1994 (99.3 per cent of households), and half had more than one set (49.9 per cent) and a VCR (57.6 per cent). However, the average electoral turnout remains much higher in Spain (73.9 per cent of eligible voters, since the death of Franco, 1977-1993) than in the United States. On average, Spaniards use the media in very different patterns (according to 1996 data from ASEP). They view only three and one-half hours of television a day (210 minutes).

The state channels still receive a third of the audience share (TVE1 at 28 per cent, TVE2 at 10 per cent), with private channels dividing up most of the rest (led by Antena 3 at 26 per cent, Tele5 at 19 per cent). Satellite channels from abroad play a much smaller role. Large differences appear especially in the printed press (according to 1996 data from FIEJ). The number of newspapers continues to grow (up 13.6 per cent from 1990 to 1994), as does daily circulation (up 36.6 per cent).

Over the same period, the number of dailies in the United States declined (by 4.5 per cent), and weekday circulation was also down (by 5.3 per cent).

Although political sociology since its founding has relied on data from statistical samples of various nations to use as indicators of political and social life, qualitative methods have also played a role. Personal essays written by citizens were considered a standard technique. In recent guides to crossnational study, half of the recommended methods require field work, and qualitative tools seem especially useful to examine subjective beliefs. Because survey data "necessarily abstracts institutions events, and processes from their unique social and cultural context", field studies become all the more important.

Autobiographical techniques have a long history in studies of the media and citizens, beginning with the groundbreaking examination of Polish peasants and immigrants to the United States. The full length autobiography has generally been used in the social sciences to study foreign or marginalized others. Bv simplifying and focusing autobiography more narrowly, researchers found a way to apply the technique to the mainstream. Blumer asked young people from many walks of life to write shorter narratives about one aspect of their experience, their memories of and reactions to movies. This technique, the limited life history, has found wide application in recent years among scholars in the social sciences and cultural studies.

The limited life history technique is especially effective for spanning time - the longitudinal section - as political culture is transmitted across generations. Life histories also impose an expanded view of political participation, not only including such elements as party affiliation and political interest included in questionnaires but also leaving open a full range of other activities, whatever participants choose to address in their narrative essays.

To find out about young Spaniards' subjective experiences with news, colleagues helped me collect life history narratives from young adults in Spain. During 1996, sixty-two undergraduates at three Spanish universities contributed their news experiences. The universities are located in three very different regions in Spain: the capital, Madrid, the industrial Navarra region, and the depressed autonomous community of Canarias. Because each of the universities draws from a wide area, the mix of participants included many other regions of Spain. The participants form what is called a "saturation sample", the qualitative standard for gathering sufficient examples. Saturation, the point at which any additional examples would add only particulars without increasing the general understanding about the group, is reached in most studies somewhere between twenty-five and thirty.

The study group is appropriate for two purposes. It first allows a close replication of the studies of U.S. college students. Second and more important, it represents the small but significant sector in Spain of the affluent and educated young. They form not only the core of up-scale audience members that news executives seek to attract and sustain but also the source for the next generation of political leaders, activists, and attentive citizens essential to democratic government.

The participants were asked to write a short life history essay, beginning with their earliest memories and continuing to their current activities. They received the same instructions as did the U.S. groups in earlier studies, translated into Spanish, one set for television news and another for newspapers. About a third of the participants agreed to write two essays, one on each medium, to allow a comparison of their ways of writing and thinking about the two.

All participants also completed a questionnaire with standard demographic, media use, and political items, the same completed by the U.S. groups but translated into Spanish. The group is not intended, of course, to be a representative sample at the morphological level. The questionnaire was collected to allow a clear comparison to the previous studies as well as to national measurements of young Spaniards. In the survey responses, the volunteers did resemble the U.S. groups from previous studies: mostly communication majors, predominantly white, and roughly two-thirds women.

Unlike the U.S. participants, a slightly larger share of Spanish volunteers haled from cities and large towns (80 per cent), with most of the remainder from smaller towns and rural areas (16 per cent). Their parents also differ, the largest share of whom attended only some high school (72 per cent of mothers, 50 per cent of fathers) and work mostly in labour and in the home.

The Spanish students reported higher levels of media use than did the Americans (the mean for each measure is shown). They read newspapers more often (5.4 days "last week") and watched newscasts more (6.1 days). More of the Spaniards said they read a national newspaper (36 per cent), local paper (40 per cent) or both (20 per cent), and none reported reading a student paper. There were no non-readers. For television news, more Spaniards reported watching local news (52 per cent) and national news (54 per cent and some watch both), but satellite and cable received no mention. There were no non-viewers.

Besides their higher attention to news, they paid slightly more attention to audio-visual media. They said they watched a bit more television on average (84 minutes "yesterday") and listened to radio somewhat more (58 minutes). In contrast, they spent substantially more time with the newspaper (31 minutes). They read more books (2.1 "last month") but fewer magazines (3.6). They also watched many more movies (8.4 viewed, plus 1.0 rented).

The participants' media use roughly matched audience statistics for urban Spaniards their age. In national surveys (all figures from 1996 ASEP data), young adults generally used print media and radio more heavily than did older adults. Young adults read newspapers more (50 per cent "yesterday") than did all adults (37 per cent), although the gap appears to be narrowing. The same share of young and older adults watched television (89 per cent), but slightly more of those under 30 watched news (76 per cent compared to 73 per cent "yesterday" for all adults). The study group, although smaller in number than the U.S. volunteers, was much more geographically diverse than either of the U.S. groups. However, the saturation sample did not yield sub-populations large enough to break out for comparison. The differing minority populations in the two countries did not permit comparison in any case.

I also gathered fifteen essays from Spanish adults older than 29, ten about newspapers and five about newscasts. These get mentioned parenthetically in the following sections. The older group, all white, split evenly by gender. They ranged from 30 to 52 years old, with the mode at 36. Their parents hold roughly the same types of jobs and attained about the same educational level as in the younger group. However, the older adults came predominantly from small towns and rural areas (53.3 per cent). They paid much more attention to newspapers, reading more days (6.3 "last week") and for longer intervals (37 minutes "yesterday"). They watched television news less often (5.3 days "last week") and spent less time with television (66 minutes "yesterday"). In fact, all their uses of media fell substantially lower (except movies rented, 4.5 "last month").

To help compare these life histories, I studied the newspaper essays separately from the television essays. For each group, I first read a small number (about a fifth) to look for the recurring themes found in the previous studies and revised the list as needed (this amounted to adding a few items). A Spanish assistant then used the translated and annotated list to code the essays for the presence or absence of each theme. To check reliability, I recoded some of the essays (20 per cent). The reliability coefficients between coders are quite good on average.

In reporting the results, I have stayed as closely as possible to the form and structure of the two earlier studies. Although lengthy, this strategy produced a wealth of description and allowed the maximum direct comparison to the studies being replicated. The analysis in the next two sections, then, weaves together three strands: qualitative readings and quotations from each group of essays, the quantitative results of coding, and related questionnaire responses.

To these dimensions I have added the following types of comparisons: with the counterpart group from the United States, with Spanish national statistics when available, and with records of important news stories since the mid-1970s, drawn from two chronicles the leading national newspapers published.

Quotations from the essays given in the following two sections identify the writer's gender, hometown size, and frequency of attending to the news medium (occasional 3 or fewer days "last week," regular 4 or 5, and habitual 6 or 7). Age is shown because I followed the Spanish norm of including adults under 30 (the U. S. statistics on young adults usually, but not always, include only 18- to 24-year-olds). Unless indicated, the writer came from a town. Partisan Newspapers and Ritual

In broad strokes, the Spanish essays on newspapers reaffirmed the centrality of daily rituals for acquiring the reading habit. Although they did not present their newspaper experiences as uniformly by periods as did the Americans, the Spaniards did provide detailed accounts of the newspaper ritual for each stage in the U.S. chronology: in early childhood at home, middle childhood in school, and transition to adulthood, with various influences and political consequences in the present.

Unlike the Americans, the Spaniards became newspaper readers (and in quotations from these essays, the writer read the newspaper habitually, unless otherwise noted). Many aspects that make the Spanish press more attractive and accessible to young adults flow from the partisan ideologies newspapers overtly espouse.

The partisan distinctiveness was echoed in the Spanish essays themselves, which on the whole seem much more varied and individualistic than the U.S. essays.

At first the newspaper simply existed in the jumble of early childhood memories. Spaniards and Americans alike said they had a hard time remembering their first glimpse of one. An urban male occasional reader, 21, wrote, "It's like trying to remember seeing abed the first time or the bathroom of your house. They've always been there and there just wasn't a first time."

A few did report a memorable first encounter: When I was five, snooping in the old family bureau, I discovered a pile of yellowed papers, gnawed by mice. I unfolded it and found before my eyes a kind of revelation: one of those newspapers from before, on sheets so large you could roll me up in them. That was the first time I saw a newspaper. -a male regular reader, 25

Many of the essays, like the U.S. group, said they experienced newspapers as a constant presence (70 per cent) throughout their upbringing. Once the newspaper emerged from the tog of early childhood, however, the initial uniformity in Spanish and U. S. experiences dissolved.' The strength of habit and family training came through strongly among the Spaniards. A majority of their essays described newspapers as a part of family routine (56.7 per cent), a share exceeding that found in the U.S. essays. None of the Spanish writers concluded from the repetitive nature of their early experience that newspapers therefore had little importance or played no role in their lives.

The Spaniards described many ways the news routine unified them with parents. Two-thirds of the essays said that their first encounters with newspapers occurred in the presence of parents (66.7 per cent), and many of those who did not cite parents instead mentioned grandparents.

The essays talked of morning rituals for purchasing bread and newspapers that made them feel part of the adult world. An urban female, 21, wrote, "When he took me to school, we used to stop at some kiosk and he gave me money so I could buy the paper. Since I was very small, it gave me the illusion of going alone to buy it, and I felt grown up."

Spaniards reported more parental encouragement than did the Americans. Quite a few essays said parents urged them to read the paper (40 per cent), and on the questionnaire a majority (66.7 per cent) said parents encouraged them either "strongly" or "somewhat" (compared to very few essay mentions and much lower ratings by the U.S. group). The Spanish parents also encouraged their children to read books (83.3 per cent, only slightly below the U.S. group), suggesting that the difference springs from their beliefs about newspapers, not about reading in general.

Some Spanish parents went beyond urging and read aloud or discussed the newspaper. Unlike the Americans, more Spaniards said their parents read to them from the newspaper (20 per cent). They also described the family having conversations based on the newspaper. I remember my father in the kitchen reading the paper while my mother served lunch.

He also, after reading something interesting, commented about it to my mother, and they both began a conversation, filled with constant exclamations. -an urban female, 20.

With all the urging they received as children, the Spaniards expressed impatience with parents (6.7 per cent) only about as often as the U.S. group, but they less often defined the paper as exclusively for adults (33.3 per cent, compared to almost half of the U.S. essays).

The gap between the child and the newspaper as an adult activity seems smaller in Spain. Responses to the format of the paper, for example, created less of an issue among the Spanish participants. Children from both countries encountered broadsheet pages as youngsters, but the Spaniards then watched the changeover to tabloid size. About a third of the essays mentioned the change (30 per cent), and none talked about continuing frustration with the large pages, as the Americans did. Instead, they remembered large broadsheets fondly as objects from childhood.

An urban female, 20, recalls, "With that enormous paper I could make the biggest paper hats you've ever seen." Although some young Spaniards mentioned the ink rubbing off, none expressed the sort of irony on the subject found in the U.S. essays. An urban female, 21, said she liked newspapers because "it didn't matter if I tore them up or spilled on them because the next morning a new one appeared in my father's hands."

The Spanish essays did not reveal the climate of conflict apparent in the U.S. stories, although the gender and power order for reading the paper worked about the same in both countries. The Spaniards mentioned fathers being first (30 per cent) a bit more often than Americans did, but the Spaniards also mentioned mothers reading first (10 per cent), or "parents" (6.7 per cent), or others, especially grandparents (13.3 per cent). (This represents a change from the previous generation, according to the older Spaniards, who said twice as often that their fathers used the newspaper first.)

Only one essay reported sibling rivalry over newspaper access. A female regular reader, 21, said "there were even fights in my house because both of us wanted to be the first to read it. In the end, what always ruled was the strong arm." Although some of the gender issues Americans discussed surely exist in Spanish home life, most of the essays did not seem troubled by the disparity between gender roles.

The Americans expressed much more conflict with the newspaper as a form and object, with its role in defining the power relationships within the family, and, most important, with the adult world it represents. Americans defined their situation by the yawning rift in their social world, between themselves as small children and the distant, sometimes incomprehensible world of grownups.

When describing the newspaper during their middle childhood years, the Americans reported resenting the pressure from parents and teachers, who nagged and cajoled at home and assigned difficult homework to make them read. The Spaniards told a strikingly different story. Parents and teachers made their expectations known through gentle persuasion, acting as models by reading and discussing news, and through in-class activities, not homework.

At home, the Spaniards said their parents would repeat a proverb - a touchstone of the transition generation - to the effect that one cannot change the world unless one knows something about it. Several essays cited the phrase. There seems to have existed a general expectation that young people would eventually read newspapers, and that was that.

The schools the participants attended appeared to have integrated newspapers into the curriculum much more than did those of the U.S. group, not only as an art medium or tool but also as content. An urban male, 23, described a reading circle, where "someone had to read a small book or story and then retell it aloud to the other children, but I remember the time when instead of books they gave us the task of looking in a newspaper for 'good news.'" Two-thirds of the Spaniards (66.7 per cent) reported schoolwork involving newspapers (more than three times the share of U.S. essays).

Where most assignments for Americans involved homework, many of those who mentioned assignments in Spain said they took place during class (80 per cent, others did not specify and only one mentioned homework). Half of those who said they used newspapers in school (55 per cent) described role-playing, games, or a publishing activity built around newspapers. In many cases, the training described appears to have sprung from something akin to a media literacy approach, in which children are armed with intellectual tools to see through or pull apart media messages. After repeating the proverb about changing the world by knowing it, an urban female, 21, said, "Little by little, from the doubts that she raised in class, I began to realise the importance, not so much of the newspapers, but of what gets reported in them."

Spanish teachers often modeled their own newspaper interest, the essays said, by mentioning what they read to students (19 per cent of those reporting school activities) and by bringing the paper to class.

The strangest thing was that my religion professor, during exams and tests, hid behind the newspaper as if absent from what was going on in the room, but when somebody opened their mouth or turned around to copy, he would call on them and threaten them with suspension. -an urban male.

Of course, the incidents where teachers simply read during exams (not included in the above percentages) added to the uses of the newspaper in school. The essayists rightfully did not consider such occasions part of their schoolwork, but they pointed to teachers' demonstrated interest in newspapers, sanctioning them as acceptable activity during certain moments of the workday.

Outside of school, only a minority of the essays described using newspapers (36.6 per cent). Paper routes - and home delivery - hardly exist in Spain, and recycling did not begin until recently. These activities received no mention. Nor did any essays mention newspapers used in churches or in scouting, an absence that reflects traditionally lower involvement in clubs and associations among Spaniards. (A third of the older Spaniards made a point of saying they never used the paper in other settings.) The few outside uses of newspapers varied extremely, with no example repeated by more than one participant.

Many participants nevertheless described newspapers as a constant presence in their school years (70 per cent). Those who did not experience newspapers as a constant typically grew up in a small town, and in fact, the smaller the city or town, the less constant a role the newspaper played (ranging from 85.7 per cent among urbanites to 60 per cent among townsfolk). (Just under half of the older participants called newspapers a constant, following the same hometown pattern.

A rural female, 33, wrote that seeing her father occasionally read the newspaper influenced her own attitude: "The fact that a person who hardly knew how to read would take the trouble to buy a paper and then spend hours reading it meant it was something important." The difference between father and daughter reflects the generational experience as people moved to urban areas and education became compulsory after 1971.) Some of the young adults did describe their parents modeling newspaper use and, for instance, mentioned that adults often conversed about what they had read in the paper (23.3 per cent).

Regarding their middle childhood, the Americans described lower institutional support for newspapers in school (but not elsewhere), expressed resentment over homework, and reported cheating to evade the assignments. The Americans presented a scene of conflict and economic activity surrounding newspapers, in contrast to the Spanish emphasis on persuasive modeling and critical training. These tendencies might have been even stronger had political circumstances not constrained them. As an urban male regular reader, 26, recalled, "My school years coincided with our transition to democracy, which meant that my teachers used the newspaper with real caution."

The Spaniards described moving smoothly into newspaper reading, where the group in the United States followed a rocky and often unsuccessful path. The few Americans who conquered what most considered a dull and ungainly product told dramatic conversion stories. Only a quarter of the Spanish participants described the newspaper as boring (26.7 per cent), and a few said they always found it interesting (6.7 per cent). They seemed satisfied that adults read newspapers and accepted reading as the mature thing to do. Several aspects of the content and format contributed to their successful transition into adult reading.

The Spaniards conceived of newspapers primarily as an information source (93.3 per cent); the Americans largely did not (5.5 per cent). (All the essays by older Spaniards defined the paper that way.) A few Spanish essays mentioned the difficulty of reading the newspapers, but lacking a store of factual knowledge did not produce the series of attempts and failures the U. S, essays described. The Spaniards usually expended not so great an effort (and showed none of the self-righteousness found among the U.S. readers):

Little by little I adopted my family's tradition of reading the newspaper over breakfast, until I got to the point where now if I don't read the paper at breakfast, it's like having coffee without sugar. By 15 1 remember being caught up completely in the tradition. -an urban female, 19

Although their progress toward more demanding content developed in parallel with Americans - from softer, more familiar stories gradually to national and international events - the Spaniards focused more on news and less on the entertainment. The comics, for instance, entered only occasionally into the Spanish narratives (which referred to a generic pastimes page containing games and puzzles).

What attracted and held the Spaniards' interest was hard news. Not all the essays addressed the subject (63.3 per cent), but of those that did a majority called news the primary draw (68.4 per cent). A smaller percentage keyed their interest to sports (21 per cent), and the remainder said they preferred other subjects, such as arts and leisure.

The tabloid format helped the Spaniards move from softer content (in the back of the single section) to serious news (in front). U.S. broadsheets actually create a barrier to that progress by separating different kinds of news physically into sections. The Spaniards often described the habit, what a male regular reader, 24, called his mania "for reading the pages backwards, that is, starting from the back."

News of local places and people attracted young people in both countries. An urban female, 21, said, "My mother always kept them on the dining room table, and I leafed through them because I liked seeing the pages with places and people I knew." Among the minority who described memories of a first story (13.3 per cent), a few recollect seeing their family or friends in the paper, just as the Americans did. I don't remember the first paper I read entirely but can recall one of the first I bought, looking for a picture of my school ping-pong team, so I started buying papers out of sheer vanity. -an urban male regular reader, 26

That closeness to home, what journalists call proximity, provided a universal hook - for some a school paper, for others a local paper - but living in Spain provides an expanded sense of the local. The Spaniards included not only such events as a plane crash in a nearby airport but occurrences throughout their country (which is no larger than a state or region of the United States), such as the Pope's visit, and even international news, such as malnutrition of children in Africa, happens fairly close by.

A sense of the newspaper as informative, an amenable format, and proximity to other countries all build on the

Spaniards' newspaper experiences in childhood. In the end, they simply became readers, often as preteens (unlike the U.S. group). "When I began to acquire a `certain taste' for the harmless vice of reading the press," said an urban male, 23, "I was about 11 years old." As young adults, a majority of the Spaniards said they read the paper habitually (53.3 per cent), and another quarter regularly (26.7 per cent). The remainder said they read occasionally, and none reported being nonreaders. (Almost all the older participants said they read the paper habitually [6.2 days "last week"].) Only one essay by a young adult contained any of the shame or embarrassment for sometimes failing to read the paper (an emotion found more often in U.S. essays).

The Spanish participants said they read the paper regularly 15.4 days), uniformly across gender, age, and parental education, with one exception: hometown size. On average, the city-dwellers said they read the paper habitually (5.7 days).

The lower rate of readership among town-dwellers (4.9 days), although not extreme, revealed the status of newspapers.

Several of those from small towns or rural areas described the newspaper as a accouterment of "the upper class," as a 25-year-old male puts it, "that is, those who read newspapers were cultured, intellectuals, and people with money." Participants from the provinces described their interest in newspapers as part of a process of self-improvement, to lift themselves out of a marginal world into the mainstream. (An essay by an older provincial male, 49, said that "newspapers had an immense attraction, they were the door opening onto a new and unknown world.")

The smooth and direct move into readership among the Spanish provides an extreme contrast to U. S. examples of bumps and failures. Both cases, however, shared a key attraction: the importance of softer, local news. Coverage touching on young people's lives in Spain, as in the United States, gave the participants the surest entrance into the newspaper reading habit.

INFLUENCES

The participants adopted a sophisticated stance toward newspapers, calm and accepting but not uncritical. They actively compared various news sources and read newspapers with a bemused skepticism and tolerance. The frequent changes in design and reduced format, as well as the ideological differences among newspapers, invited greater awareness of how journalists construct news. The Americans, by contrast, adopted a stance fraught with internal conflict before journalism they see as monolithic. The U.S. essays protested too much - how unimportant the newspaper was, how little it influenced them, and how indifferent they felt toward it - and then contradicted themselves, citing specific examples of its influence on their actions.

The Spaniards considered the press important but not as a guide to conduct. Many more of them denied the influence of newspapers on their actions (66.7 per cent) than did the Americans. The Spaniards less often called newspapers unimportant in their current lives and rarely reported an attitude of indifference. Their essays were also much more consistent. Fewer described any actions the newspaper influenced (10 per cent), and none of these went on to deny the influence (a contradiction common to the U.S. essays).

The Spaniards offered a balance, one-sixth expressed positive attitudes toward newspapers and another sixth provided specific critiques. (The essays by the older generation took this even further, most offering praise while many offered criticism, often along with praise.) Almost half the young adults replied on the questionnaire that they considered news accurate only "some of the time" (46.7 per cent), and they rated the overall job of the news media just below the midpoint (2.4 on a four-point scale) between "excellent" and "poor." Their attitudes came out in the essays:

At home we always buy one paper, not because it seems the best, since there isn't one that we like everything about. You could say that it's the one we dislike the least. Many times they publish stories in a way we disagree with, such as getting the facts wrong about a demonstration when they estimate the number of people. But each paper has its own morality, and I understand that, so I enjoy comparing newspapers. It's the easiest way to get close to the truth. -an urban female, 21

An important component of the young adults' sophistication came to light when they entered into comparisons of the various news outlets. A third of the essays did so. They compared national to local newspapers, newspapers to radio coverage of the same events, and television news to the printed press. A 20-year-old female wrote, "I figured out that simply the order that stories appear in two papers revealed a discrepancy in their editorial principles."

A male regular reader, 24, said "television has made it so these days people take a different attitude toward the press, that of critical reflection about the events carried out before our eyes." With the newsstand as the primary distribution point, the Spaniards confronted a wider array of choice and comparison each day.

They declared their skepticism much more often (46.7 per cent) than did the Americans (13.4 per cent), and a qualitative difference emerged as well. Where the Americans expressed an almost cynical doubt about newspapers, the Spaniards seemed matter of fact. Of course newspapers give a limited view of the world, the Spaniards implied, and of course they cannot be relied on completely-one cannot be gullible. "Newspapers aren't infallible Bibles whose arguments we must believe and follow in lockstep.

You have to be critical of the critics and benefit from their arguments when adopting one position or another," wrote an urban male regular reader, 26, who also thanked "the press for stimulating in me the ideal of tolerance, of listening to different opinions without prejudice, and for sharpening my critical sense, including toward the news itself." Tolerance emerged as another theme in the Spanish essays. An urban female occasional reader, 21, said, "It has helped me broaden my view of the world and see that there are a lot of people, all very different. This wider view has made me more tolerant of those around me." Such expressions, quite common in the Spanish essays, hardly entered the U.S. ones.

The Spaniards' sense of the constructedness of newspapers might result from the process of change that ended broadsheets in Spain. More than half of the essays noted changes in the visible farm of papers (56.7 per cent), and they most often cited the change in format (52.9 per cent). They said they felt surprised when papers reduced their size. One suburban female, 21, said her first impression was "that they didn't have as many things to report," but then she found "reading much more manageable." A large share also recalled the shift from black and white to colour printing (41.2 per cent). The U.S. essays hardly noted any design or format change. The Spaniards, in response to the flow of changes in their newspapers, built an expectation for more.

A female regular reader, 24, noted the "modern formats, new styles, and very different looks" add value, "so that newspapers don't get monotonous." An urban male occasional reader, 21, said, "The newspaper I read even now continues changing and searching constantly for a more agile form that allows it to reach the public in the most direct way." Such young readers conveyed a sense of riding the wave of change.

The sophisticated attitude also emerged when participants described the ways newspapers affected their moods. About half reported some type of emotional influence (56.7 per cent),5 and of these almost two-thirds said they experienced anger or disgust (64.7 per cent). In most cases, the feeling amounted to an annoyance at the depravity of humanity, but sometimes the participants said the manner of reporting, rather than the content, annoyed them.

For example, several of the essays written by those living in the Basque Country pointed out how their experience differed greatly from the impression newspapers gave of constant violence by ETA, the Basque separatist group. A few of the Spaniards said they felt fear or happiness (10 per cent), but twice as many reported sadness, usually over the state of the world. Here again, news of ETA played a role. An urban male, 23, said, "I felt terrible anguish" after reading the newspaper account of an ETA car bomb that killed two people.

Finally, a common mood among the Spaniards, absent among the Americans, described the tranquillity a newspaper encourages, for which they used the English term "relax." (This mood also turned up in essays by older adults. For example, an urban female, 36, who read regularly, described it as "a moment of leisure and introversion. It gives me a secret pleasure to read the paper abstractedly in a green space, a cafe, or a public bench in the sun.") Although the U.S. essays lacked any specific reference to relaxation, they did give a much more serene impression than did the counterpart essays on newscasts. The newspaper experiences for both countries have that tranquillity in common. Despite the presence of political violence within Spain, for instance, the Spanish newspaper essays did not mention fear as often as did the U.S. essays.

In contrast to the U.S. approach, press practices in Spain encouraged a sophisticated stance. The ideological clarity of Spanish newspapers positioned readers at the nexus of political choices, a freedom echoed in the farm of newsstand distribution, and the format and design changes clarified the inventedness of the newspaper form. The participants responded to news as mediator, not as the neutral conduit the Americans saw in the U.S. press.

The political experiences in the essays often sprang from the more strongly partisan stance in the Spanish than in the U. S. press. The Spaniards described a three-step recipe for handling the outpouring of partisan news. First, some of them used several news sources: Luckily my own political opinion doesn't derive from reading just one daily because, as I said, I usually go through several throughout the day, and... I squeeze out what I consider the most... closely adjusted to reality. -an urban male, 28.

Second, they employed their knowledge about the political leanings of each paper. "Knowing more or less the ideologies of the newspapers in my country, I try to read critically," wrote an urban female, 20, who concluded that "not all politicians are as good or as bad as they appear." Some essays listed their newspaper preference as a shorthand way of describing their own political position, rather than the other way around.

Saying one always reads El Pais, far example, reveals a preference for the left-wing liberal interpretation of events, whereas a dedication to ABC suggests a disposition to conservative and monarchist interpretations.

With a clear sense of the differences, the Spaniards said that, third, they then contrasted what they learned from the news, especially about political matters. "What I do is read and compare so that I can act in the most balanced manner, according to my personal convictions," said a suburban female, 21.

That personal compass helped them retain a discriminating distance. As a rural female, 22, put it, "Reading the newspaper has... helped me get a more critical view.... I've arrived at the conclusion that many times it's best to read without getting too caught up." Especially during elections, wrote a female regular reader, 21, "I think... the facts and opinions are the least trustworthy, due to the number of interests that hide behind that information."

Sometimes participants said the news discouraged them, especially considering what a male regular reader, 25, called "the role certain papers played in our country during recent years by denouncing cases of corruption." Disappointment with politics came more often from women. "In my political views, reading the daily paper has filled me with irony," wrote an urban female occasional reader, 21. "I think it's better to take it with humor." On the whole, the essays by women seemed slightly less politically oriented than did those by men. The difference also turned up on the questionnaire item for political interest (men 1.2 and women 1.5, on a three-point scale of "very," "somewhat," and "not at all" interested).

In the end, the competing political ideologies in a variety of newspapers, along with some citizens' skills at parsing the messages they read, built a stronger connection to politics. In fact, the young adults seemed to connect with politics more through newspapers than they did through political parties, for which they said they had little sympathy.

Only a minority expressed an affinity with any of the three main political parties, socialist PSOE, leftist IU (both 10 per cent), or conservative PP (13.7 per cent), and fully half left the item blank or wrote "none." Yet almost all rated themselves "very" (80 per cent) or "somewhat" (36.7 per cent) interested in politics.

It comes as no surprise that the Spanish participants became newspaper readers while the Americans did not. The Spaniards gave the impression of participating from their earliest years in a family project to bring them into the newspaper-reading habit at home, placing them, of course, within the minority in a country without widespread newspaper reading. The young adults remembered their parents as not pushy or nagging but encouraging, a result that confirms Mannheim's observation of how rarely didactic approaches work in transmitting values between generations.

The process comes clear in this extended example: I remember that my parents used to read me the strange and odd events that happened, from briefs on the last page, and they also explained any important news they'd read. They also urged me to read the paper.

They would say, "Oh, did you read this or that happened?" as if for me to have read it were an ordinary thing. That way they encouraged me to take the time, because it was really interesting. They still do that, but now I almost always say yes, I've already read it. What was certain was that I didn't especially like reading the paper. I could read one or two articles but I got tired right away. -an urban male, 24.

The essays also said that newspapers enjoyed substantial support from teachers. Unlike the U,S. model of homework, Spanish schools made daily newspaper reading appear painless, through in-class activities and the reinforcement of teachers' behaviour.

The media literacy approach, teaching children a critical distance from the press while emphasizing the importance of things reported there, appears to have produced more assiduous reading, rather than the opposite.

The teacher's idea for the class was for us to read a lot of papers of different ideological stripes, to analyse events from different points of view. I refer to this because it was when I changed my attitude toward newspapers. From then on, they interested me much more and I read them differently. I focused on the editorials, as well as on the political stories and their different interpretations. -a female, 27

The material side of the press encourages reading in Spain. Newspapers all have a manageable format, and almost all have reduced the problem of ink rubbing off on the hands. Regular redesigns, whatever their meaning to older readers, appealed to these young adults, who expressed impatience with papers that failed to ride the wave of change.

Clear competition at the newsstand also helped build their interest. From a wide selection - national, regional, and local dailies augmented by sports and business papers - some young adults purchased several newspapers just to see how a story was covered (this despite the high cover price, usually equivalent to more than a dollar a copy). The competition seems not to have degenerated into pandering, although a few of the essays mentioned a recent shift toward more graphic and disturbing coverage. The local paper "has tended to become more aggressive," said an urban female, 19: "All you have to do is compare the same news story in different newspapers." An urban male, 24, wrote that as newspapers try to sell serious news by running it "between curiosities and lighter news... entertainment slowly takes over."

These differences teach some important lessons for newspapers in the United States, despite the contrast in social settings and the Spaniards' exceptional access to news, education, and other advantages. Local newspaper monopolies typical in the United States probably do not encourage readership among the young, but neither do competing papers unless they have ideological differences obvious enough for readers to perceive a difference and sustain the variety. A clear ideological line, which some U.S.

editors might fear would drive readers away, apparently has had the opposite effect in Spain.

Support from parents and from teachers seems to have sprung from or responded to the sobriety of the Spanish press as well as its commitment to a political point of view regardless of economic consequences. At school, the U.S. curricula that emphasize doing the hard work of reading at home probably backfire and create resentment. On the other hand, U.S. resistance to media literacy curricula, because of fears that they will produce troublesome, critical readers, did just that in Spain, with the effect of increasing their interest in newspapers. The empowered readers read more. Finally, although they liked the smaller format and regular design change, the young Spaniards responded with suspicion to efforts to sell the news by packaging it for entertainment value. Their sophistication as readers produces just the sort of tolerance that political theorists expect from a free press in democratic societies a hopeful outcome of ideological competi tion, media literacy, and design innovation.

The similarities between the U.S. and Spanish groups, although far fewer, have more to teach. In both countries, the fate of newspapers paralleled their respective abilities to make news reading a daily ritual at home. Including newspapers as a constant presence in the schools also seems uniformly crucial. The routines of publication and the schedules of production and delivery - the temporal bases of newspapers in modern societies - are just what new electronic versions of newspapers conspicuously lack. Information without a physical form that must get manufactured on regular deadlines may float unattached to temporal processes until readers or electronic publishers invent some other ritual as a replacement.

The same content of the newspaper-another commonality-appealed to the young adults in both countries. News in the paper had to touch close to their lives in each case. Both groups found themselves drawn into the newspaper specifically (as opposed to other news sources) through stories involving people and places they knew.

Newspapers have other strengths. Americans as well as Spaniards mentioned the power of news to recognize events as important and make people seem worthy. At the same time, the content encouraged a placid response: newspapers did not in either country produce the fear incited by U.S. newscasts. In general, when the newspaper's strengths as a setter of daily ritual, as a giver of status, and as a facilitator of calm rationality combined with truly local news content that overlapped the social worlds they inhabited, young adults became readers.

The similarities in the two groups could provide a list of goals for the U.S. press: altering the regulatory environment, the structure of the industry within local and national markets, as well as the content of news and the format for presenting it. Newspapers in the United States would have to make a host of changes at every level to replicate the Spanish experience. Such a wholesale revision of the U.S. press seems well beyond reasonable expectations for printed newspapers, but perhaps not for electronic forms. The comparison of narratives from Spain and the United States does help account for the failures and successes of newsprint among young citizens, pointing to ways publishers can convey the political information needed to sustain democratic participation.

NEWSCASTS AND POLITICAL GENERATIONS

The young Americans in previous research seemed to resist the idea of writing a life history with newscasts, but the stories they related reveal various conflicts with what they considered a powerful political actor. They saw themselves as weak compared to television news, which they then attacked with all sorts of criticisms of bias, sensationalism, and triviality. The Spaniards took a greatly different view that led them to feel empowered themselves. That central story emerges from the details reported in this section.

One general observation deserves mention as preface: The forms of news they encountered seem implicated in the ways the young adults in both countries thought and talked about their experiences. Depending on which medium they described, the participants had different ways of writing. About a third of the Spaniards (twelve in all) volunteered to write two life histories, one about newspapers and the other about newscasts.

The two essays by a single writer had a consistency of skill, language, and complexity, and those who wrote at length tended to do so for both topics. However, most of the television vignettes they retold were slightly shorter (and within shorter paragraphs).

The ease of simply referring to images, as well as the abrupt shifts in topics, resulted in essays that did not run quite as long, regardless of which essay came first or whether the writer made small economies by referring in one essay to things already related in the other.

On the whole, the television essays seemed less detailed, tended to mention more images, and told less elaborate stories with thinner descriptions - a pattern similar to that found in the U.S. essays. The contrasts require more formal study because language differences make comparing essays from the two countries difficult. At least within each national setting the structures of the medium, or perhaps the habits of thought each encourages, were reflected in the ways the young adults wrote about their experiences. In short, the forms of news may delimit how people understand their political worlds.

THE NEWS RITUAL

The participants described a much stronger ritual for watching television news in Spain than in the United States. The differing historical development of television, as well as the cultural heritage in Spain, made watching newscasts a universal practice, reinforcing the importance of family routines for the success of televised news.

Compared to the history of the U.S. medium, television entered Spain later and the industry converted to colour more recently, producing among the participants a greater awareness of the television as a material objects Some of the

Spaniards (12.5 per cent) used that sense of the television set to begin and frame their essays (none of the U.S. essays did): It's easier to remember when you got your first television set or when you changed from black and white to colour (I was nine), just as it's not easy to remember when you saw a car for the first time, although you can always remember the first one you owned. -an urban male, 21

Such material memories extended to the appearance of the newscast. "I remember that they began with a clock that covered the whole screen," said another urban male, 21, "which we used to check our own to see if it was exactly on the time shown." An urban female, 21, recalled that "the broadcast had only one person and was presented about like the radio news used to be, reading from a sheet of paper." Another said the news "seemed made by hand."

In national custom, watching television news became deeply entrenched in Spain.' The midday break from work for many Spaniards traditionally runs from one and four o'clock, and the afternoon news at three consistently has therefore ranked among the highest rated television programs. "It seemed incredible that my grandparents ate lunch and dinner as fast as possible so they could watch the news," said an urban female regular viewer, 25. "At home it wasn't such an obsession, but we did always eat lunch with the national news in the background." An urban female, 19, said, "At home the television news has always been sacred, at midday as well as in the evening. Whenever the symphonic theme music came on at home, the living room fell silent."

The television ritual dated from the childhood of the young adult generation. (A majority of essays by older adults said they specifically did not watch at a routine time and place. In the Franco era, not everyone owned a television set. "The only television in my village was owned by the parish church," said a rural female occasional viewer, 41, "and we would go there to watch, paying in advance." The older adults also noted the greater appeal of news during the transition. "My interest in TV news," wrote a male regular viewer, 43, "surged as soon as the Franco dictatorship ended. Since that moment I've watched newscasts with real interest as often as possible.")

Although just about everyone adopted the news-viewing habit after Franco's death, attention to broadcast news has even older roots. An earlier generation became attracted through radio in the 1930s. Their grandchildren, the young adults in the study, described the grandparents' current habit of watching el pane and commented on the name, derived from the Spanish Civil War, when people called radio bulletins from the front el pane militar.

The strength of the family news practice produced some conflict, the essays said. Describing the news anchor, an urban female, 21, said, "How could a lady that my parents didn't even know personally get more of their attention than I, their own daughter?" Almost a third (31.3 per cent) mentioned feeling resentful of parents for their news-watching habit, a rate greatly surpassing the very few such expressions in the U.S. television essays. History here intervened with the process of adding more television sets to the home giving Americans the option to choose other programs.

Multiple television sets came later to Spain and hardly get mentioned. The participants said that in small urban apartments they had few alternatives. "For the smallest ones this began the most painful thirty minutes of the entire day> " said an urban female, 21. "It was a torture to not be allowed to talk or squeal for such a long time."

The Americans faced frustrations not only with both parents, who dictated which programme to choose, but also with their fathers, who relaxed with the news while mothers cleaned up. When such differences appeared in their essays, the Spaniards either did not remark on or did not make much of them. The Spanish state monopoly until the 1990s had no commercial competition, making the news on Television Espanola (TVE1 or La Primera) the news.e A further U.S. frustration, with the racism of newscasts, received no mention at all among the Spaniards.

A combination of some gender equality and fewer contested role norms tended to mute the feminist reaction to news watching in Spain. In many cases participants described home routines that included women and men equally. Newscasts themselves also included women.

The state channel had female anchors from the participants' earliest memories. Since the addition of a second state channel and three private channels, women continue in anchor positions, although usually in secondary posts (presenting the sports segment, for example, or the weather, both of which appear in national newscasts).

The Spanish women also accepted male prerogatives with tolerance. A suburban female regular viewer, 25, said that "it was one of the few things my father always wanted to watch, because the rest of the programs on television didn't interest him much."

Even when the essays mentioned being told to be silent during the news (21.9 per cent), the demand reiterated the communal quality of the activity.

An urban male, 24, said, "I remember that when it didn't interest me and I'd start to talk, my grandparents and parents would all go `Shhh!' and I had to be quiet." No essays mentioned parents getting angry in the authoritative way found in the U.S. cases. The Spanish group also recalled that conversation reinforced the news-watching ritual (9.4 per cent), which hardly received notice in the U.S. group.

During the midday meal, someone in the family would bring up a topic of conversation and refer to what they would see on television.

That way I kept getting more interested in the news and in what happened in the world, because if not, I would never understand the conversations at home. -an urban female, 20 Frustrations the Americans felt led them to a feel indifference toward newscasts. Even with the relatively high level of childhood frustration, only some of the Spaniards expressed indifference (9.4 per cent). The ritual in Spain had largely the opposite effect. An urban male, 24, wrote, "A lot of times I could stand watching the newscast because, if all the grown-ups were full of interest and anticipation, they must have been expecting something."

OUTSIDE THE HOME

The Americans described a variety of ways institutions reinforced news watching. Many remembered watching newscasts in school, usually aimed at having fun and entertainment.

The Spanish essays revealed much less institutional activity supporting television news. A majority said newscasts never had any role at all during school (71.9 per cent). (An even larger share of older Spaniards agreed.) "It's true that in some courses like language arts they covered some things about news," wrote an urban male, 21, "but they were almost always related to newspapers rather than to televised stories."

When they mentioned in-school experiences, only a minority said they ever watched news at school (9.4 per cent). A few mentioned role-playing (6.3 per cent). One participant, 24, said her class had an assignment to "act out the work of television journalists, although without knowing anything about the technical process." Such tasks took a fairly serious tone, not meant to entertain.

The activity the Spaniards most often cited, class discussion (9.4 per cent), trained them to think critically and present articulate arguments about the news. Teachers, often in language arts classes, explained the ways newscasters "employed the language," said a 24-year-old participant. The approach went without mention in the U.S. essays, where the only discussion they noted happened in the school yard.

For homework, fewer of the Spaniards reported assignments involving television news (9.4 per cent, and 56.3 per cent denied receiving such assignments). (Even more of the older Spaniards concurred.) A few young adults who did have homework described how their families worked with them. One participant asked to watch a news story on an assigned subject said I sat with my father, and with great patience he started to translate the news into a more understandable language.... But he not only told me what they said but also tried to reconstruct the history, so I could contextualize the news story. -an urban female, 21 Although not in schools, watching the news did occur in other public places, the essays emphasized. An urban female, 19, said, "I discovered that the newscast was sacred not only at my house, but anywhere else you went - everybody was paying attention, at my grandmother's, my friends' houses. or any restaurant or cafeteria."

The newscast ritual emerged primarily outside of school life in Spain. The television essays mentioned class discussions, role-play, and homework assignments much less often than the newspaper essays did. The symbolic environment of Spain in that respect matched what the U.S. groups described. While reaching a much wider audience, Spanish newscasts received a much lower level of support that did newspapers in the cultural values the essays described.

GENERATIONAL MEMORY

Television news emerged in the previous study as a force that-through an initial major news story - helped young adults identify with their generation. The U.S. essays focused on the explosion of the space shuttle Challenger as the event to catch attention. Coming from a wider span of ages (eleven years instead of six), the Spanish essays did not agree on a single first event. In those recalling a first story (43.8 per cent), three major events stand out.

The story most often cited (12.5 per cent), the death of Generalisimo Franco, lasted more than a month in 1975, prolonged as doctors went to extraordinary measures under pressure from those wishing to extend the Falange regime. The final announcement left a strong impression:

I do remember one image... that had an impact. It was of Carlos Arias Navarro [the head of government] crying before the camera as he announced the death of Franco. I've seen that image many other times, but I believe that the reiteration has served to reinforce in memory that first time it appeared. -an urban male, 24

The young adults also said they (like the U.S. group) shared a universal response with family and friends. A 24-year-old female remarked that after the announcement, "I recall my parents' faces marked with fear for what would happen next."

The event occurred very early in the lives of many participants, some of whom instead referred to one of two subsequent incidents (each 9.4 per cent). Regarding one, the attempted coup d'etat in 1981, a rural female, 22, said, "I remember having seen the news about the golpe de estado of February 23." The essays cited the image of Lieutenant Colonel Antonio Tejero firing shots in the chambers of parliament, with the TVE1 cameras broadcasting live. Others cited, without elaboration, the election of Felipe Gonzalez and the socialist party (PSOE) in 1982.

The important moments in Spain's transition to democracy contain the qualities also found in the U. S. first-story accounts. The essays did not for the most part describe the event, but instead merely pointed to its name or date or principal protagonist. In most cases, the Spaniards said they experienced the event as communal, not in the schools, where the U.S. students watched the shuttle explode, but at home with the family. Both groups remembered the event primarily as visual - in Spain an image of Franco, the king, the colonel, or Felipe Gonzalez, with another telling detail such as tears or senators diving for cover. Finally, the element of surprise came through in both groups. Even for Franco's death the actual moment, although not unexpected, caught some families with one member away, adding fear to the surprise.

Among the other first news events they recalled, a few mentioned the space shuttle explosion that played so prominently in the U.S. group. Whatever the event, the participants all assigned similar meanings to their first news story. Besides defining the event as universally shared and understood, they centered the retelling on the operation and importance of the news media. Repetition also played an important role. "I no longer remember if I saw it the year it happened." said a 19-year-old female.

"They repeat it almost every year." Finally, the essays follow a pattern of mentioning discussion, which reinforced the event, its significance, its universal interpretation and emotional charge. The shared understanding of a key moment (and in some cases the same moment) in their interaction makes television news central to forming a generation's identity.

BECOMING A VIEWER

A majority of the U.S. television group reported regular or occasional news viewing, and the group's essays generally did not describe any rites of passage leading to a commitment as a viewer. None of the U.S. television essays told a story of trying to join the audience and failing, unlike their counterpart newspaper essays. Although less tortured than the accounts of the U.S. newspaper group, the television essays by Americans reported a variety of tensions and conflicts.

Many recalled their parents urging them on, and some complained about the nagging. Others said they faced social pressure from overachieving relatives or friends. Those who acquired the habit wrote with derogatory language - far from the self-righteous attitude among the U.S. newspaper readers - identifying their high level of news viewing as an addiction, with binges or other extreme swings from time to time. Little wonder they developed an inconsistent and desultory habit of attending to newscasts.

The Spaniards acquired a much higher commitment to watching the news, without much anxiety or complaint. According to the questionnaire, they watched daily for the most part.ll Many identified themselves as habitual viewers (78.1 per cent], and of these, most said they watched every day (84 per cent of habitual viewers). Regular viewers made up the next largest group (18.8 per cent), only one reported viewing only occasionally, and none reported not watching at all. The only difficulty they cited, newscasters' use of complex language, turns up infrequently. "It was a challenge to connect with what they tried to say, and keeping up to date was a difficult task," said an urban female, 20. "I think only now am I really understanding the news."

The Spaniards said they reached high levels of viewership without much parental urging. Only a minority of the essays said their parents gave any overt encouragement (18.8 per cent), and nearly as many said their parents did not encourage them at all (12.5 per cent). They rated the level of parental encouragement at the midpoint (3 per cent) on the questionnaire, indicating their parents neither encouraged nor discouraged them. The neutral rating makes sense. With the custom of news watching a given, parents had little reason to urge it on the young. A majority called the news a constant, repetitive presence during their middle and late childhood (78.1 per cent).

The content of news programming more often provided the impulse. Several essays mentioned one particular programme: "I remember from a very young age my parents watching `Informe Semanal.' I didn't know what it was, but there were some reports I liked," said an urban female, 21. "At home 'Informe Semanal' is something of an institution." The Saturday evening programme appears to have had the same traditional position among Spanish television news magazines as held in the United States by "60 Minutes" (which no U.S. essay mentioned). The Spanish programme runs more to documentary without a hard news treatment:

One Saturday, during those cold, boring winters of my adolescence, I found myself wide-eyed, watching a story from "Informe Semanal" and without realizing it I got caught up in those reports. I still didn't like the regular newscasts, but on Saturdays I had a regular date to get to know the world. - a female regular viewer. Most participants did not mention the age at which they began watching

news for their own interest, rather than as part of the family ritual. Those who did, specified an age ranging from 9 to 16, Of course, a strong family tradition made the issue moot in most cases. The essays more often said when the news they watched daily simply began to interest them. Some called their own progression normal. "I've always chosen freely the programs that were broadcast," wrote a suburban female regular viewer, 25. "At first I liked the children's shows, later I preferred movies, and finally news programs began to interest me."

In sum, the Spaniards wrote without the disparaging comments of the U.S. newscast viewers and without the self-righteous tones of the U.S. newspaper readers. None of the Spaniards expressed regrets, apologies, or hostility for failing to view (of course, all but two watched news at least regularly). From a young age, the participants considered news viewing an activity for adults (37.5 per cent of the essays mentioned this explicitly), and the general tenor of the writing seems to accept the news as the natural avenue toward adulthood. The routine at home grew uneventfully into an adult habit.

FORM AND CONTENT

The young Americans previously studied did not recall many changes in the look of news. They considered newscasts information, especially appreciated for its visual form, and they had regrets for missing the show. Their preference for news and weather (in that order) reinforced the sense of the centrality of news.

In contrast, the Spaniards considered newscasts with somewhat more reserve. They less often equated television news with information (78.1 per cent) or remarked on missing the broadcasts (perhaps because they simply missed it infrequently). Several essays did highlight the value of the visual content of news, just as the Americans did. An urban female, 21, cited the example of getting a sense of other countries. "With the visuals, it's much easier to remember," she said.

The Spaniards, however, had more awareness of its constructed look, commenting more often on the changes in the newscast (40 per cent). The end of the dictatorship brought a general thaw in the style of newscasting. "Back then," said one urban female, 21, "the news was cold and distant from the viewer." (The older Spaniards remembered the old broadcasts vividly.

"The news, back in the time of Franco, was censored and very filtered, and seemed gray and terribly discouraging to me," wrote a 40-year-old male. "They presented a Spain in positive stories that seemed dull and ingenuous, and an exterior world in negative ones, as somewhat dangerous....")

The entry of commercial channels opened the state television stations to competitive pressures, with a resulting increase in sensationalism. A few of the young adults noted specific visual and technological changes in the previous five years, but mostly they commented on the accompanying shift in the tenor of news content, from the values of serious knowledge to the values of entertainment, a transformation that mimics U.S. newscasts.

Everything now seems more like a variety show, like something serious in content but perfectly planned to keep viewers watching the station. The package shines brighter all the time. The coif of the anchor and the smile of the co-anchor contrast with the quantity of negative images and stories. It's quite depressing to watch the news these days. -an urban male, 24

Just over half the Spanish essays expressed a preference for a particular content (56.3 per cent), and weather (the Americans' second favourite segment) figured hardly at all (6.3 per cent). In both countries, news topped the list. For some Spaniards, the interest started early, as it did for a 22-year-old female, who wrote, "I found it enjoyable to know what happened in places with odd names, although at first I didn't understand a thing."

News shared first preference with sports (both 28.1 per cent) among all participants, but by gender the males (like their U.S. counterparts) mentioned sports most often (37.5 per cent, and not one called news a top preference).

The women, on the other hand, listed news most often (37.5 per cent) followed by sports (25 per cent), a notable attraction not shared by U.S. women. In some cases, the writers credited interest in sports with leading to their commitment to watch all the newscast, just as in the U.S. examples.

"Little by little I began to pick what interested me, at first sports more than anything else," wrote a rural female, 22. "Later I began watching the entire newscast."

The Spaniards acquired the habit of viewing with relative ease, primarily through the news and sports, but they also acquired a critical distance. Besides a sense of how journalists construct news (a result of recent Spanish media history), their response to sports stands in contrast to the Americans' second choice: weather. Sports covers invented games, where weather supposedly reports reality.

INFLUENCES

The Spanish essays were reticent to talk about their moods in detail, and fewer of them said that television news changed their emotional states (53.1 per cent) than did the Americans. Spanish television, at least before the 1990s when commercial stations appeared, did not emphasize danger and violence, and the essays did not refer to many cases of fear during childhood.

The Spaniards, even more often than the Americans, listed the various emotions they felt without elaborating. When they did specify, the essays gave examples of human suffering, just as the Americans did. For example, an urban female, 21, wrote, "The images of the charred bodies affected me so much I didn't watch the programme again for several years."

The emotion the Spaniards most often cited, anger (25 per cent), appeared more frequently for women (29.2 per cent) than for men (12.5 per cent), just as in the U.S. group. An urban female, 21, wrote, "The images of terrorist attacks and resulting activities always affect me, but instead of fear, they make me feel anger and helplessness, and that sensation stays with me all day." The participants sometimes directed their anger toward government policies and politicians.

"The story that made me mad, not that long ago and I believe it angered not only me but all of Spain - was the coverage of corruption," said a rural female occasional viewer, 23. (The story she cited enters in the next section.) Anger also focused on the newscasts themselves. An urban male, 21, said the news "provokes my indignation because of the way the stories are treated, usually from the most macabre angle."

Next often the Spaniards cited fear (21.9 per cent), but at less than half the rate of the Americans. In contrast to the U.S. group (in which women, especially from the cities, expressed fear strongly), the Spaniards had no major gap between the numbers of men and women reporting fear or its qualitative expressions.

In a typical example, a 26-year-old female regular viewer said, "When the news reports come out about anorexia or depression, the statistics on the incidence of these illnesses are frightening." Such statements cited fear without expressing much emotion.

Sadness, the Americans' most frequent emotion, the Spaniards mentioned least frequently (6.3 per cent), citing happiness twice as often (12.5 per cent). Every instance of these two feelings came from an essay by a woman (in the U.S. group, only women said they ever felt sad, but men expressed happiness more often than did women).

In their emotions, the U.S. group tended to passivity, with men understated in their responses, and women experiencing more volatility. The Spaniards, male as well as female, took a somewhat more active stance, reacting most frequently with anger and newscasts and their content (while understating the passive emotions such as fear and sadness). That pattern extended as well into the actions they took in response to newscasts.

A substantial minority of the Spaniards said television news did have an influence on their actions (34.4 per cent), but none mentioned any changes in dress, hairstyle, or tone of voice - the authoritative airs that some U.S. women said they imitated. Nor did the Spaniards mention news affecting any decisions about their present or future jobs or family. They reported only one action that newscasts influenced: using information in conversations.

If there is something that stands out from watching news on television, it's the comments we make afterward, whether in the family, with friends or around other people. We have the custom of commenting on a news story and exchanging opinions about it. -an urban male, 23

Another important difference in how the news activated the Spaniards but left the Americans reactive appeared in the precautions they said they took. The tenor of fear did not come through among the Spaniards, who mentioned no precautions and did not appear to share the U.S. fear that one wrong move might spoil their lives.

As a result, a majority of the Spaniards (53.2 per cent) maintained that television news did not influence their actions. Like the Americans, they seemed dismissive of the idea that news might affect them. Unlike the Americans, they did not then contradict themselves by listing specific ways the news affected their appearance and actions, including major life decisions.

POLITICS AND MEDIA

The young Americans writing about television news reported a limited interest in politics to match their moderate viewing habits. Unlike their elders, they told no stories of using the news to take political actions.

The young adults tended to define themselves as ineffectual and relatively powerless, seeing television news (often mentioned with the generic phrase "news media") as a potent political actor. Some essays mentioned observing cynicism in themselves or in peers as a response to media power and their own political impotence. Although they gave a positive overall rating to the job news outlets do, they saw entertainment values corrupting the news. Somehow the media, they believed, supplanted political parties and weakened political discourse, limiting their own options. Some of the Americans saw their only option as a choice between television news and newspapers.

The essays from Spain revealed a stronger interest in politics, which also turned up in the questionnaire. The group gave itself a mean rating between "very" and "somewhat" interested in politics (1.5 on a three-point scale). Although higher than the national average, the rating reflects the group's median age (21), when Spanish youth have the highest political interest (Institute de la Juventud, 1991). The participants also linked their political interest with media use. In the questionnaire, those "very" interested in politics watched news habitually (6 days "last week"), and those "somewhat" interested said they watched slightly less (5.5 days "last week"). None reported being "not at all" interested in politics.

The Spaniards most often mentioned a type of action they call a political decision, which they usually defined as making a choice between political alternatives. Some essays also mentioned voting, and several specified other actions. "These days the news still has an impact on me," said a female regular viewer, 26, "and perhaps those are what in a given moment made me try working in a non-governmental organization or making a donation or whatever else to help out." Such levels of participation match survey results (Institute de la Juventud, 1991), in which a majority of 18- to 29-year-olds said they voted in elections (69.2 per cent) and about half said they usually followed political stories in the media (51.9 per cent). Consonant with other statistics, only a small share of participants reported joining associations (13.8 per cent).

When they wrote about politics, the participants considered the use of power central, and they saw themselves, not television news, as capable of exercising power. The exception, a 20-year-old female, remarked, "Everyone knows perfectly well how important a politician's image is when televised. It's the only medium that they can count on to reach the entire population and share their ideas." Even this passage places the politicians, not the journalists, at centre stage and lacks the sort of cynicism found among some Americans. Instead, the Spaniards appear to play down the importance of the news media generally and television news particularly in their political world. They rated the overall job the news media do in Spain (2.4) lower as a result.

An urban male, 21, said, "More than a few times the newscasts give too much importance to an exchange of insults between politicians." The Spaniards saw the shift toward spectacle in television news as confirmation of their judgment that television news can play only a partial role in their political thinking.

Such a critical stance toward television news appears to go hand in hand with their own sense of potency and independence. The Spaniards emphasized their own position as decision-makers. "I think the stories get too little coverage to be used as the only base for information," said an urban female, 21. More than a quarter of the essays described comparing the various news media (28.1 per cent). A rural female, 22, said that newscasts led her "to take a more critical view, since the different ways of presenting stories on the different television networks give you contradictory images.

Only after thinking about them can you then form your own opinion." The essays also brought newspapers into the discussion. "I always like to watch several newscasts to see the different ways journalists have of narrating the stories," said a suburban female regular viewer, 25. "I also like to contrast this with the press." The Spaniards did not treat newscasts and newspapers as competitors, between which to choose. Instead each news outlet had a use.

As did their compatriots who wrote about newspapers, the television group also took a sophisticated attitude, judging television news harshly but also acknowledging its usefulness. I've always thought that assimilating information from newscasts is relatively complex. The bombardment of information is so rapid it's difficult to absorb what they say. Now I also believe it's much more powerful seeing images on television than reading them in the paper.

Television touches my emotional fibre as a spectator. a suburban female regular viewer, 25.

The essays most often cited one political topic: the corruption scandals surrounding the former socialist (PSOE) government (a current issue in the news just after the 1996 election). Revelations by news outlets illustrated the importance of a free press in Spanish democracy, the essays said. More than half of the essays talked about the value of television news (56.3 per cent) since the transition to democracy. The scandal coverage, followed by a substantial young adult vote against the socialists, appeared to have especially enhanced the participants' sense of power to make political decisions, independent from the older generation that repeatedly elected socialist governments.

Instead of concluding that the media have somehow supplanted political parties and weakened political discourse, the Spaniards discounted the role of newscasts as only one source among many. They emphasized their own thinking, as well as their ongoing political discussions with family and friends.

MEDIA CRITICISM

Complaints about bias in media coverage played prominently among the Americans. Women and members of minority groups such as African Americans included examples of discrimination in their essays and vented their harsh judgments of newscasts as a result.

Similar complaints of bias did not play so prominent a role among the Spanish group. Several participants from the Basque region, however, did decry the false impression television reports gave of life in their communities.

A person from Jain, for example, who sees the news, must think that in the Basque country and Navarra we all go around armed and that it's almost like Bosnia. But if you live here, you realise that's not reality. -a suburban female regular viewer, 22

In general, however, the essays did not censure newscasts for discrimination. The only example parallel to the U.S. criticisms involved images of women. A suburban female regular viewer, 25, wrote: "I remember seeing a room full of men. One of them brought in a girl of seven or eight. They tied her with esparto rope... and proceeded to cut off her clitoris." The essay described this "montage of images," intended to expose discrimination, as an example of the cruelty to women "they show on television every day." Several women complained of the recent turn of television toward shocking or violent news. The essays dated the shift to the arrival of competition. They denounced the new commercial channels for trying to attract viewers without considering the repercussions:

What I like least about TV news is how very morbid they are, how, when something happens, they thoughtlessly show it all without thinking of the consequences. They only care about being as dramatic as possible, and sometimes the scenes they show... can harm the people involved. -an urban female, 19.

Although not as prominent as in the U.S. essays, such complaints mark a shift in the meaning of television news to the Spaniards. Both groups appear to share a sense that news has become degraded under commercial pressures. The transformation that the Americans noted, however, has just begun entering the situation the Spaniards describe.

The experience of television news among the Spaniards presents myriad contrasts to the U.S. group. Many of the differences result from the distinct historical contexts in the two countries.

The recent change from dictatorship helped produce a more widespread custom of news watching, which some attendant resentment hardly weakens. More of the young Spaniards became viewers without much overt parental encouragement and with little support from the schools. Instead the reinforcement of daily practice built a deep commitment.

The Spaniards, despite their constant attention to television news, tended to discount its importance. Changes in news form gave them a greater awareness of the constructedness of the newscast.

The Americans, by contrast, saw their preferred content (news and weather) as information about a factual reality and responded with sadness and fear. The Spanish group reacted to news with anger, a relatively active emotion, and the women expressed less fear. In general, the Spaniards presented themselves as more independent of television news. It influenced their actions less often, although they reported more conversations about it than the Americans did.

The most intriguing differences occurred in the political realm. The young Spaniards, at least in the particular moment after an election, took more interest in politics. They not only engaged in discussion but saw political decisions as theirs to make. They followed politics and watched television news more than the Americans did, but at the same time they had a lower opinion of the news media. Where some in the U.S. group felt powerless, the Spaniards did not.

They described themselves as free to make choices and saw an array of options for informing themselves. The Americans instead tended to see the necessity of choosing between television and newspapers, and some of them saw the media as powerful. By rejecting this view, the Spaniards avoided falling into the cynicism found among the Americans.

The U.S. television news industry cannot, of course, replicate the national historical experience of Spain, but the different experiences the Spaniards reported can recommend practices for U.S. newscasters interested in creating a high level of commitment to and critical independence from news. The Spanish example suggests a reasonable alternative to the U.S. definition of a news market, in which television must compete with newspapers in a winnertake-all contest. Such a view probably does not contribute to young adults' sense of their own options. In Spain the media cooperate as a way of competing in the news arena.

Newscasts commonly highlight newspaper stories, show images of the pages, and then go on to illustrate alternative points of view. The practice teaches viewers to read newspapers, watch the newscast, and listen to radio with the intent to learn more by comparing and drawing their own conclusions. It is tempting to attribute the cross-fertilization among news media to the growing consolidation of media outlets in Spain.

However, the television news segments highlight the main stories of all the principal newspapers. In the United States, as a result of cross-ownership such as the Chicago Tribune and the WGN super-station, newscasts plug only the company's own newspaper and Web version. The case clearly differs in Spain, where anchors present news as a cooperative endeavor in which each medium has its use. Newspapers provide flexibility in time - they await the opportune moment - but their efficiency and convenience define newspapers as private reading. Television news has a programme schedule, and that inflexibility in time helps build a family ritual, although it also makes newscasts ephemeral.

By emphasizing and promoting alternative sources, the U. S. news media could provide a sense of abundance and variety similar to what the young Spaniards note. The sacrifice each medium in Spain makes in its own position as an authoritative source is small. The cooperative spirit does not dispense with competition but highlights it, producing a rising tide of news coverage that lifts all ships, for the young as well as for newspapers, electronic news, and newscasts. The young gain a sense of independence freedom to explore and make decisions. In the bargain, the news outlets get what they need most, viewers (and readers) who stay attentive and critically aware.

SIMILARITIES

The experiences of the U.S. and Spanish groups do have some important parallels. In both settings, a ritual at home supplied the most powerful and universal meanings of newscasts. Viewers acquired the practice through the rhythms of childhood experience. The temporal quality, then, came not just from the news as something new, but in the daily-ness of the process, especially in Spain. The ritual also involved the presence of parents, who shared in witnessing both the news and the family watching the news. In this sense, news watching depends on generational experience. The older generation, in Spain as in the United States, appears to have transmitted the practice through daily example more than through preachment, as predicted. Schools probably cannot reproduce the experience.

The young generation also brought its common experience to the news, and, in turn, the news of both countries contributed to the memories of the new political generation. The experience of being caught up in a national event occurred in both countries, which tends to confirm the generationbuilding effect of television news. In some cases, young adults in both countries shared the same initial news event. The international reach of some major stories appears to tie young people in what may be an emerging trend toward actual generations, to use Mannheim's term, that cross national boundaries. That first news story does more than initiate the young generation's memory. At the same time, the common experience of the two generations, in the presence of news, ties them together in the national political identity, although as Mannheim predicted, their qualitative experiences of the event differ.

At the centre of television news stands the image. The young viewers valued the images of people and places they would not otherwise know. Such images helped them define what belongs within the nation as well as without, to the familiar us and the foreign them. The everyday procedures of news work do not often manufacture the kinds of images vital for linking young people to news. The events that tie the young generation to the old and fuse them all into national consciousness usually happen unexpectedly and overtake the newscasters at the same time. The element of surprise makes a difference. The news that marks a generation's memory transcends the daily routine of news and leaps outside the boundaries of the newscast as a temporal ritual.

One final commonality, the shift away from serious content and toward the rhythms and style of entertainment in the newscast, plagued both countries. The transformation, quite advanced in America, appears implicated in the dispirited and cynical attitudes among young citizens. The changes young adults observed in Spain presage a similar reaction among the generation to come. The stronger ritual in Spain, as well as the custom of comparing news outlets, has built sturdy links between generations, at least for the young adults studied here. However, the move toward sensational coverage and ratings competition seems most likely, in the long run, to harm Spanish broadcasters - their own reputation and position in the constellation of news options.

When developing the life history technique in the early twentieth century, Herbert Blumer attempted to create a lens for looking at the facts of his participants' childhood encounters with movies. The idea was simple: just ask them. The critique of empiricism in the intervening years suggests that life narratives, rather than simply reflecting the past, instead operate as a primary tool in the construction of identity in the present. The stories young adults wrote for this study do reveal the occasional event from history, such as the military coup in Spain, but their importance lies elsewhere. The stories give insight into subjective responses, the meanings and values young citizens assign to events in past.

Their narratives are public documents, not revelations of private goings on. The method of collecting written stories, despite the consistent offer of anonymity, generates an official version of events as the participants would like them seen. The picture they offer of themselves as audience members represents their ideal, along with a frank admission in many cases of how they fall short of that model. In their experiences as citizens and members of media audiences, the young adults depict themselves as public persons. That image comes as close as possible to citizenship, making life histories an appropriate tool for understanding how the young adults explain their identities as citizens.

In short, life narratives reveal not historical facts (although they allude to them) but symbolic interpretations, which in turn influence how the young act out their citizenship. The success of the news industry in the United States and elsewhere depends on a range of decisions, from editorial content to corporate strategy, which rarely take into account the symbolic worth of the enterprise. As young Americans abandoned news over the past twenty years, the loss, although financial in the short run, has symbolic weight in the long run. Yet research has not usually examined that elusive quality, the subjective value of news.

A cross-national comparison of how young citizens understand the news helps fill the gap. The contrasts between subjective experiences in Spain and the United States shed light on the consequences of a news arena organized for market competition. Some things that U.S. journalists avoid most assiduously may in fact provide antidotes to the declining role of newspapers in the political life of young Americans and to their disregard for newscasts as an alternative.

An explicit ideological position seems foremost among them. Reporting that consistently covers events from two opposing sides puts journalists in the role of neutral arbiter and leaves citizens out of the decision-making loop, as mere spectators. In the United States, the ideology of balance makes for powerful journalists but weakened young citizens, who respond by disengaging and in some cases turning cynical. Taking a political position and speaking consistently from it has had the opposite effect in Spain.

Another activity that U.S. journalists avoid may suggest a second remedy: a willingness to talk directly about the competition, its news decisions and ideological aims. When news organizations compete mainly in the market, mentioning the competition becomes a taboo, an unseemly intrusion of money matters into the high-minded business of public information.

Fairly uniform coverage, which accompanies the silence about competitors, enhances the authority of journalists as professional news-handlers and leaves citizens with branded versions of what amounts to the same news product. In the United States, the limited choices reduce young citizens to mere consumers, who respond with boredom and indifference. Talking about the many points of view available in competing news outlets creates a vibrant news arena with the opposite effect among elite young adults in Spain.

The similarities in subjective experience between Spain and the United States suggest further remedies. In both countries the key that opens newspaper reading and news watching to more young citizens is daily ritual, observed in the example of parents and teachers. Didactic methods such as those employed in recent Newspaper Association of

America campaigns seem ill-advised. The results reported here imply that the campaigns would have better success if built from in-school activities rather than homework, and in any case, getting parents to engage with news daily seems essential, and school work ancillary.

As news has become more professional in the United States, journalists have moved away from reporting the local and the particular, preferring to cover more significant and impressive events. In all the groups studied so far, however, young citizens report that local events most sparked their interest. The trends in U.S. journalism go against the subjective preference for news that stays close to young citizens' social worlds, reporting on familiar people and nearby places. Re-focusing on the local community, as the recent public journalism movement proposes, may help slow the decline in interest among young citizens.

In the context of remedies, it bears repeating that in the groups from both countries, models of entertainment and commercialism for news produce a similar negative response. The young adults' interpretations bring to mind the logic of the traffic jam. When passing an accident, drivers may prefer not to look but cannot resist. Despite their mounting frustration over so-called "gaper's delay," each car slows down at the scene of mayhem (which always reveals less than it promises).

Young adults react to shocking and entertaining news in much the same way, looking against their better will, but resenting their brief union with the crowd. For the purveyors of news, any short term gain in ratings or circulation from such coverage only feeds a longterm malady: the weakening subjective sense of the value first of news to citizens and then of citizenship itself.

All these recommendations interrelate. In the end, the U.S, news industry would be wise to target older adults primarily, organizing all efforts around building a daily habit. Whatever the cost in the near term, seriousness will build a more lasting commitment. Techniques that draw from entertainment and advance commercialism may attract momentary attention from a young audience while doing damage to parents' willingness to incorporate news into daily living, thus sacrificing the next generation of viewers and readers. U.S. news businesses likewise would benefit by making their usually unspoken ideological stands overt, contrasting themselves clearly and openly to other news outlets.

Whether motivated by politeness or professional brotherhood, journalists who fail to highlight honest disagreements about news in effect devalue not only political ideology but also the news itself. News deserves better. Variety and conflict between news organizations create, paradoxically, a cooperative news arena, increasing interest among the public rather than limiting the audience for news.

BUILDING THEORY

Besides the policy implications of the research, the Spanish case study and the comparison with the U.S. studies also contribute to theory. Three principal insights deserve elaboration, two that advance existing theories generations and political participation - and one that builds grounded concepts from subjective experience.

Similarities between the Spaniards and Americans help clarify the role of news in the formation and structure of generations. First, the young adults in each country share memories of particular moments in their national history covered in the news, especially, in the case of Spain, the events in the transition to democracy. That groups from both countries also share memories spanning national borders - such as the explosion of the space shuttle - suggests the emergence of cross-national generations, which were a conceptual impossibility at the time Mannheim wrote. Although probably not sufficient to form an actual generation, their common experience does point to an emerging global news arena and a potential internationalization of citizenship.

Second, the college students in each country might form a distinct unit within their own national generation. A next step should investigate groups of young adults from other socioeconomic levels. In the United States those who enter college form a large unit, but further study could profitably compare them with others who do not. Additional study seems especially appropriate in Spain, where fewer young citizens attend universities and read newspapers. That need does not, however, reduce the importance of an initial comparison of elites in the two countries.

The present study sheds light, for instance, on the persistent puzzle of participation in Spain. How could a citizenry deemed passive on many survey measures accomplish and sustain so successful a transition from dictatorship to democracy? The evidence presented here contradicts the statistics for the population as a whole and expands the understanding of surveys focusing on youth (Instituto de la Juventud, 1991). Instead of the picture of a post-transition generation hopelessly disengaged from politics, the participants (unlike their U.S. counterparts) knowledgeably and willingly tackle political issues, foreign and domestic, while disparaging political parties and even their own government. Clearly the general indicators of knowledge, involvement, and efficacy fail to measure the dimensions of a subjective environment where, to paraphrase the classic statement by V S. Pritchett, nothing mediates - no association, party, medium, state, or church - between Spaniards and whatever power directs their world.

Capturing the particular moment of transition in Spanish history, contrary to expectation, does not diminish the importance of such results. Besides the obvious ways that the transition heightened citizens' sense of the importance of politics and their own decisions, the evidence suggests that the transition generation acted with circumspection, constraining their tendency to criticism when modeling media literacy. Nevertheless, further study should compare young adults in other countries where transitions have occurred, such as Brazil.

Finally, the study suggests a concept grounded in the contrast between young Spanish citizens and their counterparts in the United States. The comparison reveals a pattern in which several aspects of the participants' responses tend to cluster together in what can be termed a subjective posture. On one hand stand many of the Americans, whom the earlier studies describe as responding with indifference to politics and activism, with resentment toward the media, and with a sense of fear and powerlessness. Another posture turns up in the essays by Spaniards, who have considerable interest in politics leading to activism, view the media with a detached but critical eye, and respond to news by comparing and making choices among political options. The two postures, or clusters of subjective responses, seem to mark endpoints on a continuum.

Certain kinds of enrichment or impoverishment define that range, which, for lack of a better term, might be called subjective affluence. The term affluence, of course, refers here to something other than material poverty. Both countries are relatively well off, and the groups studied enjoy substantial economic advantages. Their differing postures, where the observed personal responses cluster, have striking parallels, however, within the surrounding media environment.

The Americans experienced an arena for news driven by commercial competition. The news media avoid taking overt ideological stands, in favour of a uniform standard of coverage. A market mentality furthermore drives news outlets to employ the techniques of entertainment, along with an emphasis on private tragedy and public violence, to make the news more captivating (that is, to win higher ratings or circulation). The Spaniards experienced a very different news arena. The driving force of partisan ideology aims to present an politically coherent depiction of public affairs, and, moreover, holds up examples of other news media and their differing news judgments.

Of all the evidence presented, recent changes in Spain support most strongly the interpretation that these two arenas mark (in lived experienced) the endpoints on a continuum. Participants described a shift within the Spanish arena toward the U. S. version of things. They bore witness not only to external events, as media outlets Americanize, but also to subjective events, as the young Spaniards themselves responded to that changing media environment. The subjective postures in the two countries link, not to their material prospects in this case, but with their responses to the symbolic arena. The subjective postures and the news arenas interact and together define the relative wealth of the subjective environment.

In short, subjective affluence describes a symbolic continuum independent to some degree from economic affluence. Despite material abundance, the Americans experience a symbolic poverty, brought on by trends that now have begun spreading to Spain. Further study of subjective affluence could clarify the complex relationships emerging between news and citizens, while examining the long-term consequences for trust and interest in the press and in politics.

Chapter 7

Writing for Professional Publication

With the collapse of earlier certainties, the last two decades have witnessed serious soul-searching among art historians about the future of the discipline. This is strikingly expressed by Hans Belting in two of his theoretical works-one with the melancholy title The End of the History of Art?-accepting the demise of art history as a grand Hegelian narrative. There is, he points out, a progressive disjunction between the awareness of the enormous diversity of art forms and practices and the narrow focus of canonical art histories. However, his fear that the canon looks increasingly vulnerable may be somewhat premature.

Take, for instance, Art since 1900, the magisterial volume on the avant-garde published in 2004. The book raises immensely important questions that demand engagement. The four authors display intellectual sophistication, an exemplary attention to detail, and a masterly grasp of the broader picture of Western avant-garde art in the twentieth century. Because of its importance, the work has been reviewed widely and its underlying arguments scrutinized and dismantled, raising a great many urgent critical and historical issues relevant to our times. I think we must recognize the advances made by this work, which brings into question the triumphalist discourse of modernism in the opening decades of the twentieth century. It should further be acknowledged that a wide-ranging text of this sort for a general readership cannot hope to include everything.

Nonetheless, perhaps because my own work has dealt with artists in the periphery, I would have liked to have seen the authors filling more of the gaps in our knowledge of world art. The book contains few references to notable artists living outside Europe and the United States who have made significant contributions to the global processes of modernity.

It would have been desirable to see even a brief mention of artists such as Jamini Roy, whose innovative formalism based on a primitivist reimagining of the folk art of India powerfully mediated between the global and the local; the savage, spiky images of the Mexican primitivist Wifredo Lam; the amoebic shapes of the Brazilian avant-garde painter Tarsila do Amarai; and, more recently, Everlyn Nicodemus's profoundly moving representations of global genocide and the expansive work of African artists shown at Africa Remix, a recent exhibition at the Hayward Gallery, London.

The Mexican muralists are discussed, but one could run the danger of concluding from this volume that except for this major movement, there has been no worthwhile art of political resistance in the non-Western world, notwithstanding significant artistic expressions in Asia and Africa of cultural resistance to Western dominance. Art since 1900 touches on a few isolated samples of postwar diaspora art and Asian avant-garde movements, but these owe their presence more to what they mean to the West than for their intrinsic worth. In consequence, they tend to come off as bit players in the master narrative. Thus, despite the above inclusions, the canon is not significantly enlarged. Rather, the non-Western artists are brought in primarily on account of their compatibility with the avant-garde discourse in the West.

This is not to discount the book's very wide range of topics. Among its considerable merits is that, within the parameters of its own definition of modernism, it rigorously documents the internal debates in the West on the predicament of modernity, mapping successfully its complex, dialogic, oppositional, and agonistic agenda, foregrounding its intellectual wherewithal, such as psychoanalysis, social history of art, formalism, structuralism, and poststructuralism.

It will consequently remain a valuable document to the last century's insider-outsider politics of modernism from the Euro-American perspective. I point this out only because the authors in fact distance themselves from the hollow universalism of the colonial period, as expressed in Hal Foster's admirable attempts to negotiate "between diverse cultural space-times."

However, since the authors aim to deal with "art" as a universal category, readers will inevitably demand much of these scholars-who inspired a generation of students in exposing the knowledge-power nexus of twentieth-century modernism. For this reason, none of the issues raised here would be problematic if the title of the book were, for instance, Western Avant-Garde Art since 1900 or Western Art since 1900.

The book's wider global ambitions nonetheless offer me a starting point to situate its "universalist" canon within an epistemological framework that goes back to the Enlightenment. The book follows a well-trodden path that equates Western norms with global values, having the unintended consequence of excluding the art of the periphery. Take the example of a recent standard history of world photography: not a single Chinese, Indian, or African photographer features in it, not, for instance, the stunning colour photographs of Raghubir Singh, nor the elegant black-and-white studio portraits of the African photographer Seydou Keïta, whose work could well compare with that of August Sander.

Similarly, the work of the Indian-Hungarian Amrita Sher-Gil, a highly original woman painter who worked in the context of global modernism, is generally written out of world histories of women artists. Such faith in the universal is not unique to art history, though it creates its own specific inclusions. Take the world of fashion. We are led to believe that today it embraces with enthusiasm all ethnic groups in an unprecedented expansion of the canon of beauty.

Yet what comes across is the fact that representations of multiethnic supermodels are homogenized within the prevailing Western classical framework of beauty. Looking at economics, we see that models of development, based on a Western definition of well-being, are presented as a panacea to the developing world irrespective of the values and needs of specific regions. I use these analogies merely to demonstrate the pervasive hold of "hegemonic" universality.

Despite its serious intentions, the "universalist" project of art history remains trapped within the constraints of Western epistemology, which cannot be remedied simply by a culturally determined self-reflexivity. The wide acceptance of the Western modernist canon as self-evidently universal (even in non-Western regions, I must add) does not give sufficient weight to the role of convention in artistic production." In the social sciences, this use of the universal for the specific is described as an unmarked case.

Modernism in this sense is an "unmarked case" that implicitly stands for "Western" modernism. By this token, a qualifying epithet becomes necessary to speak of any other: East European modernism, Chinese modernism, Indian modernism, and so on. It is perhaps no accident that following Immanuel Kant's a priori view of aesthetics, the concept "art" is often regarded as neutral and disinterested, which systematically ignores the implications of race, gender, sexual orientation, and even class (by the latter I mean all forms of folk and popular art that are excluded from the master narrative). The universal canon of art subsumes either the classical canon or the modernist canon that supplanted it in the twentieth century.

THE SHOCK OF THE NEW

The embedded hierarchy implied by the modernist canon and its impact on contemporary art of regions regarded as the cultural periphery can be understood only in historical terms. In the late nineteenth century, the modernist revolution began to alter European sensibilities, gradually spreading to other regions throughout the twentieth, shaping global perceptions of contemporary art and literature, a transformation that has left few societies untouched. Imagine the profound shock on first encountering Pablo Picasso's Les demoiselles d'Avignon, or the frisson given by Marcel Duchamp's Fountain, a porcelain urinal signed R. Mutt.

Even from this distance in time, we can still sense the dislocation and bewilderment with which the general public greeted these radical assaults on their vision and sensibility. Nor is it difficult to be impressed by the radical outlook of the early Cubists, Expressionists, and Surrealists, who declared war on bourgeois values and bourgeois artistic models, the portentous pompiers peintres of the Victorian era.

Adrian Stokes argues that The Bathers by Paul Cézanne, which inspired Picasso's Demoiselles d'Avignon, encouraged artists Io turn to African sculpture in repudiation of classical taste. This prompts him to speculate "in the most far-fetched manner whether one day it will be possible to claim for The Bathers that it is among the first and perhaps the greatest works of a deeply founded cosmopolitan art which was to pre-figure the eventual evolution of a multi-racial society."

Surrealism, with its distaste for colonial rule, enjoyed a mutually beneficial cross-fertilization with black cultural resistance, as suggested by the friendship between André Breton and the Martinique poet and intellectual Aimé Césaire. Indeed, it is only in the liberal atmosphere of bohemian Paris that the creative genius of the black chanteuse Josephine Baker could flourish, the Jazz Age and "negrophilia" helping to release Europe from its sterile exclusivity.

Today the preeminence of modernist art is universally assured, as its controlling canon and market mechanism hold the so-called peripheries in its thrall or in its grip, depending on one's point of view. Even postmodern and postcolonial thinking which arose partly in revolt against the avant-garde in the twilight years of the last century, was a child of this worldwide movement, though a child in revolt against some of its fundamental tenets.

These enormous achievements of the heroic age of the avant-garde cannot be gainsaid, as the modernist technology of art, not to mention the formal language and syntax of Cubism, allowed artists in far-flung regions to devise new ways to image the visible world. One of the favourite projects of the colonial powers in the nineteenth century was to inculcate "good taste" in the subject nations through the introduction of academic naturalism and classical standards.

Therefore, the revolt of the Western avant-garde against academic naturalism and its attendant ideology was openly welcomed by the subject nations, who were concerned with formulating their own resistance to the colonial order. Above all, modernism's experimental attitude that constantly sought to push intellectual frontiers, its ideology of emancipatory innovation, and its agonistic relation to tradition and authority released new energies in artists raised in a more traditional mode.

In short, its revolutionary message fur- nished ammunition for cultural resistance to colonial em- pires, as each colonized nation deployed the language of modernism to fight its own particular cultural corner. In the Indian Empire, for instance, the nationalist artists asserted their own cultural identity against the colonial-capitalist complex.

Non-Western nations were no less persuaded by the Western theorists' critical engagement within modernism that kept it on its toes, so to speak, preventing it from becoming complacent and formulaic in the aftermath of its public acceptance.

Marxists have taken the lead in interrogating the troubled relation between modernity and tradition, between the social usefulness of art and the avant-garde aesthetics of autonomy, and between high art and the mass culture of consumption in capitalist societies. Walter Benjamin's idea of mechanical reproducibility helped undermine the "aura" of originality in modernist innovations, while Carl Einstein's primitivism sought to restore the symbolic dimension of collective life within the avant-garde.

In 1939, in answer to the Soviet critics' condemnation of bourgeois formalism, Clement Greenberg deployed the very same Marxian critical apparatus to defend the modernist aesthetics of autonomy against kitsch; he provided a fresh definition of the avantgarde as a historical agency that resisted the consumer culture of capitalist society.

The instrumentalist explanation of the social meaning of art as a reflection of class-consciousness and ideology was replaced by a new generation of critical historians of art led by T. J. Clark (and indirectly inspired by Meyer Schapiro) with a more nuanced "against the grain" interpretation of artistic creation, which stressed the instability of ideologies and the complex relation of artists to the totality of a historical situation. Repudiating a simplistic polarity of high and low art, Thomas Crow posits a dialogic relation between high art and the leisure industry of market capitalism, in which "advanced artists make unsettling equations between high and low, which dislocate the apparently fixed terms of that hierarchy into new and persuasive configurations...."

In an essay, Rosalind Krauss explores Auguste Rodin's production of multiple copies to challenge the much-vaunted originality of the modernists. Hal Foster offers us two influential formulations of postmodernism-one that is complicit with capitalism and the other as a form of resistance to it, his own work eloquently articulating the latter position.

THE PICASSO MANQUÉ SYNDROME

These critical interventions by Clark, Krauss, and others have been of seminal importance in tempering the triumphalism of the avant-garde, highlighting the fractures and contradictions of modernity and its complex relation with tradition, all of which have, of course, inspired art practices not only in the centre but also in the periphery.

However, as argued by David Craven, critical interventions of major thinkers from the periphery in art history are lacking, which by their absence contribute to the erasure of nonmetropolitan art practices within the "universalist" canon. The discipline of art history has yet to change in any substantive manner the implicit evaluation of non-Western modernism as derivative and devoid of originality. Two cases highlight, for instance, the glaring difference in art historical assessments of the use of material from a culture outside one's own. The first is the exhibition "Primitivism" in 20th Century Art: Affinity of the Tribal and the Modern, held in New York in 1985, and the critical interventions surrounding the exhibition; the second is what I call the Picasso manqué syndrome.

"Primitivism" in 20th Century Art was an impressive exhibition mounted at the Museum of Modern Art in New York. Its goal was to highlight the formal similarities between ethnographic art and Western modernism. The exhibition, which sought to overcome the "debased" notion of causal influence by treating ethnographic objects as possessing aesthetic merit, described the "primitive" motifs in the works of Picasso and other iconic modernists as a reflection of the "affinities" between modern and "tribal" art that transcended time and space.

Among its reviews, Foster's and James Clifford's stand out for laying bare the contradictions of this ambitious curatorial exercise. Foster focused on the show's anodyne formalist juxtaposition of the tribal and the modern and its attempts to assimilate tribal culture to Enlightenment values. Such an approach, he showed us, had the effect of reducing primitivism's disruptive potentials, its raw power as a fetishistic discourse, which the Surrealists had exploited brilliantly.

The anthropologist Clifford commented on the exhibition's erasure of colonial violence, which had wrenched African and Oceanic objects from their social contexts for display in European museums, by its projection of a neutral formalist "allegory of affinities."

For me it is quite telling that the organizers of "Primitivism" in 20th Century Art wished to underline the fact that the artistic "borrowings" of Picasso and other modernists from simple "primitive" cultures did not amount to a debt to these societies. On the contrary, the European "discovery" of ethnographic art redeemed these fetishist objects for the modern world and elevated them to the level of high art. Importantly, the New York exhibition was at pains to emphasize that the selected pairings of modern and tribal objects demonstrated the common denominators of these arts that were independent of direct influence.

What is crucial to realise is that Picasso's borrowings from "simple" ethnographic objects in no way compromised his cultural integrity as an artist. A noted authority, writing a decade later on Vladimir Tatlin's discovery of a tribal mask in Picasso's studio, could thus exclaim that "it is one of the wonders of our age that such a simple tribal artifact, which could justifiably be called primitive, should have given birth indirectly to Russian Constructivism, one of the most technically visionary of all twentieth-century art movements."

As opposed to appropriations by the Western avant-garde, let us now see what happens to the artist as a colonial subject who responds to an intellectual product of the "dominant" European culture.

The widely held view that modern art beyond Europe and the United States is at best a derivative exercise reflects the implicit assertion of the "intellectual property rights" of the West. In 1959, the English art historian William George Archer published India and Modern Art, which remains a classic example of colonialist art history.

Even though the work was written nearly half a century ago, I believe its underlying assumptions about the lack of originality of non-Western modernism continue to be symptomatic of a widespread bias. Archer posed a pertinent question: Can modern art be appropriated by Indians, and if so, in what manner? In answer to this, he provided a succinct analysis of the paintings made between 1921 and 1928 by the pioneering Indian modernist Gaganendranath Tagore, who was among the first Indian painters to adapt the revolutionary syntax of Cubism.

Archer claimed that such appropriation must be "absorbed into the blood stream" of that society to be a genuine item. But as the next defining passage makes clear, this had failed miserably in the case of the Indian artist:

His style was, at first sight, not unlike the early followers of Braque and Picasso.... Yet apart from their very evident lack of power-a power which in some mysterious way was present in the work of Braque and Picasso-Gogonendranath's pictures were actually no more than stylised illustrations...

weak as art, but what was more important, they were un-Indian.... As a result, his pictures, despite their modernistic manner, had an air of trivial irrelevance.

Elsewhere I have contended that Archer failed to comprehend the Indian artist's achievement in deploying the flexible syntax of Cubism in order to create miniature watercolors of poetic intensity that were meaningful in the colonialnationalist milieu of India. Let me explain.

Analytic Cubism, which destroyed the conventions of illusionistic naturalism, helped to restore the internal cohesion of a picture so that it ceased to be a window on the external world. Artists worldwide were drawn to Cubism's flexible nonfigurative syntax, which could be put to different uses, but they were not concerned with the formal revolution of Analytic Cubism as such.

To take an example pertinent to my argument, the motivation behind the Western Expressionists Franz Marc, Lyonel Feininger, or Georg Grosz and the Indian artist Gaganendranath was analogous: objects could be distorted and fragmented to produce dazzling patterns.

Although they shared this formal language, the specific cultural contexts of the Central European artists and Gaganendranath were as different as their artistic aims, not to mention their different artistic agendas.

The German avant-garde critic Max Osborn, reviewing an exhibition of modern Indian art in Berlin in 1923, quite perceptively drew out the affinities between Gaganendranath and Feininger in their indifference to the formal implications of Analytic Cubism.

The Indian artist epitomizes the decontextualizing tendency of the age, shared as much by artists in the centre as in the periphery: styles past and present could be appropriated to generate strikingly new meanings.

As his critique of Gaganendranath makes clear, Archer follows Roger Fry's notion of "significant form" as the antithesis to weak "feminine" anecdotal painting.

In addition, the word "power" in the passage expresses his primitivist longing for the "masculine" formalism and virile geometry of Indian tribal art. However, the overwhelming reason for Archer's dismissive evaluation of Gaganendranath's "Cubist" works lay in the Indian painter's use of the visual language of a culture to which he did not belong.

In other words, Gaganendranath suffered a loss of self in becoming a colonial hybrid. We can find interesting parallels in "Primitivism" in 20th Century Art, which while reifying tribal artifacts as timeless high art erased Third World modernisms, denying the existence of contemporary tribal artists in the name of authentic traditional art. Interestingly, according to Shelley Errington, genuine living "primitive" art ceased to exist in the twentieth century for complex reasons, such objects becoming denizens of the corridors of European ethnographic museums or objects of a nationalist tourist industry.

Unlike Picasso, whose use of African sources did not compromise his integrity as a European artist, Gaganendranath's use of Cubism resulted in the loss of self as an Indian. I have called the complex discourse of power, authority, and hierarchy involved in the study of the non-Western avant-garde the Picasso manqué syndrome, as Archer's endeavor consisted almost entirely of tracing Picasso's putative influence.

Inevitably, he reached the conclusion that Gaganendranath was a Cubist manqué, and his derivative works, based on a cultural misreading, were simply puerile imitations of the Spanish master. In short, the use of Cubism, a product of the dominant West, by an Indian artist who belonged to the colonized world, immediately locked him into a dependent relationship, the colonized mimicking the superior art of the colonizer.

Archer's analysis of modern art in India rests on reductionist criteria employed by art historians to describe the reception of Western art in the periphery: while successful imitation was a form of aping, imperfect imitation represented a failure of learning.

If it seems that there are no limits to what Western artists can appropriate from the peripheries, let me turn to what the

Western canon suppresses. The relation of the early abstract painters to Eastern thought arouses strong emotions.

The facts of the case are not so much in dispute as their implication and significance for the rise of abstract art. In other words, what importance can we attach to the role of these ideas in the paintings of Piet Mondrian, Kazimir Malevich, and Wassily Kandinsky, the three iconic figures of modernism? The formalists dismiss such interest as at best inconsequential and at worst an aberration; the transcendentalists affirm the central role of Eastern thought in nonfigurative art, sustained by Sixten Ringbom's painstaking research on the connection between Theosophy and abstract art, along with the contributions of other scholars.

This interest culminated in 1986 in the ambitious exhibition The Spiritual in Art: Abstract Painting 1890-1985, held in Chicago, Los Angeles, and finally the Hague.

The extent to which the abstract painters absorbed Eastern thought, discovered via Theosophy, is seen to be compromised because of that movement's dabbling in the occult. Yet surely it is possible to separate the wheat from the chaff and discern the genuine elements of Buddhist and Hindu philosophy in Theosophy that colored the intellectual makeup of these artists.

Piet Mondrian is known to have admired the mystical poem Bhagavad Gita and the philosophy of the Upanishads, and he treasured the Indian mystic Jiddu Krislinamurti's "little book" until his death. In 1914 Mondrian recorded in his notebook that he was developing the idea that art belonged to a higher spiritual realm that transcended the natural, a sentiment that owed as much to Neoplatonism as to the Upanishads.

Mondrian also believed that the elementary forms were abstract, and they were the constituent elements of nonobjective art. Nonfigurative art has been described as an alliance of aesthetics and mysticism, "the essential stages of Mondrian's move from representation to pure abstraction." One of the striking concepts for Mondrian as well as other pioneers of abstraction was the metaphysical idea of the absolute, which enabled them to break with what they saw as the last vestiges of mimesis, proclaiming the reality as belonging to the spiritual.

Strikingly, the concept of nature was considered relative to the spiritual absolute, as the imperfect material world was to the perfection of mathematics. The idea recalls the definition of mathematics in ancient Indian thought, though the absolute is also a core Hegelian notion ultimately going back to Plato. Again, in the Upanishads, the Absolute (Brahman) is imagined as noncorporeal, the very antithesis of materiality and impermanence, ideas close to Mondrian's interpretation of the absolute, as his denial of the self paralleled the dissolution of reality in the Upanishads. Absolute purity, divested of all the material associations, chief among them illusionism, could not be achieved within empiricist foundations.

John Golding is the most recent scholar to have recourse to the aesthetics of autonomy in order to reiterate the essentially formalist foundations of abstract art. In his Mellon Lecture of 1997, he argued that "at its best and most profound, abstract painting is heavily imbued with meaning, with content, and that, in order to make this content palpable, new formal pictorial innovations must be found to express it." Rightly considering Mondrian's encounter with Cubism as the turning point in his oeuvre, Golding then asserts that the artist's purest and austere quest for ideal simplicity to be uncontaminated by spiritual elements. Yet almost in the same breath, as an aside, Golding remarks that Mondrian's rejection of Renaissance materialism was predicated on equating flatness with spirituality.

The work of Cézanne, Cubism, and Futurism were welldocumented formative influences for Kazimir Malevich. However, as he moved toward pure abstraction he began to search for a philosophy that he felt most resonated with its spirit. The celebrated Indian savant Swami Vivekananda's Chicago lectures, published in 1904, introduced the Russian painter to the Upanishads, which certainly made some, and I would maintain substantial, contribution to his idea of pure geometry, the absolute, and the illusory nature of the threedimensional universe, the Upanishadic maya.

He defined Suprematism's "zero of form" as "objectlessness" rather than abstraction as such, which is again reminiscent of the Upanishadic sunyata (state of nought) and notions of consciousness, infinity, and the self. I do not wish to labour the point, except to mention that in ancient Indian sacred geometry, unlike the restless circle, the square is the ultimate and ideal form and the site of the absolute (Brahmasthana), because of its essential stasis. One cannot help recall that the most original creations of Malevich were based on the square, the painting The Black Square being the ultimate expression. These metaphysical ideas were no less important than his interest in Futurism and formalist theories.

The evidence that Kandinsky's spiritual progress from the mystical Russian faith to Eastern philosophy, including yogic meditation, paralleled the dissolution of corporeal form in his art is even more persuasive. Although publicly reticent about his debt to Eastern thought, Kandinsky was prepared to express it in sympathetic company.

When Michael Sadler, a champion of modernist art in Britain, and his son visited the artist in Germany in 1912, they were "so fascinated by [his] mystical outlook that they missed the last train...." Golding, recognizing the unique importance of the modernist text On the Spiritual in Art but unconvinced about ideas from outside the discourse of modernism, is puzzled by what to him seems an anomaly in the Russian's worldview. Art since 1900 simply dismisses the "unwelcome religious flavour" of Kandinsky's On the Spiritual in Art.

Both formalists and transcendentalists marshal strong arguments in support of their particular point of view. The presence of the purely formalist Western aspects in abstract painting, its part of the art historical continuum, and "exotic" Eastern spiritual elements are viewed as essentially agonistic and incompatible.

The insistence on the truth of one to the exclusion of the other rules out the possibility of the coexistence of contradictory elements in an individual's mental makeup. In the pages of the avant-garde journal De Stijl, for instance, idealist aesthetics, industrial mechanics, Utopian politics, and rationalism intermingled with notions of spirituality. The history of the avant-garde has contributed to the disjunction between rationalism and irrationalism, writes Néstor García Canclini, who proposes that a theory of art that transcends the antagonism between thought and intuition would contribute to a reconfiguration of the dilemmas of the late twentieth century.

One argument in favour of the formalists is that Eastern thought was filtered through the garbled preachings of Helena Blavatsky, the cofounder, with Henry Steel Olcott, of Theosophy. As a movement, Theosophy attracted controversy, and Mme Blavatsky was occasionally accused of charlatanism. And yet its more philosophical aspects had influenced a number of leading late-nineteenth- and twentiethcentury figures, among them the feminist Annie Besant.

However, even allowing for the limitations of Theosophy, it is more to the point to explain the attraction these antimaterialist doctrines held for these artists. If Eastern thought fired the artists' imagination with the promise of an alternative intellectual standpoint, why was there a need for such an alternative in the first place?

By the mid-nineteenth century, the crisis of capitalism gave rise to a series of social thinkers from John Ruskin, William Morris, Lev Tolstoy, and Karl Marx to a whole range of Utopian critics of urban modernity. Many artists rebelled as much against Victorian materialism as against mimetic art; some sought to restore the integrated community that had been lost with the rise of urban modernity and had led to the alienation of individuals from society. To many, nonindustrial societies held out the promise of social integration.

Modernists, especially abstract painters, who "felt" at home in this world, sought affinities with the "decorative" art of the "primitive" and non-Western peoples untouched by "materialistic" Renaissance naturalism. That is when they turned to Eastern, particularly Indian, philosophy, which is described by David Pan as "the intellectual context of the abstract method." In light of creative needs that went beyond mere fashion, they engaged critically with Eastern philosophy rather than merely reproducing Eastern spiritual concepts in their works.

They found sustenance in a form of syncretism that offered fresh existential and epistemologica! possibilities. It is this vision of primitivism that served as an alternative to Enlightenment rationality. These artists viewed the distinction between the primitive and the modern as the difference between the spiritual and the material dimensions of human existence.

Charles W. Haxthausen has explored the writings of Wilhelm Hausenstein, one of the German "expressionist" critics who longed for the restoration of an integrated German critics to overcome the alienation between artist and society. The goal of this avant-garde theory "was an anonymous, collective art, integrated with the praxis of life..." Kandinsky and Marc, editors of the journal Blaue Reiter, were characterized by Haxthausen as "romantic anti-capitalists" who saw avant-garde art as heralding a new age of spirituality parallel to Eastern thought.

Colonial mentality deems cultural transmissions to be a one-way process flowing from the Occident, but fascination with the East has periodically surfaced in the West in different guises. In the eighteenth century, it gave rise to the Oriental Renaissance, which was in many ways as influential as the "first" Renaissance. The following passage in J. J. Clarke may well apply to the controversy over abstract artists' debt to the East.

There is a persistent reluctance to accept that the West could ever have borrowed anything of significance from the East, or to see the place of Eastern thought within the Western tradition... as only a trivial part of a wider reaction against the modern world.

For some the Orient is still associated with shady occultist flirtations, the unconscious rumblings of the repressed irrational urges of a culture that has placed its faith in scientific rationalism.

ART AND THE PATHOLOGY OF INFLUENCE

The above debate seems to hinge on the question of influence, and influence has been the key epistemic tool, implicitly or explicitly, in the asymmetrical valuations of cultural exchanges between Eastern and Western art.

As an art historical category, though, influence ignores significant aspects of cultural encounters, especially the enriching value of the cross-fertilization of cultures that has nourished societies since time immemorial.

These exchanges of ideas and forms need not necessarily be interpreted through ideas of domination and dependence. Rudolf Wittkower, the great authority on the migration of symbols across ancient cultures, traced the fascinating story of how the West received and transformed images and motifs from the Orient in an interaction that had no basis in political competition.

In this respect, we can learn useful lessons from historians of material culture, who seek to study in a less value-laden way the global exchange of artifacts of material culture.

They include within their purview not only objects of high art but also ceramics, glass, metalwork, textiles, and furnishings. Drawing on the theoretical perspective of the knowledge economy, they analyse the transmission of technical skills across borders, setting them in a historical framework as an aspect of global connection.

The advent of modernism in Asia, Africa, and Latin America could thus be studied as the transfer of technology, which in other fields is accepted as part of the global process of cross-fertilization.

However, such a perception is already defined by a discourse of power, colored by assertions of Western superiority and consequent feelings of inferiority, resignation, denial, and resistance on the part of non-Western nations.

In the nineteenth century, this political dimension was exacerbated during a period of the West's ascendancy, when peoples were ranked within a global hierarchy of chain of being, race, and evolution. Borrowing from outside the West was inconceivable to the Victorians, who would concede only the Greeks and the Romans as the twin classical giants on whose shoulders European civilization stood. It was seen in the field of science, which was in awe of classical empiricism as the mainspring of the experimental method.

Yet it was the union of empiricism with the Hindu place value system of numbers that laid the foundations of the great scientific revolution that came to fruition only in the eighteenth century.

Nor should one ignore the enormous contributions of the Chinese to Western technology' - paper, printing press, distillery, gunpowder, and the compass, to name the most obvious.

It would be reasonable to accept that the triumph of modern science was a product of a historical situation in the eighteenth century that drew on different traditions, including those that were extraneous to the West but thoroughly internalized. But because of the part the classical world played in European cultural formation (Bildung), the Greek heritage was increasingly taken to be the sole contributor to European parthenogenesis.

In the context of this pervasive ideology of progress, "borrowing" implied the dependence of the inferior culture on the superior and dominant one, an idea nowhere more ubiquitous than in the field of art. It was as natural for the colonized to imitate as it was inconceivable for the colonizer to take part in this exercise.

This may have something to do with Johann Joachim Winckelmann's epithet "noble simplicity and quiet grandeur" for classical art, which swayed generations, including seminal thinkers such as Georg Wilhelm Friedrich Hegel and Marx.

Notions of stylistic influence acquired a special significance for colonial art historians, who were obsessed with tracing the Wrestern grammar of nonWestern modernisms and ranking them within a universalist world order. I can do no better than quote Michael Baxandall's powerful indictment here, describing the obsession with stylistic influence as a curse, or remind ourselves of Harold Bloom's celebrated phrase the "anxiety of influence."

Baxandall writes in Patterns of Intention that artistic influence seems to reverse the active-passive relationship, "which the historical actoi experiences, and the inferential beholder will wish to take into account." He further argues that responding to circumstance, the artist makes an intentional selection from a range of sources. This is a purposeful activity on the artist's part, which involves making conscious choices.

If we discard stylistic genealogy, what can we put in its place? The overdetermined analysis based on the relationship of dependence between the borrower and his or her source is slowly being undermined even by historians of European art.

In an absorbing account of Jacques-Louis David's workshop, Thomas Crow uses the term "emulation" to illuminate the master-pupil relationship in which David paid a moving tribute to his late pupil Jean-Germain Drouais as not only his equal but also someone worthy of emulation. Elizabeth Cropper also deploys emulation to challenge influence as a convenient analytic tool.

Drawing on Thomas Greene's reading of the Italian Humanists, who attempted to set up an active dialogue with ancient classical authors, Cropper explores the "intertextual" character of artistic styles, which engages with past models in a dialectical and even agonistic mode. Such conscious heuristic imitation advertises its derivations, defining itself by asserting its distance from diese sources.

Gaganendranath's relation with Cubism was similarly heuristic. He admired the movement yet felt distanced from it culturally, making it perfectly clear that he was not seeking to reproduce the French Cubists. He once explained to the journalist Kanhaiyalal Vakil that "the new technique is really wonderful as a stimulant."

Nonetheless, the Indian painter's visual conventions continued within the bounds of Oriental art, not least the miniature scale of his works. The visiting English painter William Rothenstein confirmed this when he mentioned that Gaganendranath remained an Oriental "miniaturist with an eye for exquisite lapidary details."

Equally, despite grumbles from the nationalists for abandoning his earlier "Orientalist" style, the artist insisted that Cubism had simply "enabled me to [express] better with my new technique... than I used to do with my old methods." I propose here another explanatory tool for understanding the generation of social and cultural meaning within the context of colonial art.

The concept of paradigm change, postulated by Thomas Kuhn in the history of science, provides a convincing argument for change through adoption. As Kuhn seeks to demonstrate, knowledge develops in a succession of tradition-bound periods, punctuated by revolutionary breaks or, in his term, paradigm shifts.

These shifts occur when a system breaks down, or when anomalies in one paradigm force new paradigms to emerge. New paradigms function by challenging the norms of a given practice that now seems constricting and vulnerable to challenge. The new paradigm in its turn marginalizes practices that no longer conform to their criteria.

The advent of academic naturalism during the colonial era was the first great revolutionary break in India that profoundly transformed art institutions, practices, patronage, genres, materials, as well as artistic style, moving from flat two-dimensional pictures to illusionist naturalism.

The paradigm change ushered in by colonial rule simply made the earlier practice that tied artists to private patronage obsolete. Artists now emerged as independent professionals who depended more on public support and recognition. This phase lasted from the 1850s to about the 1920s.

In the 1920s, the tensions between academic artists and the nationalist purveyors of a Pan-Asian nonnaturalist mode, known as oriental art, forced a second revolutionary break. Artists such as Gaganendranath sought to emancipate themselves from the constrictive and artificial polarity between the two modes of artistic representation, namely, academic naturalism and "decorative" Orientalism.

The language of modernism, signifying changes in artistic imperatives in a rapidly globalizing world, offered the Indian avant-garde a new visual means to challenge the previous artistic paradigm centering on mimetic representation.

Archer had the whole weight of art history behind him in his evaluation of Gaganendranath's paintings. The modernist canon encompasses a great deal more than a simple matter of influence, as its powerful teleology constructs a whole world of belongings and exclusions, the epicenter and its outlying regions.

The linear interpretation of art history boasts a long and distinguished tradition, going back to Giorgio Vasari, whose Lives of the Most Eminent Architects, Painters and Sculptors of Italy created the master narrative for Renaissance art, based on the conquest of visual representation.

Additionally, the stylistic categories, drawn from classical norms, that motivated Vasari 's notion of artistic progress automatically excluded those art forms that did not conform to them. The Vasarian master narrative defined Florence, Rome, and Venice as centers of innovation, categorizing other regions in Italy as sites of delayed growth and imitation.

As it has been argued in studies of Renaissance art inspired by Vasari, periphery is not a matter of geography but of art history.

Vasari did not just valorize the three centers within Italy, he also displayed prejudice against the art of other nations. In the late eighteenth century, Winckelmann, whose own preference was for Greek art, reconfigured and reified these prejudices by formulating climatic, national, and racial differences in art as objective facts.

Vasarian teleology enjoyed the added confidence of a positivist art history in the nineteenth century, as evolutionary doctrines enabled art historians to map world art from its putative "primitive" base to its triumphal climax in Victorian history painting, with Oriental art occupying the intervening space.sBy this token, Indian miniature painting, a species of Oriental art, though charming in itself, was assigned a respectable middle rank in world art. The nationalist response to colonial art history in India was to develop a decorative form of Oriental art in repudiation of academic naturalism.

To be sure, the Western avant-garde was in the forefront of challenging the hegemonic claims of academic art, and its revolutionary message provided inspiration for the avantgarde in the colonized countries. But the implied hierarchy in the relation between centre and periphery could not be so easily resolved.

In the cultural economy of global modernity, all artistic productions in Asia, Africa, and Latin America became marginal to the preoccupations of the core, that is, the art of Paris and later postwar London or New York. Set against the originary discourse of the avant-garde, emanating from these metropolitan centers, other modernisms were silenced as derivative and suffering from a time lag because of their geographic locations.

Yet the significant point is that the centre-periphery relation is not only one of geography but also of power and authority that implicates race, gender, and sexual orientation. Viewed from this perspective, the concept of the peripher)' assumes important theoretical significance. Modernism created its own tacit exclusions and inclusions, instances of which are scattered throughout Art since 1900.

Chapter 8

A Counter Discourse of Modernism

With such a powerfully embedded ideology that privileges certain definitions of art to the exclusion of others, how can we shift the centre of gravity of the modernist discourse? We need to destabilize Vasarian concepts of artistic centre and periphery while loosening the linearity of art history, something given unique authority in Hegel's theory of artistic progress as the inevitable unfolding of the world spirit. First, we must seek explanatory tools that adequately describe art practices and their social and cultural milieus in the so-called outlying areas, taking into account the peculiar contextual needs and expressions of regional artistic productions and consumptions, along with the local assertions of global concerns.

I propose below some tentative strategies for recovering the counter discourse of modernism, largely drawn from my own work on Indian modernism covering several decades, which I hope will be of relevance to other "peripheral" regions, as well as help fashion more nuanced art histories drawing on the richness of truly global experiences.

At the outset, I must acknowledge the efforts of recent scholars to find strategies of empowerment through new readings of the avant-garde in Asia, Africa, and Latin America. Visual studies and postcolonial theory have made valuable contributions toward destabilizing the modernist canon and challenging hierarchy and value in art history, prising open the narrow empirical connoisseurship-focused discipline of art history involving analysis of style, iconography, and documentation.

Its own practice owes debts to a postMarxian discursive approach based on semiotics, poststructuralism, and psychoanalysis.

The theorists of visual culture seek to erase the distinction between the fine arts and a range of material objects that had been excluded from the canon, thereby seeking to destroy the exclusivity of the concept of high "art." Keith Moxey makes a valuable point in support of the inclusive concept of "visual culture" that is not restricted to what is generally defined as high art in the West, which tends to perpetuate the global inequality in power relations.

His view is analogous to Pierre Bourdieu's pertinent comment that modes of representations are essentially expressions of political conflicts. John Clark, basing his view on the semiotic theory expounded by Umberto Eco, describes Western modernism as a "closed" system of discourse, which cannot accommodate new modernist discourses to which the regions beyond the West have given rise. And yet the most exciting aspect of modernisms across the globe is their plurality, heterogeneity, and difference, a "messy" asymmetrical quality that makes them all the more vital and replete with possibilities.

Geeta Kapur seeks to restore the Indian artist's agency through what she terms a radical restructuring of the international avant-garde. Wifredo Lam, as an artist of multiple heritage, is "a deft juggler of cultural modes, as a potent symbol of the intermixing of cultures that will flower in our increasingly 'multicultural' civilization," as described by Jason Edward Kaufman. The Tanzania!) artist, writer, and activist Everlyn Nicodemus develops the notion of "mutual appropriation," contending that "our urge for change and modernization is as universal as our sense of tradition."

A most persuasive tool for unsettling the hegemonic canon has been the concept of hybridity. Among Latin American scholars, Néstor García Canclini uses the concept to propose "multi-temporal heterogeneities," while Gerardo

Mosquera sets forth the notion of decentralized international culture to argue that the peripheries are ceasing to be defined entirely by the notion of tradition.

They are emerging as multiple centers of international culture as well as strengthening local developments in a constant process of cultural hybridization. Hybridity, a biological term, is theorized by Homi K. Bhabha in order to empower the diaspora thrown up by global migration that automatically generates situations of inclusion and exclusion.

"An interstitial passage between fixed identifications," he writes, "opens up the possibility of a cultural hybridity that entertains difference without an assumed or imposed hierarchy."

The compelling nature of his formulation for art history and its promise lie as much in challenging the essentialism of cultural difference asserted by the colonial order as in countering the monolithic discourse of the avant-garde.

Some concerns have been raised about the theory regarding its limited ability to explain the role of artistic agency and the transformation of material culture through the integration of foreign elements. "Because of its semantic associations and resonances," Andrew Causey, for instance, cautions, "hybridity is a metaphor that diffuses agency and unintentionally masks possible relations of power."

While the theory of hybridity undoubtedly offers empowerment to the minorities of multiple heritage who are marginalized by what are characterized as "insiders" rooted in a culture, there are artists to whom the concept of hybridity can hardly do justice. For these artists outside the West, national identity has furnished a language of resistance to colonial art, especially in a period when many Asian, African, and Latin American countries were struggling to create a counternarrative in answer to the dominant canon.

A group of Latin American art historians were unhappy with Art since 1900 precisely because it failed to recognize that in the countries south of the United States, modernism, modernity, and modernization have been intimately tied to the construction of cultural identity or relate to the disjunction "where the dreams and desires of modernity are fully developed but modernization is not yet wholly established."

However valuable hybridity is, an unintended consequence of valorizing it to the exclusion of other possibilities would be to consign to oblivion artists such as Roy by the very fact of their not resisting through an "interstitial" narrative. But they, too, are major players in the global process of modernity. The difficulties of studying contemporary art forms that do not conform to a particular avant-garde discourse have led art historians to propose alternative modernisms or regional modernisms. One of the thoughtful recent contributions to the enlarging of the canon has been a set of essays entitled Cosmopolitan Modernisms, edited by Kobena Mercer, who comments on the unanticipated consequences of the global processes of modernity that create a two-way traffic between the West and the rest.

COSMOPOLITAN PRIMITIVISM

Modernism is generally presented as a hypostatic image, beyond time and space. Yet the Western avant-garde, with all its achievements, we may remind ourselves, has been historically situated with its own set of conventions, even though its experience can and has enriched other traditions. Therefore, we may renounce Art History in the sense used by Hans Belting but pay closer attention to particular art histories, the contexts of their ideologies, contradictions, and fractures in their engagement with modernity.

To my mind, multiple local possibilities illuminate the global processes of modernity more effectively than a grand globalizing narrative, which is more likely than not to perpetuate a relationship of power. My particular field, as I have indicated, is the rise of the avant-garde in India in the 1920s, and I have tried to show that its history can be meaningfully mapped within the context of nationalist resistance to the British Empire. It is possible to formulate concepts that will address the particular interactions between global modernity, artistic production, and the construction of national identity not just in India but also in regions that seek to resist the colonial-capitalist cultural dominance.

This inflected narrative of global modernity, I would argue, clearly yields another possible way of restoring the artist's agency in the context of colonial empires, and that is by analyzing art practices and reception as a cultural document that is historically situated. One serious criticism of influence as an analytic tool is that it views artists as passive agents of transmission rather than active agents with the ability to exercise choice.

A little while ago I raised the question of centre and periphery in connection with Vasarian categories. But centre-periphery also relates to the wider politics of the colonial order. One of the powerful aspects of modern nationalism has been the interplay of the global and the local in the urban space of colonial culture, led by the Westerneducated intelligentsia, who acted as surrogates for the nation. Colonial expansion gave rise to the worldwide phenomenon of the hybrid cosmopolis, often favoring port cities or entrepôts for the circulation of material goods mediated by local merchants and middlemen.

These cosmopolitan cities emerged as flourishing centers of cultural exchange. I want to use the example of Calcutta as a hybrid metropolis here to explain the role of this urban centre in the growth of the first avant-garde tendency in India.

As the capital of British India, it became the locus of colonial encounters, its Bengali inhabitants emerging as beneficiaries as well as interlocutors of colonial culture. In the nineteenth century, the Bengal renaissance pioneered Indian modernity, a hybrid intellectual enterprise underpinned by a dialogic relation between the colonial language, English, and the modernized vernacular, Bengali. English as the colonial medium of instruction gave Bengali elite access to the Enlightenment, opening up a window to the West, prompting one of the finest flowerings of a modern literary tradition. The great poet Rabindranath Tagore, possibly the bestknown cultural figure in the interbellum years, was a product of the Bengal renaissance.

Modernity, which followed European expansion in India, gave rise to a globally "imagined community" based on print capitalism; its membership was as vast as it was anonymous, no longer having the need for face-to-face communication and yet sharing a corpus of ideas on modernity. The Bengali intelligentsia admirably demonstrates the negotiation of the wider cosmopolitan modernity through the printed medium, since it had a limited acquaintance with expatriate Europeans and even less so with distant Britain. To explain this community's critical engagement with modern thought, I put forward the notion of the "virtual cosmopolis" here.

This was essentially a hybrid city of the imagination, which engendered elective affinities between the elites of the centre and the periphery on the level of intellect and creativity.

Their shared outlook was possible not only through the printed media but also through major hegemonic languages, such as English in the case of the Bengalis in India, as well as French and Spanish disseminated through colonial encounters. In sum, the colonial intelligentsia negotiated their transactions with modernity essentially by means of virtual cosmopolitanism.

Cosmopolitanism is an inevitable consequence of global technology transfers and communication and transport revolutions.

Arjun Appadurai, who theorizes globalization, draws our attention to the contradictory pulls of homogenization and heterogenization, to which the colonial orders, based in European capitals and spread throughout the nonWestern world, gave rise." Mercer prefers the term "cosmopolitan," as a sharper conceptual tool in the study of worldwide interactions of artistic modernism, to the confusing array of terms such as "global," "international," "cross-cultural," and "culturally diverse."

In sympathy with Aristotelian universals, the philosopher Kvvame Anthony Appiah views cosmopolitan values as the thread that ties human beings together. He rejects both the politics of difference and nationalist fabrications of exclusive claims to cultural patrimony, reiterating everyone's right to share the common human heritage. He has faith in the ability of the individual to transcend parochialism, to demand to be a citizen of the world.

While the imaginary citizen may find this desirable, he or she may not have the wherewithal to achieve such a world affiliation. Power and authority confer visibility and inclusion, in the historically uneven relation between centre and peripher)', allegorized in the mutual relationship of Luis Buñuel and Jorge Luis Borges.

Borges once asserted, "I believe... our patrimony is the universe; we should essay all themes and we cannot limit ourselves to purely Argentinian subjects in order to be Argentinian." In his autobiography, My Last Sigh, the Spanish filmmaker found the Argentinian guilty of self-absorption and pretension, inflicting the ultimate snub with the telling aside, "as we say in Spanish."

In the context of the present global diaspora, recognizing the outcome of forced migration, exile, and other border crossings, James Clifford puts forward "discrepant cosmopolitanism" as a notion of "cosmopoli tan ism-from-below" that generates lived experiences of unfinished local and global identities. This cosmopolitan mode of the powerless and the disadvantaged refers essentially to globalization from below.

Even though I am speaking of an elite in India who are not physically dispossessed, my definition of virtual cosmopolitanism is closer to Clifford's than to Appiah's because of the uneven power relation between centre and periphery, and between the colonial powers and the subject nations in my period of study. Of course, the cosmopolitan ideal can be full of ambiguities, and being well versed in cosmopolitanism often may connote imbibing the values of the hegemonic centre or of the colonial regime.

However, the important point I want to make here is that asymmetrical power relations do not prevent the free flow and cross-fertilization of ideas on the level of "virtuality," as has happened across the globe in the age of knowledge and communications revolution in the previous century.

How does virtual cosmopolitanism enable the periphery, whether formerly colonized or not, to contribute to the project of modernity on an intellectual level? One of the most creative ideas developed by Indian avant-garde artists in the 1920s in their exercise of virtual cosmopolitanism was to develop an empowering concept of primitivism. It enabled them to construct their resistance to urban industrial capitalism and the ideology of progress, the cornerstone of colonial empires. Jamini Roy, with whom I began, was one of the most striking exponents of artistic primitivism in India, but the tendency spawned other remarkable figures as well.

Primitivism, we are aware, represents the romantic longing of a complex society for the simplicity of premodern existence. The crisis of the industrial age, which was traced back to Enlightenment rationality, made nineteenth-century Utopians embrace primitivism with fervor. Though primitivism helped temper the relentless progressivism of colonial-industrial modernity, one cannot ignore the inner tensions and contradictions within the concept, described by Edward Said as "the age-old antetype of Europe... a fecund night out of which European rationality developed." Primitivism stands charged with complicity in sustaining colonial hegemony in its representations of the non-West and in its consumption of primitive ait.

It is characterized as a fetishistic discourse that evokes simultaneous fear of and desire for the Other. Western artists have been both primitivism 's beneficiaries, in terms of an enlarged formal armory, and its unwitting victims, because by "articulating their own fantasies about the meaning of the objects and about the peoples who created them, artists have been party to the erasure of the self-representations of colonized peoples in favour of Western representations of their realities." Nonetheless, as Foster points out, the avant-garde's identification with the primitive, "however imaged as dark, feminine, and profligate, remained identification with white, patriarchal, bourgeois society."

We have already encountered some of the best-known cases of primitivism inspiring the avant-garde, which declared its allegiance to primitive art, children's art, and the art of the mentally ill.

The naïveté of primitive art is a myth. African art, for instance, is governed by strict aesthetic conventions, but the potent myth helped emancipate Western artists from the constraints of classical taste, bringing about a remarkable paradigm shift. The other primitivism, we may remind ourselves, was the critical modernism of nonobjective art. For the avant-garde, the artistic discourse of primitivism opened up the possibility of aesthetic globalization as part of art historical consciousness.

The very ambiguities, instabilities, and fractures within primitivism provided the colonized a singular weapon with which to interrogate the capitalist/colonial world of modernity, enabling them to produce a counter modern discourse of resistance.

In the West, the very flexibility of primitivism offered endless possibilities, ranging from "going native" to a radical questioning of Western positivism." What the periphery did was to turn the outward "gaze" of Europe back to the West itself, deploying the very same device of cultural criticism to interrogate the urban-industrial values of the colonial empires. In many ways, Mahatma Gandhi was the most profound "primitivist" critic of the twentieth century. In 1909, his revolutionary booklet Hind Siuaraj, or Indian Home Rule set out his anticolonial resistance based on a critique of Western civilization as a slave to the machine.

Thus, primitivism as a critical form of modernity formed a bridge between Eastern and Western critics of industrial capitalism that affected the peripheries no less than the West. Primitivists did not deny the importance of technology in contemporary life; they simply refused to accept the teleological certainty of modernity."

The politicized "rural ism" that emerged in the 1920s in India was the particular Indian expression of a global response to modernity, as the definition of nationhood shifted from the pan-Indian to the local. It inspired a whole generation of artisLS, among whom Jamini Roy was the most original. One of Roy's initial concepts was a series of moral contrasts he made between rural and urban values; rural honesty pitted against urban "decadence." His aim was to restore through art the precolonial community that had been severed from national life during British rule, alienating the elite from its cultural roots. The intimate connection between the vitality of an artistic tradition and its mythological richness became the central plank in his theory of collective art. Through the folk idiom, Roy sought to restore the link between art and society, thereby repudiating artistic individualism and the "aura" of a work of art, the twin hallmarks of colonial art.

These were the structural affinities between Roy's primitivism and the avant-garde critics of modernity in the West such as Hausenstein, although they arrived at their respective critiques of modernity through different routes. Another feature shared by Roy and the Western primitivists was the rejection of universale, whether from a unifying "capitalist" or from a "nationalist" perspective. Roy argued that the mythology that nourished a community art had of necessity to be local and timeless.

Roy's belief in political heterogeneity, his insistence on "locality" as the site of the nation, and his preference for multiple aesthetic possibilities were uncannily similar to the ideas of the German Expressionists. I call these similarities structural affinities in a virtual global community, since neither knew the existence of the other.

At the same time, one must recognize the important differences between the primitivism of the centre and the periphery. The Western primitivists were chiefly concerned with the predicament of urban existence, whereas Indian artists used primitivism as an effective weapon against colonial culture.

While Western primitivists aimed at merging art with life in a disavowal of the aesthetics of autonomy, they never ceased to believe in the unique quality of aesthetic experience. Roy endeavored to erase it, deliberately seeking to subvert the distinction between individual and collaborative contribution in a work of art.

Roy's objective of making the signature meaningless was his playful way of undercutting what Walter Benjamin called the "aura" of a masterpiece. In addition, he turned his studio into a workshop to reproduce his works cheaply. What the cognoscenti simply failed to grasp was Roy's emergence as a radical critic of colonialism through his art. The Indian painter deliberately eschewed artistic individualism and the notion of artistic progress, the two "flagships" of colonial art.

But this is not what necessarily made him the most remarkable painter of pre-independence India. Roy's search for the formal equivalent to his primitivist ideology eventually led him to the Bengali village scroll painting, the pat, which afforded an ideal synthesis of formalist strength and political theory. Through intense concentration and a ruthless ability to pare the inessential details, Jamini Roy created an avant-garde art of a monumental simplicity and deep social commitment.

TOWARD A NEW ART HISTORY

Its being attempted here to recuperate the importance of the artistic modernisms of Asia, Africa, Latin America, and Australia, which are regarded as derivative of the W'estern avantgarde.

Communication and transport revolutions, massive population displacements, and other global processes led to the intense cross-fertilization of cultures and the growth of cosmopolitan values, chief among them the emergence of new art forms.

In the West, avant-garde art, nourished by ethnographic arts and Eastern thought, broke away from the constraints of academic naturalism and classical taste. Modernism spread worldwide because of the West's dominance, and yet modernism's radical message inspired non-Western regions to create their own art of resistance against the colonial order.

Despite its radical agenda, the Western avant-garde failed to take into account either the progressive heterogenization of art or the richness and creativity of art practices in the peripheries.

Its limitations stem from the monolithic, linear narrative of an art history that does not allow for difference, in part a reflection of the unequal power relations between centre and periphery. My argument contributes to the recent debates on the need to shift the centre of gravity from the originary discourse to a more heterogeneous definition of global modernism, incorporating the changes that have taken place in the twentieth century. It responds to the challenge of transnational art, calling into question the "purity" of the modernist canon and the consequent imputation of the derivative character of the periphery.

The rich variety of contemporary art around the world and its powerful advocates have, of course, helped to blunt the self-assurance of the canon; my conviction remains that old ideas will continue to seep out of the fault lines unless we consciously interrogate old ideas and their colonial antecedents and seek to replace them with a more inclusive art history.

In the final analysis, the new art history will be enriched through a contextuaily grounded study of nonWestern modernism that engages with the socially constructed meaning of artistic production. This will go a long way toward contesting the commonplace that peripheral modernisms are merely attempts to catch up with the originary avant-garde discourse.

Surrealism in art, poetry, and literature uses numerous techniques and games to provide inspiration. Many of these are said to free imagination by producing a creative process free of conscious control. The importance of the unconscious as a source of inspiration is central to the nature of surrealism.

The Surrealist movement has been a fractious one since its inception. The value and role of the various techniques has been one of many subjects of disagreement. Some Surrealists consider automatism and games to be sources of inspiration only, while others consider them starting points for finished works. Others consider the items created through automatism to be finished works themselves, needing no further refinement.

An echo poem is a poem written using a technique invented by Aurélien Dauguet in 1972. The poem is composed by one or more persons, working together in a process as follows. The first "stanza" of the poem is written on the left-hand column of a piece of paper divided into two columns. Then the "opposite" of the first stanza, opposite in whatever sense is appropriate to the poem, is composed in the right-hand column of the page. The writing is done automatically and often the "opposite" stanza is composed of a sound correspondence to the first stanza.

For a longer work, the third stanza can then begin in the left-hand column as an "opposite" or a sound correspondence to what preceded it in the right-hand column. Then the fourth stanza might be an "opposite" or sound correspondence to what preceded it in the left-hand column, and so forth. When the poem is completed, the opposite of the last phrase, line, or sentence, generally serves as the title.

This is unrelated to the non-Surrealist echo verse form which appears as a dialogue between the questions of a character and the answers of the nymph Echo.

ECLABOUSSURE

Eclaboussure is a process in Surrealist painting where oil paints or watercolours are laid down and water or turpentine is splattered, then soaked up to reveal random splatters or dots where the media was removed. This technique gives the appearance of space and atmosphere. It was used in paintings by Remedios Varo.

ENTOPTIC GRAPHOMANIA

Entoptic graphomania is a surrealist and automatic method of drawing in which dots are made at the sites of impurities in a blank sheet of paper, and lines are then made between the dots; these can be either "curved lines... or straight lines." Ithell Colquhoun described its results as "the most austere kind of geometric abstraction." It is apparently to be distinguished from other "entoptic" methods of drawing or art-making.

The method was invented by Dolfi Trost, who as the subtitle of his 1945 book ("*Vision dans le cristal. Oniromancie obsessionelle. Et neuf graphomanies entoptiques*") suggests, included nine examples therein.

This method of "indecipherable writing" (see below) was supposedly an example of "surautomatism," the controversial theory put forward by Trost and Gherashim Luca in which surrealist methods would be practiced that "went beyond" automatism.

In *Dialectique de Dialectique* they had proposed the further radicalization of surrealist automatism by abandoning images produced by artistic techniques in favour of those "resulting from rigorously applied scientific procedures," allegedly cutting the notion of "artist" out of the process of creating images and replacing it with chance and scientific rigour.

However, the question has arisen whether an algorithm should be used to determine in what order to connect the dots to maintain the "automatic" nature of the method. The method has been compared to the "voronoi mathematical progression."

The general argument of this book is that the role of the creative, 'artistic' imagination has been regrettably neglected in courses of professional education. It is based on several years' experience of courses for professional practitioners, where participants explore and represent their professional practice through 'artistic', 'imaginative' forms of writing, in particular, 'fiction'.

We usually think of the term 'fiction' as referring to events that didn't actually happen, characters who don't actually exist, i.e. a sort of 'fantasy'—as opposed to the 'facts' or 'theory' of 'non-fiction'. And that is indeed part of what this book is about—exploring experience by *imagining* 'stories'. But the word 'fiction' also has a broader meaning, derived from its Latin origin, 'fingere'—meaning 'to shape, to fashion, to mould', and it is this meaning which is more central to our argument.

So writing 'fictions', in the title above, refers generally to the process of exploring and reflecting on the meanings of experience by representing it in forms of writing which have been shaped by the writer's imagination. By 'imagination' we don't just mean general mental agility and resourcefulness; we mean specifically the creative faculty which shapes the raw material of experience into *artistic* form.

Of course, the artistic imagination uses many different media (paint, music, dance, sculpture, and so on) and so our general argument could, in principle, be expanded and adapted to suggest the value of all these media in exploring the meanings of our professional experience. But we focus on just one medium—writing.

We celebrate the learning potential of the writing process, but suggest that the largely analytical forms of writing in which we are usually asked to explore and represent our understanding of experience are too limited: they do not draw on artistic and imaginative capacities which we all possess, so that many people are prevented from doing justice to the power and subtlety of their thinking.

Hence, our argument is not simply that the artistic imagination could play a larger role in professional learning, but that it *should* do so.

Most of the book is centred on examples of imaginative work by a range of professional practitioners (nurses, social workers, schoolteachers, managers, university lecturers, counsellors) exploring their practice by means of stories, poems, satires, fictionalised descriptions, etc. We begin with these examples almost immediately, but this brief prologue provides a preliminary statement, a general summary and a 'menu' for what is to follow.

In an important respect, this book is a challenge—a challenge to current conceptions of the role of imaginative literature in society and in education. The world of literary art is conventionally seen as the specialist realm of famous novelists, dramatists and poets, in which the rest of us think of ourselves as merely spectators.

But let us remember that the term 'artistry' is regularly applied to common features of our everyday performances. There is, we say, an 'art' to parenting, to packing a suitcase, to driving a car, to organising a party, and—of course—to the skilful practices of nursing, social work, teaching, management, and so on.

The 'artistry' of reflective practice, says Donald Schön, refers to that close link between expert action and understanding which occurs whenever we deal sensitively and effectively with 'situations of uncertainty, instability, uniqueness, and value-conflict'. In other words, 'artistry' is required on all those many occasions when there is no simple general rule, no single 'right way' of doing things.

And yet, in spite of Schön's repeated references to the artistry of skilful professional performance, he nowhere suggests that artistic means of expression might be valuable or appropriate as a way of representing practitioners' understanding of their work.

But if many (or even most) people regularly demonstrate a capacity for artistry in their actions, why should we not assume that they can use artistic means for expressing their understandings of those actions?

And indeed, our work suggests that professional practitioners do indeed have a capacity for representing and exploring their professional lives in the artistic medium of fiction, which they themselves find both surprising and impressive. The examples presented in this and the following chapters are intended to show the scope and nature of their work and to indicate its professional value.

In this way our argument is fundamentally about widening access to advanced qualifications: it introduces formats for representing professional understanding which enable practitioners to draw on the full range of their cultural resources and the full range of their capacities (including imaginative empathy), rather than requiring them always to present their understandings within the restricted but normally dominant modes of 'description' and 'analysis'.

In our work over the past six years, we have developed two approaches to the use of imaginative writing as a medium for reflection: first, the writing and sharing of short fictional stories; and second, the production of what we term 'patchwork texts', in which different forms of writing are 'shaped', 'fashioned' and assembled to explore the relationship between a variety of perspectives.

Both approaches involve the sharing of short pieces of writing, so that writers can learn from several readers how their writing may be interpreted in different ways, and incorporate this learning as a 'critical commentary' on their original text.

In their different ways, both stories and patchwork texts take advantage of the 'openness' of artistic representations of meaning; they shape experience into meanings which are purposeful and yet ambiguous and inevitably incomplete, and they represent experience in such a way that the form itself suggests that interpretations are open to question and critique.

In this sense, then, they both use the methods of 'fiction' (shaping experience through artistic form) to represent the 'uncertainty, instability, uniqueness and value-conflict' which, as Schön says, is characteristic of professional work. These two approaches to the use of fiction as a method for professional reflection are introduced separately in the next two sections of this chapter.

Let us take a look through this window of the university building and see what is going on. At one end of the room is the usual whiteboard and overhead projector, and a litter of furniture is pushed to the edges to create a space for three separate circles of five or six chairs.

The people occupying the chairs may be social workers, or nurses, or teachers, or health visitors, or school teachers, or university lecturers, or managers, or counsellors, or doctors. And what they are doing—with great concentration—is reading and discussing the 'stories' concerning their professional work which they have written since the previous session, a week ago, when the idea was introduced and the task explained.

At the moment this group is reading a story by Christine Dale, a social worker. It is neatly typed on two sides of A4, about 800 words, and is called 'Great expectations', and can be summed up as follows:

A client has a dream in which a social worker arrives bathed in light, a fairy godmother figure, called Pandora. The client's children are Red Riding Hood, Cinderella and Jack (of beanstalk fame), and in complaining to the social worker of her difficulties with them, she comically turns the three fairy stories of children's heroic initiative upside down to provide symptoms of 'problem' behaviour! ('Jack will not do as he's told.... He's dug up the few flowers that we had and planted this bloody great plant in the back yard.')

The fairy godmother social worker opens her bag and brings out magical gifts for the children—a coach and six white horses. The children step into it and wave to their mother. At this point the client is awakened from her dream by a knocking on the door: 'It's probably that bloody social worker again.'

Now the group have finished reading and start to discuss what they think the story is saying, while Christine listens and makes notes. Clearly, it is about the unrealistic expectations to which the social work profession is subjected. As though they could suddenly wave a wand and change clients' lives!

And anyway, what would happen if such dreams could be realised, since the client seems to have an excessively negative view of her children, and seems even to want them to vanish! Furthermore, the fairy godmother social worker is called Pandora, and her ability to produce limitless gifts from her capacious bag (like Mary Poppins) is actually very worrying, because when Pandora's box was opened, all the evils of humankind were let loose, leaving us only 'hope'.

So this seems to be a story about the dangers of unrealistic expectations on both sides: social workers' powers are limited, and that is as it should be: professionals and clients are both liable to be misled by their 'dreams'. There is a lot of careful poring over the text to see what it actually says, and much serious discussion of the nature of the professional role—as it is and as it is idealised—as well as considerable laughter. The two sessions on story-writing came at the beginning of a course where the participants' main task was the compilation of a 'journal' of reflections on their professional work. The purpose of the story sessions was to broaden their sense of what might be important themes to look for in their own interpretations of events. The suggestion, the previous week, that they should write a fictional story based on their professional life had initially been greeted, as usual, with anxiety.

They associated 'writing' with, on the one hand, producing a professional case report, or on the other, an academic essay or perhaps making descriptive entries in a diary. The notion of a 'story' offered a somewhat worrying form of liberation from these familiar formats and often evoked distant but still powerful memories of not being 'good at' a school subject with the curious title 'English'. Writing 'stories', they had assumed, was either for children or for 'specialists'—Jane Austen, perhaps, or Graham Greene, or Barbara Cartland.

Once upon a time (so the story goes) everyone used to be a story-teller. Every traveller, from nearby or afar, was expected to have a tale to tell; personal experience was recreated and represented, shaped, framed and structured into performances for collective entertainment. And not only travellers: there was pleasure to be gained from celebrating the familiar—anecdotes concerning local events and characters and myths embodying timeless patterns of experience.

So stories were exchanged—round the fire, in the shade of a tree, in the village inn and in the workshop—to pass the time on a journey (Chaucer's *Canterbury Tales*) or even while waiting for an outbreak of plague to abate (Boccaccio's *Decameron*). But, this story continues, that happy time is now past. The popular and universal art of story-telling has been extinguished by the passive habits of reading professionally published novels and watching the products of the film and TV industry.

This is a popular myth of cultural decline, feeding the pleasures of nostalgia as we shake our heads lamenting lost arts, skills and forms of social relationship.

But there is another, contrasting story—that the art of the story is alive and well. In the offices and canteens of workplaces, in the staffrooms of schools, colleges and universities; in pubs and parks, on beaches and round dinner tables; stories are told of the bizarre/comical/extraordinary/ 'typical'/ depressing/delightful behaviour of acquaintances, relatives, colleagues, bosses, customers, students, clients and patients.

The specialisation of life in modern societies means that we are all travellers in realms unknown to some of our neighbours, while the mass media remind us endlessly of the themes which provide a framework of general significance both for public events and for individual experience: technological progress and social suffering, oppression and resistance, catastrophe and hope, glamour and sleaze, the investigation of wrongdoing and incompetence, and (above all) issues of justice and injustice.

Moreover, our ancient ability to tell stories orally is now enhanced by our familiarity with the written narrative. And whereas the oral narrative has to have a simplicity and directness to be immediately understood there and then by the listener, the structure of the written text can be more complex and allusive, because it can be re-read, pondered at length, and analysed in the light of alternative interpretations.

A 'high tech' version of this latter story is also gaining ground, in which stories are shared by e-mail or the internet. At the press of a key or the click of a mouse my story is transmitted to any number of readers, over any distance; and—within minutes—my printer is reeling off their various responses for me to ponder.

Hence the feasibility and the value of writing and sharing stories in a course aiming to develop a 'reflective' understanding of professional experience. The first time I tried out the idea, I shared students' initial anxiety. Now, years later, I can respond to their worries by saying, confidently: 'You will be amazed at how "interesting" you will find other people's stories and how interesting they will find yours. You will also be taken aback at the "quality" of the writing, although that will not be the point at issue because you will be discussing "non-judgementally" what the story seems to mean, what effect it has on you, its professional significance.' Although the initial hesitancy is real, the responses afterwards are immediately enthusiastic. Here are the evaluative comments written by the group we have just been observing:

A story always moves towards an ending. Even though the ending is often ambiguous ('open-ended'), it still represents some sort of temporary closure on a train of thought; the ending is, after all, very often the focus of the shaping process at work. So the question is: how do we 're-open' the ending of a story, in order to continue the reflective exploration that the story has started?

This leads to an important practical question: how can we put together a course of professional reflection in which the process of shaping experience through fiction is continued over a period of several weeks? And our answer is: by constructing a 'patchwork text'.

A patchwork text may start from, or include, a story, but it includes a variety of different forms of writing, each of which provides a further perspective on the others. What defines a patchwork as an artistic medium is that its overall pattern is gradually assembled from smaller pieces, each of which has its own individual pattern.

Thus, just as a patchwork fabric is a texture built from a variety of textures, and a design built up from a variety of sub-designs, a patchwork text is a fiction which is shaped at two levels, or twice over.

Each piece is shaped in itself, but then there is the shaping of the overall meaning, as contrasting pieces of writing are put together, creating unity from the subtle parallels or stark contrasts between them. In the construction of a patchwork fabric this unified design is often planned from the outset, but sometimes each new segment is improvised, as in 'crazy patchwork' where the unity and balance of the overall texture and design emerge gradually and even retrospectively. It is this latter process which is mirrored in the patchwork texts produced for our reflective writing courses.

By way of introducing a further perspective on the concept of the patchwork text, here, to begin with, is a pleasant scene. A narrator is telling us a story—sitting there in front of us and holding our attention—creating for us through her words the people and events she is recounting.

We hang on her words, and she transports us, portraying for us the world she describes with such skill (in selecting and presenting vivid and evocative details) that it seems to become a reality—she makes us feel that we are actually there.

But then, to spoil this pleasant scene, a worry arises: is there not an element of falsity at work here? Because this is, after all, only her view of the story; its reality is a creation, not a description. So if we the readers come to accept this story as reality, we are deceived; and if the story-teller is convinced by her own skill into thinking that her story is the only story, then she also is deceived.

Then, to confuse matters further, here come the philosophers, telling us that there is no such thing as an accurate representation anyway; that all descriptions and narrations are selective—based on value judgements which can never be absolutely justified and which will be shared by some people but never by everyone.

So, the argument runs, our narrator should not deceive us (and herself) by creating the illusion that this story is *the* story, but should make it clear (through the form of the narration) that there are many possible stories, that no story is ever the only story.

Consequently, we should not think of narrators as encompassing an 'overall' perspective within a single authoritative 'voice', and narrators should not think of themselves in this way. Instead, a narrative should recognise that it is merely assembling a variety of voices and perspectives into a 'multi-voiced' text, presenting contrasting points of view through the eyes and voices of different characters, as though they were contributing to a sort of documentary, or as though they were actors in a drama.

Of course, the long tradition of the directly persuasive, single-voiced 'realistic' narrative is still very much with us.

But the less familiar concept of the multi-voiced text (what we have called the patchwork text) has the merit of drawing attention directly to that essential process of fiction which makes it so appropriate a method for exploring the meanings of experience: collecting different aspects and interpretations of events and examining the relationships between them.

Indeed, the argument for the value of the patchwork text could be made more strongly and more generally: its flexibility, together with its essential characteristic of seeking a provisional unity within varied material, make it in many ways a more 'natural' format for the presentation of complex understandings than the sustained analytical essay which has come to play such a dominant role in educational assessment processes.

More precisely, whereas the analytical essay focuses exclusively on cognitive and logical skills (and thus favours the special talents of a minority) the patchwork text enables students also to draw on their imaginative, empathetic, affective and aesthetic modes of understanding, and thus takes more account of current theories of the variegated structure and distribution of human capacities.

Perhaps, therefore, the patchwork text may be, in quite general terms, a more appropriate format for representing the complexity of understanding in a society which hopes to provide 'higher education' as an opportunity for the *majority* of its citizens.

So, how do participants in the reflective writing courses set about constructing a patchwork text? What happens is this. The course participants form small working groups of four or five members, which remain constant throughout the course. Each week everyone brings along several copies of a short piece of writing—a description, an account of an incident, a story, a poem, a dialogue (remembered or imagined), etc. To begin with, interpretations of the meaning of the piece are exchanged by the readers; but then further questions are raised.

How might these events be portrayed from a different point of view? Or, what might be thought of as, perhaps, 'missing' from this piece of writing? Consequently, what is the next piece of writing going to be, which might explore this missing dimension? In this way the group sharing process suggests to the participants how they might continue their writing and their reflections.

The assignment submitted at the end of the course is a selection from the various pieces of writing, arranged in a sequence which may or may not be the order in which they were written, together with a final commentary which analyses the unifying theme(s) underlying the different pieces.

Here, as illustrations, are summaries of two contrasting patchwork texts produced within the reflective writing courses. The texts usually consist of five or six pieces of writing, each about a page or two long, sometimes with short linking commentaries.

ASSESSMENT: 'DREAM OR REALITY?' BY LIZ MORRIS

Liz Morris is a nursing sister with responsibility for the care of all the patients in one ward of a hospital.

The first piece in Liz's patchwork is called 'Dream or reality: the stroke'. John awakes in a strange environment and wonders where he is.

He realises he is in hospital but he does not understand why and has no memory of how he got there. He tries to shout for help, but no words come. He tries to get out of bed to go home to find his wife, but finds that one of his legs will not function.

when the nurses reached him his numb leg was trapped in the cot side and he was half hanging out of the bed. They untangled him and hurled him back up the bed. 'You mustn't do that, Trevor,' they told him, 'You'll hurt yourself.' And then they went. John was left alone.

He goes to sleep hoping to wake and find it was all a dream. When he wakes up and finds his wife there he thinks it was indeed a dream. But why is his wife weeping? 'He reached out to comfort her but his arm would not move. [She] reached out to stroke his hand and he too began to cry'.

The next piece is called 'Dream or reality: 5.30'. A nurse awakes and sees her alarm clock showing 5.30. The beginning of another hectic day. A dizzying round of endless work is described 'with two staff off sick and no help available'. Suddenly:

> she noticed one of the patients climbing over the cot sides. 'Oh no,' she thought, 'Not geriatric gymnastics, not now!' Quickly she called for help and deftly put him back to bed. 'You mustn't do that, Trevor,' she said, wincing slightly as she recalled he preferred to be called John. Still that wasn't important right now, she had other priorities.

Exhausted, she falls asleep and then wakes to find her alarm clock showing 5.30. Thinking that the day has not yet begun she is relieved at the thought that it had all been a dream. But then she realises that the time is 5.30 in the afternoon, and that it has not been a dream.

Then there is a 'Commentary' in which Liz draws attention to the acute shortage of resources in hospitals: nurses are overstretched and cannot offer the care they know they ought to provide, so that the emotional needs of patients like John go unrecognised.

Medical care has become 'a consumer-led industry' with managers always 'on the look out for increased productivity from less staff'. In the final piece of her patchwork, Liz analyses the implications of the previous pieces of writing and provides an overall commentary on the problems of managing a hospital ward.

She also notes that, although the individual pieces convey rather negative messages, she actually believes that the situation contains an 'exciting' opportunity for nurses to respond actively and positively. The crucial challenge is how to balance optimism and pessimism.

It is interesting that Liz finds that the 'dream/reality' theme which evokes very directly the patient's vulnerability in the first piece has a resonance for the wider situation, and uses it for her general title. Medical practice, and management decision-making are both forms of 'assessment': are they perhaps both currently based on 'dreams' and delusions, such as the supposed parallel between nursing and the production and marketing of food?

Both this example and the next show how the fictional process of the patchwork text combines imaginary scenes and events with factual analytical writing. But we should not forget that this is true of fiction in general, and very obviously so in some cases, e.g. the whole of the science fiction genre, the many passages of historical analysis in the novels of George Eliot, and (to take a modern example) the extended accounts of the physics of ice and snow formations in Peter Hoeg's novel *Miss Smilla's Feeling For Snow.*

Matthew Stewart is a forensic nurse working in a special hospital for patients whose mental health problems render them dangerous to others and/or who have committed violent offences. 'Behaviour therapy' is a controversial form of treatment based on theories of 'conditioning' in the training of animals.

Matthew's first piece has the punning title 'Personal effects'. In the first section the abstract, 'kindly' voice of 'behaviour therapy' speaks:

I can change your behaviour, make you a better person, loved (or at least tolerated) by Society. I can mould your behaviour like a potter working his clay.... Of course it may take time and a little bit of hard work, but a myriad of our animal cousins have pulled levers, escaped from boxes, negotiated mazes and salivated into jars to demonstrate the validity of my claims. Give it a try.

There's nothing to lose, is there?

In the second section a patient replies: I don't want to change. I don't give a damn if I'm loved or tolerated.... Who are you to decide what I should or should not do? Who are you to steal from me a part of *my* individuality, to steal that which helps make me me. I don't want to give it a try; there's plenty to lose, not least my very identity.

The second piece is an imaginary interview which brings out the powerful prejudices and emotions of the 'average citizen'. Although the self-righteous anger is shocking, there is no mistaking its insidious appeal:

When I think of some of the things they've done it makes my blood boil. I know what I'd do with them.... lock them up for good as far away from civilisation as we can find.

Otherwise they just get let out and the next thing you know another self-respecting citizen drops dead with some nutter's knife in his back. The Victorians weren't daft: lock them away in a nice big building with high walls and let normal people get on with their lives with one less worry on their minds...

Would you be in favour then of some form of treatment based on punishment?

Well that seems to me a much more logical approach. For a start that's the way the world works: you do something wrong, you face the consequences.... Whereas you guys set up an environment which bears no resemblance to reality?

In fact it turns the real world on its head. Instead of sending someone to prison and punishing them you take them off to your little holiday camp and say, 'Here's twelve quid a week; take care how you spend it'.

What about the research that suggests that punishment is not effective?

Bollocks.

Next comes an imaginary interview with 'a psychologist':

What do you think of behaviour therapy?

Well, when I was studying I didn't believe in its use at all; but since working here and seeing how effectively it works in a lot of cases I think it certainly must have a place.

Do you really get consent or do you just bribe people with a suitable reward?

It's the same thing really. We offer a reward and the client chooses to either have his reward, by not displaying a targeted behaviour, or chooses to forfeit that reward and instead display the behaviour. Voilà: consent.

The next 'interview', with 'a liberal and enlightened citizen', picks up the moral ambiguity just revealed by the psychological rationale:

It's a difficult one. I mean, where do you stop? ...You're changing the way someone acts, thinks even, against their will.... The fact that, in some cases, it works is not really the issue. If someone displayed a problem behaviour, picking their nose for instance, a simple and *very* effective approach to eradicate the problem would be double amputa-tion somewhere above the wrists. Effectiveness, therefore, I trust you agree, is not necessarily a justification.

The next piece presents the point of view of 'a nurse', who recognises the potential value of the treatment but expresses reservations. It can easily be overused, leading to treatment programmes which ignore the 'possible causes of challenging behaviour'.

Some forms of behaviour offend some sections of society but don't necessarily affect a person's ability to function. So 'who decides what we use it for? Who plays God, if you like'.

Having thus displayed a variety of perspectives on the issue, with all their sometimes frightening ambiguities, crudities and contradictions, Matthew's final piece is his own analysis, drawing on some of the current literature on the subject and arguing that treatment policy must 'steer a course between the polarised views of the persons from the earlier passages'.

So, we have had a brief preliminary glimpse at the two sorts of work that this book will describe—the use of a single story and the use of patchwork texts where imaginary scenarios are continued, analysed and contrasted with other scenarios.

But there is already a substantial tradition of work under the label of 'reflective writing', with which many readers may be familiar. So how do the ideas presented here relate to this tradition? To answer this question, and thus to complete our introduction, let us briefly consider how the two approaches we have just outlined relate to, differ from, and expand upon other more familiar forms of writing frequently used to promote 'reflection' on professional experience.

Writing Fictions as a Contribution to 'Methods' for Reflection

The publication of Schön's *The Reflective Practitioner* in

1983 was followed by several other highly influential books also emphasising the personal, experiential, explorative and—above all—the reflective nature of professional understanding; in particular.

But although these texts (and others influenced by them) frequently invoke the term 'artistic' along with their basic terminology of critical reflection and reinterpretation of experience, they do not include the artistic, imaginative shaping of experience through the writing of fiction among their basic repertoire of activities.

Our argument, in contrast, is that the operation of the artistic imagination through the writing of fiction can be understood, precisely, as a mode of critical reflection upon, and reinterpretation of, experience. This section will therefore review briefly the basic activities proposed in the seminal texts listed above in order to consider how the process of writing and sharing fiction would complement and enrich them.

Keeping a Journal

Journals, in one form or another, are advocated as a general process for capturing the details of experience. When Walker elaborates what he calls the 'diversity' of forms of 'writing as an aid to reflection', he gives the following list: 'journals, diaries, record books, portfolios, verbatims, sociological diaries, dossiers, and logs'. However, what is common to all these formats, with the possible exception of the 'sociological diary', is the absence of an explicit awareness of the process of *shaping* experience through selection and interpretation.

Each journal entry is of course selected and shaped, but the fragmentary and chronological structure of the journal as a format means that it does not, in itself, help us become aware of exactly how we have selected and shaped—nor, therefore, of the alternative selections and shapings that might be worth considering.

In contrast, if one's reflective writing is conceived as a form of fictional shaping, then entries in a journal are considered as a set of possible components of a patchwork text, constructed consciously to raise issues by placing discordant elements side by side and thereby pointing directly to ambiguities and alternatives in need of clarification.

Writing in Order to Structure Experience

Walker's mention of a 'sociological' diary suggests, implicitly at least, a recognition that reflection needs a guiding structure. Other examples of this from the 'reflective practitioner' texts are: the analysis of parallel experiences and options, the analysis of metaphors as a way of linking specific experiences to general cultural themes, and the use of repertory grids to make explicit one's assumptions and values. Heron presents the process in general terms as: description followed by conceptualisation, considering alternatives and seeking theoretical explanations.

More precisely, instructions are often given for writing a 'critical incident', which moves from 'what happened' through personal analysis (What did I feel? What was I trying to achieve?) and analysis of alternatives (What other choices did I have?) to analysis of learning. Broadly similar instructions are given by David Tripp, with the addition of a final phase in which one is asked to 'classify' the incident in terms of theoretical categories.

The limitation of these approaches is that the basic method seems to be a form of unassisted self-questioning, a purely 'rational' mode of introspection with no procedures for tapping into one's imaginative resources.

And, unlike the process of writing a story and collecting different readings of it, or building up a patchwork text from a series of contrasts and reflection on those contrasts, these methods do not involve consciously shaping the original representation of the experience. It is therefore not clear how the initial description will provoke the recognition of alternative interpretations.

Our argument here, in other words, is that although we agree wholeheartedly with the objectives proposed here, we think that the methods they propose are 'difficult', and that if, instead, writing fiction is the starting point for the work, it is more likely that writers will easily come across a line of thought that they did not initially have in mind.

Sharing Interpretations of Experience

The general notion that reflection is facilitated by sharing accounts of experiences is emphasised in Main's account of cooperative learning strategies and Candy *et al.'s* description of 'learning conversations'.

More specifically, both Brookfield's and Tripp's approaches to critical incident analysis recognise the limitations of introspection. Tripp emphasises that incidents must be written with an audience in mind, since the knowledge that one is writing for others creates 'the discipline of anticipating what others would need to know, how they might react, what they might criticise'.

For Brookfield, the point of reflecting upon critical incidents is to expose one's assumptions, and he asks practitioners to describe an incident to a group of colleagues, who then suggest what assumptions (about 'good practice') are embedded in the writer's presentation.

Again, we would argue that where the accounts being shared are presented as 'fictional' stories, a specific freedom is provided for readers to bring their own interpretations to bear on the text; the openness with which a story conveys its meaning anticipates and welcomes alternative readings in a way that an analytical description does not. As Bruner says:

Fiction places events in a wider 'horizon' of possibilities.... Skilful narrative.... highlights subjective states, attenuating circumstances, alternative possibilities.... To make a *story* good, it would seem, you must make it somewhat uncertain, somehow open to variant readings.

The fictional format thus provides an immediate creative opportunity for the reader, and it also provides protection for the writer. The ambiguity of a story means that there is uncertainty as to where the writer stands in relation to the text. Discussion about the meaning of the text does not, therefore, put the writer 'in the dock', whereas writing a descriptive account of one's practice and then awaiting others' views as to its underlying assumptions (as Brookfield proposes) is potentially highly threatening.

The same potential emotional danger is present in the process of videotaping role-plays for interpretation by a group of peers. In contrast, the relative safety of sharing a fictional story (as opposed to a descriptive account) has been specifically noted by participants in our fiction-based workshops and reflective writing courses, often with surprise and relief.

The question, then, for autobiographical writing, is: how does one balance the need for emotional safety against the educational purpose of going beyond one's starting points?

A fictional story also may well be, in many ways, a partial prevarication, which is why readers' interpretations can often tell writers something they themselves had not 'noticed'. But a fictional story does not necessarily need to be written with self-protection in mind—as Abbs implies is often the case with autobiography.

On the contrary, its status as a product of imagination means that writing a fiction sets us free—to range over the possibilities implicit in our experience, secure in the knowledge that no-one will be able to 'pin down' any particular motive, opinion or action as that of the author.

This brings us to the end of our introductory outline. We have presented our basic argument—that current forms of writing in courses intended to foster the reflective analysis of experience have ignored the great educational potential locked in our creative capacity for writing fictions—either in the form of stories or more complex patchwork texts. We have given a preliminary indication of what practitioners' fictions are like, and of their value as explorations of professional practices and understandings.

And we have indicated how such forms of writing would both enrich and facilitate the writing activities conventionally undertaken. Clearly, we have raised a host of questions and so far given only the sketchiest of answers to a very few of them. What is the general rationale for writing and sharing fictions as a mode of reflection on professional practice?

What is the relationship between educational processes, imaginative creation, and the interpretation of imaginative representations of experience? What is the relation between 'fictional' accounts and 'factual' accounts of experience, between the particular and the general, and (most importantly) between 'imagination', 'reflection' and the development of professional knowledge?

But on the whole our book is organised to enable the work produced by the course participants to speak for itself; so the next two chapters present a wealth of examples—first of stories and then of patchwork texts. We hope that these examples will begin at least to provide support for the arguments and claims that have been put forward so far.

Bibliography

Brand Stewart. The Media Lab: Inventing the Future at MIT. New York: Viking, 2000

Calvert, J. (2004) Interview with Hugo de Burgh, 28 May 2003.

Englewood Cliffs, N.J. The Fourth Estate.: Prentice-Hall, 2000

Foot, P. (1973) Who Killed Hanratty? St Albans: Panther.

Hulteng John L. The News Media: What Makes Them Tick? Englewood Cliffs, N.J.: Prentice-Hall, 2001

Kerlinger Fred N. Foundations of Behavioral Research. New York: Holt, Rinehart and Winston, 2002

Lloyd, D. (2005) Talk to the students of the MA Investigative Journalism course at Nottingham Trent University, 19 February 2002.

Lavine John M., and Daniel B. Wackman. Managing Media Organizations. New York: Longman, 2004

Meyer Philip. Precision Journalism: A Reporter's Introduction to Social Science Methods. Bloomington: Indiana University Press, 2003

Sellers Leonard L., and William L. Rivers (editors). Mass Media Issues: Articles and Commentaries. Englewood Cliffs, N:J.: Prentice-Hall, 2001

Ullmann, J. and Colbert, J. (2000) The Reporter's Handbook: An Investigator's Guide to Documents and Techniques, 2nd edn. New York: St Martin's Press.

Wallraff, G. (2002) The Undesirable Journalist. London: Pluto.

Willis Jim. Surviving in the Newspaper Business: Newspaper Management in Turbulent Times. New York: Praeger Publishers, 2003

Index

R

S

T

V

W